S0-BRN-311

LANDMARK VISITORS GUIDE

Lake District

Norman Buckley

Following more than forty years as a frequent visitor, Norman Buckley has lived in the Lake District since 1990, indulging his enthusiasm for this unique area, its history and its landscape.

For the past ten years he has been a prolific writer of guide books of various kinds; this is his fourth and much the most comprehensive Lake District guide, previous books having concentrated on routes for walkers and the exploration of towns and villages. In partnership with his wife June, Norman has also written several books linking recommended walks and tea shops in various parts of Britain, with more to come. He is a keen environmentalist, holding post-graduate diplomas in Environmental Management and in Lake District Studies from the Universities of Liverpool and Lancaster respectively.

Acknowledgement
To my wife June, who not only contributed the sections on Accommodation, Eating Out and Beatrix Potter, but also provided a great deal of wide-ranging support throughout the whole period of the research and writing of this book.

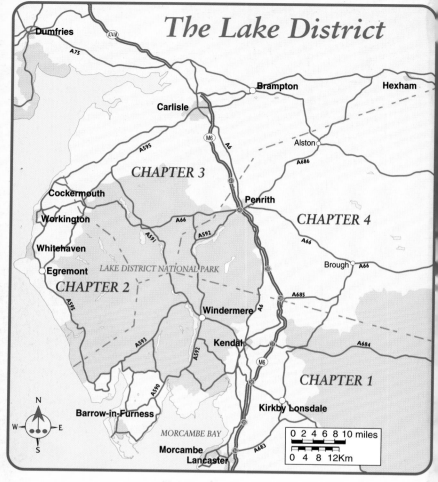

The Lake District

Note on the Maps
The maps drawn for each chapter, whilst comprehensive, are not intended to be used as route maps, but rather to locate the main towns, villages and points of interest. For exploration, visitors are recommended to use the 1:50,000 (approximately 1¼ inch to the mile) Ordnance Survey 'Landranger' maps.

Dedication
Landmark Publishing thanks Michael Bell of Bells Bookshop, Halifax, Yorks (01422 365468) for supplying the material upon which the maps in this book are based.

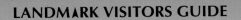

LANDMARK VISITORS GUIDE

Lake District

Norman Buckley

Contents

INTRODUCTION

WELCOME TO THE LAKE DISTRICT

The Lake District is one of the most popular areas for visitors in the country. In all seasons, people come to explore its fells and valleys, whether in spring when wild daffodils may be seen in many areas, in the balmy days of summer, or autumn when the changing foliage brings a richness to the colours of the fells and lakes. Even in winter, a dusting of snow on the fells creates scenes of memorable beauty.

In addition to the fells, valleys and lakes, there are the literary attractions which draw visitors from all around the world who come in large numbers to see for themselves the homes of Beatrix Potter and William Wordsworth.

There is much to see and much to do, all of it set against a backdrop of magnificent scenery protected by the National Park and the area's major landowner,

Above: The Windermere "Steamer" arriving at Waterhead Pier, Ambleside.

the National Trust. The Lake District attracts visitors back time and time again, often several times a year. The Lakeland experience endears and endures despite the passage of the years.

Yes, there is always a welcome in the Lake District, to new visitors and old friends alike. Even if it pours down while you are there, your enthusiasm to return will not be dampened. In that sense, the Lake District can readily claim to be the complete holiday destination.

THE BACKGROUND

How the Lake District was formed

Since geologist Jonathan Otley produced, in 1820, the first real definition of Lake District geology, the subject has always attracted interest. For the layman it is probably enough to know that the formation of the district involved a complex mixture of the laying down of marine sediments and volcanic activity, with later compressive movements forcing the land above water and into a great dome-shaped mound.

The oldest rock, about 470 million years, is the **Skiddaw Slate**, forming the northern part of the district from Loweswater to Blencathra, with an isolated mass at Black Combe in the far south-west. Next came lava and ash from volcanic eruptions, forming the **Borrowdale Volcanic Series** of the rough, craggy, central core. A covering of **Coniston Limestone** followed, now seen only as a very narrow, occasionally outcropping, band running south-west to north-east from the Duddon Estuary almost to Shap. Much more important in relation to the present landscape is the next sedimental phase, the variety of rocks formed over 400 million years ago during the **Silurian Period**, present right across the southern part of the district and responsible for the comparatively soft, gentle countryside seen around Hawkshead and Windermere.

Repeated earth movements took place and another sinking beneath the sea resulted in thick coverings of carboniferous limestone and, later, sandstone. During the time of this latter covering, desert conditions prevailed for a few million years. **Erosion** has removed the limestone from all except a rim around the area, best seen at Scout Scar near Kendal or Whitbarrow Scar, well to the south. Likewise most of the sandstone has gone; the fringe remains are very impressive in the cliffs at St Bees and were used in the construction of Furness Abbey and much of the town of Penrith.

Further uplifting, perhaps 60 million years ago, eventually produced the now recognisable dome shape, with fissures which became the origins of the present valleys spreading out like the spokes of a wheel. During the last million years – recent times by geological standards – the repeated southerly extension of the polar ice cap brought great sheets of ice over the Lakeland peaks, with intervening periods of milder climate during which the ice retreated. The grinding, scouring and plucking of the moving ice had a profound effect on the landscape, producing the **classic glacial features** such as U-shaped valleys (Great Langdale, Langstrath) with hanging valleys (corries) high up the valley walls, moraines and drumlins. It is a mere 10,000 years since the final retreat of the ice left the area ready for the first appearance of man.

Human Occupation

To our eyes this **Palaeolithic Age** (Old Stone Age) landscape would have seemed intolerably dreary and desolate. It has been compared with parts of Norway as they exist today; fauna and flora were very sparse, with much reindeer moss and a few stunted birch trees slowly creeping in around the fringes. Human activity was confined to a few wandering hunter-gatherer bands, probably following the herds of reindeer known to have been present at the time.

As the climate improved between 8000 and 5000 BC, during the **Mesolithic Age** (Middle Stone Age), diversified forest gradually took over, covering the mountains to a high level. There is evidence of a more settled form of occupation in favoured areas such as the fringes between mountains and coast, where there was a more plentiful and diverse supply of food, including fish. By about 3500 BC – the **Neolithic Age** (New Stone Age) – the hunter-gatherers began to clear the forests on the margins of the district, increasing the grassland, initiating their transformation into farmers. The **first cultivation** of cereals started a few hundred years later.

By the time of the Bronze Age, from about 2200 BC, there was no tree cover on the higher ground, and it is during this period that most of the surviving **prehistoric monuments** were constructed. Most noteworthy are the avenue of standing stones at Shap, the large stone circles at Castlerigg, near Keswick and at Swinside, the array of small stone circles on Burnmoor, Eskdale, and the henge monuments at Eamont Bridge, south of Penrith.

The axe factory in the scree-filled gully beside Pike of Stickle in Langdale, **Lakeland's first industry**, came into use at this time. A particularly hard band of Borrowdale Volcanic rock produced a flint-like stone which could be shaped by rough chipping on site, followed by a final polish with coarse sandstone particles on the coast. The axes were produced in large numbers and exported great distances.

Many hut circles from the **late Neolithic** and the **Bronze Ages** can still be identified; some of them in remote high situations were probably the first of the seasonally occupied 'sheilings' or summer dwellings, a pattern of farming whereby livestock was taken to high pastures for summer grazing under supervision, and moved back to more sheltered lower areas during the winter. This practice continued in Lakeland into medieval times. Similar farming activities continued throughout the **Iron Age**, ebbing and flowing with changes in climate, and with a more coherent tribalism evidenced by the construction of hill forts, the largest of which is found on Carrock Fell.

The Romans

The Romans arrived in an area which had been farmed for 3,000 to 4,000 years, the resident population at the time being part of the huge Brigantes tribe. As this tribe was loosely spread over most of northern England, local chieftains must have wielded considerable power. Initially, in AD 79, Agricola

Above: Lanrigg, Grasmere, one of the many lovely small country hotels.
Middle: Wasdale Hall, now a youth hostel.
Below: The Three Shires Inn, Little Langdale, takes guests.

Above left: *Crinkle Crags in Winter.* **Above right**: *Stone Arthur from Butterlip How YH, Easedale road, Grasmere.* **Below**: *Try an unusual way of seeing the lakes – from a hot air balloon. These went up near Hawkshead.*

subdued only the eastern part of the district, bypassing the remainder on his way to and from Scotland. Full Roman control was imposed gradually over the next 50 years or so, when most of the forts and other known sites were constructed. Apart from a little mining and the use of the port of Ravenglass, the Roman occupation was very much a military presence, having minimal effect on the lives of the indigenous people who carried on as before with the essential struggle to exist by farming this harsh area.

The Dark Ages

Following the Roman departure early in the 5th century came the so-called Dark Ages, which were very important in the formation of today's Lakeland landscape.

The examination of fossilised pollen preserved in the sediments of lakes and tarns has yielded valuable information about the trees, wild plants and cultivation from prehistory onwards. In the 6th century, cultivation and its associated settlement spread higher into the uplands than at any time before or since, resulting in over-exploitation and consequent soil erosion. Coupling this with the arrival of a wetter climate, the inevitable result was abandonment of marginal settlements and a retreat to the valleys, leaving the hilltops largely as we see them today, covered with large blanket bogs.

In lower areas there was some regeneration of woodland at this time.

Merger by **local tribal chieftains** formed the Celtic kingdom of Rheged, probably centred on Carlisle. As Rheged declined in the latter part of the 6th century, the Anglian kingdom of Northumbria expanded westwards and there was a relatively bloodless takeover as incomers merged with the existing population. From the 7th to the 10th centuries the district remained under Anglian influence. As Northumbria itself collapsed under the pressure of Danish invaders, the British kingdom of Strathclyde pushed southwards from its Scottish heartland, absorbing much of what is now Cumbria. At about the same time seaborne **Norse invaders**, who had been living in Ireland and the Scottish Western Isles, arrived in considerable numbers, quickly infiltrating and settling wherever they could find unoccupied land capable of being farmed. A later Scottish invasion in 1061 desecrated large parts of what later became Westmorland and north Lancashire.

Place names

The successive colonisation by Anglians from the east, Scots from the north and Norse from the sea may be traced by the examination of place names (see page 38). Most important are those names of Norse origin which indicate: a summer pasture – names ending in 'er; ergh;

scale; set; side', a clearing in woodland – names ending in 'thwaite' or a farmstead – names ending in 'by'. Progressive colonisation of the dales by the Norse can often be traced, early sheilings (summer pastures) being later converted into permanent farmsteads.

The Normans

The arrival of the Norman conquerors was considerably delayed; by the time of the Domesday Book in 1086, only the southern fringes of the district were recorded and it was 1092 before William Rufus captured Carlisle and brought stability to the area. The strong castle which William himself then built at Carlisle was of great importance in discouraging further Scottish invasion. Early in the next century King Henry I divided Cumbria into a series of large baronies, with **castles** such as Cockermouth, Penrith, Egremont and Kendal providing defence in depth across the district.

Christianity

There is a scarcity of evidence of very early Christianity in the Lake District although church dedications do give clues about the activity of well known saints in the area. No less than eight churches in the northern part of Cumbria are dedicated to **St Kentigern** (or Mungo), who moved south from his Strathclyde homeland to convert the heathens of this mountainous area. One of these is the important church at Crosthwaite, Keswick. Another early saint active in the area was St Ninian, whilst St Wilfrid also has the odd dedication. Standing lonely by the shore of Bassenthwaite Lake is the small church dedicated to **St Bega**; the great sandstone cliff of St Bees's Head is close to the spot where she allegedly landed after leaving her home in Ireland. In all these cases of church dedications the present buildings are, of course, of much later date than the saints themselves.

The names of **ancient wells** also provide clues to early Christianity although, as with St Patrick's at Glenridding, subsequent folklore is usually unsupported by any real evidence of origin or of involvement with a saint. Very few of today's churches have structural elements which pre-date the Norman conquest, although a circular or oval shape to a churchyard is very often significant in indicating an **early Christian site**. The most notable structure is a little way outside the Lake District at Morland, south-east of Penrith, where the tower is a fine example of Anglo-Saxon architecture. Several Anglo-Saxon **monastic sites** have been identified, those at Dacre and Heversham having documentary evidence. Other sites have produced **carved stones**, generally parts of crosses. The best surviving example is at Irton, north of Ravenglass; other fragments have been found in the vicinity of later churches, in some cases built into the fabric of the church, tending to indicate that the site was originally monastic.

The arrival of the Vikings disrupted the Anglo-Saxon monasteries, although the incoming settlers were quickly converted to Christianity. Subsequent **Viking sculpture** was widely distributed throughout the area and, unlike the Anglo-Saxon, was not confined to monastic sites. The cross at Gosforth is a wonderful example of the transitional period, combining the Crucifixion with Norse pagan mythology. Other important Norse survivals are the **'hogback' gravestones**, clearly seen in the churches and churchyards at Dearham, Lowther and Penrith.

Farming

Following the Norman conquest and the establishment of the feudal overlords, the great 'forests' were designated as their hunting preserves. At the same time, farming settlement was pushed further into the remote parts of the district, setting the basic pattern with which we are familiar today. Large **dairy farms** ('vaccaries') were established by the overlord himself on land retained in his direct control towards the heads of several of the valleys, that at Gatesgarth, Buttermere being documented from very early times. **Population growth** in the 12th and 13th centuries coincided with much conversion of summer pastures into **permanent farms**, with more grazing being wrested from the rough hillsides. Not surprisingly, woodland dwindled, largely due to the intensive grazing of the flocks of sheep and herds of pigs. Trades such as charcoal burning, iron smelting, tanning, mining and weaving all flourished. In the south of the district Furness Abbey became the dominant landowner, playing a leading role in many of these developments.

Further expansion was, however, curtailed by Scottish raids, by the arrival of the Black Death in 1348–9, and by later outbreaks of plague, livestock diseases and harvest failure, collectively producing deserted settlements, impoverished inhabitants, with fields reverting to the wild over a period of a hundred years or so.

Recovery from the mid 15th to the late 16th centuries was largely related to the development of the **woollen cloth industry** based on Kendal. Land was once more in demand and fellside was again taken into small, hard-won 'intakes'. With recovery of the **woodland industries**, particularly the demand for charcoal for the smelting of iron and other ores, areas were fenced to exclude livestock and coppicing was developed as a means of managing and retaining surviving forest.

Particular to the Lake District farming environment was the

Above: Ashness Fell from Ashness Bridge. **Below left**: the old slate quarry at Tilberthwaite Gill. **Below right**: Elterwater with the Langdale Pikes in the distance.

rise of the 'statesmen' (estates men) from the mid 16th to the mid 18th centuries. In most essentials these largely independent farmers were similar to the yeomen of other parts of the country. Their customary tenure of the land, usually quite small in extent, gave them near freehold status and thus great power over the development of that land and, collectively, on the evolution of the landscape. Townend, at Troutbeck, now in the care of the National Trust, is a good example of a statesman's house which remained in the same family for more than 300 years. In valley bottoms 'town fields' were shared between several farmers. Oats and barley were extensively grown on the better quality land, whilst on the unfenced fell sides grazing was shared in accordance with rules laid down and enforced by Manor Courts. Towards the end of the period the numerous farms in each valley were already being amalgamated into larger units; the process accelerated in the 19th and 20th centuries. Some of the abandoned farmsteads can still be identified.

The valley bottom open fields were gradually partitioned and enclosed by the dry stone walls which are such a feature of the present day landscape. **Parliamentary enclosure** – whereby large areas of open common grazing land were divided to create individually-owned fields – reached the district in the latter half of the 18th century,

firstly on low moorland fringing the district proper, but reaching many more central areas of high ground by the mid 19th century. Scarcity and inflated grain prices of the period of the Napoleonic Wars brought more land under the plough than ever before or since. No land which is truly Lake District is now used for arable crops, but the 'ridge and furrow' undulations remain as evidence of previous ploughing in many places.

Gentrification

Whilst the farming landscape has remained, with continuous but subtle change to field shapes and to farm buildings, a few **grand houses**, with extensive parkland, have been superimposed, largely contemporary with the 'discovery' of the scenic attraction of the district in the late 18th century. Notable examples are the Round House on Belle Isle, Windermere (1774), followed by Lyulph's Tower, Ullswater, and several beside Derwentwater. From the mid 19th century the **cotton magnates** and other successful tycoons of Manchester and its district were following this lead by building lesser but often still impressive villas in favoured positions, particularly close to Windermere, where the **newly-arrived railway** provided swift communication to and from their businesses. Many of these houses are now used as hotels; examples are the Belsfield, in Bowness, the Langdale Chase and the Merewood, both between Windermere and Ambleside.

The 'Discovery' of the Lake District

The previously virtually unknown Lake District was 'discovered' by some discerning and intrepid travellers – **the first tourists** – in the latter half of the 18th century. There had been one or two earlier visits, for example by Daniel Defoe, who described the landscape as 'barren and frightful' and 'of no use or advantage either to man or beast'. This set the tone for the tours by, *inter alia*, Dr John Brown, a local vicar who wrote *Description of the Lake and Vale of Keswick* in 1767, Thomas Gray (of *Elegy* fame) and William Gilpin who became the popular authority on the 'picturesque' approach to landscape. Their writings promoted considerable interest among the leisured classes of the time. Mountains continued to be described as 'horrid' or 'dreadful' by these sensitive souls, but the more gentle vales and lakes were regarded as 'delicious views', to be analysed piece by piece and described in meticulous detail. Thus was born the **'picturesque' movement**, the refined tourists viewing the scenery through a Claude glass, a little mirror in which scenes were framed in order to create the best picture.

Thomas West published the first *Guide to the Lake District* in 1778, advocating 'viewing stations' from which visitors could admire the best views in each area. Inevitably, many painters and engravers of the time flocked to Lakeland, often regarding it as their duty to re-arrange the natural features sufficiently to achieve an improved balance for the picturesque or to exaggerate the mountains in order to emphasise the horror. The finest pictures of the district were painted by J.M.W. Turner. However, there are many others which are of great interest, not least in illustrating the attitudes of these early visitors themselves.

Industrial History

Quarrying

Apart from the production of the stone axes in Langdale, early industry in Lakeland comprised the extraction of various minerals and the localised quarrying of stone for building purposes.

Over the centuries quarrying has continued into modern times in many parts of the district. The particular qualities of some of the Borrowdale Volcanic Series rocks, notably the cleavage into thin **slates** and the range of attractive colours, resulted in great expansion of this industry in the 19th century, with the development of sizeable quarries in comparatively remote places such as Kentmere, Troutbeck, Kirkstone and Langdale. The latter two quarries are still worked. Although nature eventually provides some cover when quarries are exhausted, the impact on the landscape of the digging, blasting and tunnelling has been, and remains, considerable. The Tilberthwaite area, near Coniston, shows the greatest concentration of scars from generations of quarrying.

The geological intrusions of **granite**, mostly found on the fringe of the area, have been extensively quarried for building blocks and roadstone, still providing a major industry at Shap. Others at Threlkeld and in Eskdale have closed down.

The ring of carboniferous **limestone** which surrounds the district has also been of industrial importance. Blocks from Scout Scar near Kendal and from Whitbarrow Scar in the south have provided the large runner stones for gunpowder mills and, more importantly, the former has provided the building material for much of Kendal, in consequence locally known as the Old Grey Town. Lime for agricultural use, for mortar and for limewash, was produced by burning the stone in small kilns, the ruins of some of which can still be seen. A few kilns can also be found on or adjacent to the narrow band of Coniston Limestone which crosses the district.

Quarrying of the remains of the red **sandstone** was confined to the coastal strip near St Bees and the vicinity of Penrith. It can be seen in the buildings of these areas, often as lintels, quoin stones and decorative blocks. The long disused quarries have generally blended into the landscape.

Mining

The varied rocks of Lakeland contain a wealth of minerals including iron, copper, lead and small amounts of gold and silver. The extraction of these minerals from such difficult terrain has ebbed and flowed over several centuries. Early workings were always from the surface – the 'stopes' still apparent above Coppermines Valley near Coniston – with tunnels or 'levels' later being driven into the hillsides to follow the mineral veins underground. The levels provided drainage and ventilation as well as access and many can still be found. The harsh climate, the rough mountain country and the hazards of primitive working underground compounded the difficulty, danger and expense of extraction.

German miners were brought to the Keswick and Coniston areas in Elizabethan times by the Company of Mines Royal. **Copper** was the main objective and large smelters were constructed at Brigham on the River Greta near Keswick. Early to mid 19th-century revival of the copper industry brought Cornish miners to the Lake District, the Coppermines Valley becoming a huge industrial

Above: Tarn Howes. *Middle*: The World of Beatrix Potter Attraction in Bowness, one of several dedicated to the authoress and her books. *Below*: The Lakes have a wide variety of attractions. This is the Ravenglass and Eskdale Railway at Ravenglass.

complex, of which abandoned workings, levels, shafts, pit wheels, mill races and buildings remain as evidence. The Coniston branch railway line of 1859 was constructed to meet the need to transport large quantities of ore to a smelter at St Helen's in Lancashire.

Lead was also worked by the German miners of the 16th century, particularly in the Newlands Valley, south-west of Keswick. Again, this industry was intensified in the second half of the 19th century, coinciding with the enormous demand for lead for roofs and plumbing systems in the rapidly expanding towns of the northern industrial areas. There were smelters at Stoneycroft near Keswick and near Hartsop Hall, south of Patterdale. The scars of former lead mining are still widespread in the Caldbeck area, in Newlands and, most notably, at the large Greenside mine above Glenridding, closed as recently as 1962. The toxicity of the waste from lead mining ensures that spoil heaps remain largely free of masking vegetation.

Iron ore (haematite) is present in most of the types of Lake District rock and has been extensively worked since well before the arrival of the Romans. **Smelting** was carried out in primitive 'bloomeries', tiny clay and stone furnaces where the necessary temperatures were achieved by the use of hand operated bellows, with charcoal as the fuel. As charcoal was bulky and fragile to carry, the ore was carried to bloomeries sited close to the woodland which produced the charcoal.

A later development was the 'bloomsmithy', with water power and mechanical hammers much increasing the output. Many of these early smelting sites have been identified by the deposits of slag and by associated place names, e.g. Cinder Hill and Smithy Beck.

Early in the 18th century the first **blast furnaces** were set up at several sites in the district including Cunsey on the western side of Windermere, Backbarrow near Newby Bridge and Duddon Bridge. The increased output of these furnaces consumed vast quantities of charcoal. With a late conversion to coke firing, the Backbarrow furnace continued in use until 1966. The remains of the Duddon Bridge furnace have been taken into the care of the National Park Authority as a scheduled ancient monument.

Rich deposits of the ore were concentrated in the carboniferous limestone of West Cumbria, where the extensive abandoned 19th and 20th-century workings have been filled and re-graded, changing much of the landscape over a large area inland from Workington and Whitehaven. In the 19th century this area, together with the Millom district, was covered with excavations, factories, workers' houses, mineral railways and spoil heaps. Despite the modern improvements, many of these industrial remains are still very evident. Millom is a Victorian town built on the wealth created by iron, whilst villages such as Pica are typical of the mining era. The Florence Mine at Egremont is open to visitors.

The still-thriving **pencil industry** of Keswick was founded on the graphite extracted since Elizabethan times from a mine near Seathwaite, in Borrowdale. Today, the graphite used in the factory is imported.

Woodland

Woodland-related industries have long flourished in Lakeland. The south of the district in particular has large areas of deciduous woodland rich in oak, beech, ash, hazel, birch, alder and sycamore, providing raw material for the building of houses and ships, with an array of other traditional uses which included the brushwood and the bark of the trees. Particularly important was **coppicing** – the cutting down of a tree in such a way that re-growth is encouraged in the form of multiple shoots. After 15 years the shoots are about 6 metres (20 feet) long and 12 centimetres (5 inches) in thickness, ready for cutting and use. The tree's root system is stimulated into further growth to repeat the process and the wood has become a renewable resource for use in **charcoal** production for smelting, brewing, tanning and a variety of constructional purposes. The charcoal burning has left large numbers of 'pitsteads' – circular clearings or platforms of about 6 metres (20 feet) diameter on which a mound of coppiced timber was carefully constructed and then fired. Controlled combustion, with air largely excluded, and constant attention by the burners was needed to produce good quality charcoal in a few days.

Charcoal was also an essential ingredient of **gunpowder**, in great demand in an area with so many mines and quarries. By the mid 19th century there were five gunpowder mills in operation within or close to the district, that at Elterwater being the most central and probably the best known. These large industries also needed copious supplies of water to power the many waterwheels and large sites to accommodate the wheel pits, the tramways, the storage buildings and the blast walls. As accidents were not uncommon with such a volatile substance, the works were well spaced in order to reduce the damage resulting from such an occurrence.

More gentle woodland-based trades included the making of woven baskets or 'swills', besom brushes and clothes pegs. Many towns and villages had **tanneries** using tree bark; Kendal is still the home of a well known shoe factory.

Mills

There were more than 60 bobbin mills in use early in the 19th century, providing the millions of **wooden bobbins** required by the booming Lancashire cotton industry. The concentration of these mills in the south of the district resulted from the combination of abundant water power, coppiced woodland providing the right type of wood, ready access to Lancashire and many existing buildings capable of modification for the purpose. The bobbin-turning lathes and associated machinery were also made locally, by Fell at Troutbeck Bridge (now the Royal Mail sorting office) and Braithwaite at Crook. The decline of the cotton trade and the introduction of plastic bobbins soon destroyed the industry, though the last mill, at Stott Park, a short distance north of Lakeside, closed only in 1971. Happily, this mill has been preserved as a working museum.

From medieval times, sheep farming and the consequent woollen industry centred on Kendal, meant that small-scale **fulling mills** were common in Lakeland by the sides of the rivers and larger streams, often close to the equally small **corn mills**, serving the local communities. Hand spinning and weaving of the wool was a contemporary domestic craft. Ambleside has an obvious former mill area by the side of Stock Ghyll, close to the main street. A little further upstream another, larger, mill area has been redeveloped with modern housing. As the **industrial revolution** reached the district, the spinning and weaving of wool, cotton and flax were carried out in larger factories, often on the site previously occupied by a fulling mill. Because of the geography, such large mills were on the fringes, at Staveley, Kendal, Ulverston and Cockermouth. The fine late 18th-century example at Barley Bridge, Staveley has a typically varied history of cotton, wool, bobbins and paper packaging. These larger mills became the centre of mill communities, with terraced housing for the workers close by.

Paper mills developed from the late 17th century, the scale much increasing after the middle of the following century, with the banks of the River Kent between Staveley and Kendal being particularly noted for this trade. The huge mill at Burneside is the surviving example.

TRANSPORT

Roads

The mountainous countryside and the limited importance of the Lake District to the Romans restricted even those doughty road-builders to comparatively few routes, the lines of most of which are only partially confirmed. A particular puzzle is the famous route over the

Above: Fell Foot at the southern end of Windermere, one of many attractions around the lake. *Below*: The National Park Visitor Centre at Brockhole, Windermere.

summit of High Street, reaching an altitude of more than 610m (2,600 feet). The much more obvious parallel route over the present-day Kirkstone Pass is better in all respects and is now known to have been used by the Romans. The central section of the road from Galava (Waterhead, Ambleside) via the Hard Knott Pass and fort to Ravenglass is obvious and well-confirmed as Roman, but most of the remainder of this road and its eastern continuation to Watercrook, south of Kendal, is still conjectural. From Papcastle (Cockermouth) the lines of the roads to the north-east to Carlisle and north-west to Maryport are confirmed, but to the south-east the road heading for Troutbeck, Whitbarrow and Penrith has long sections which rank only as 'probable line'.

After the Romans, although there was no actual road construction until comparatively modern times, the routes in use today were gradually established by the movements of people, livestock and, importantly, **packhorses**, for trade purposes. In such a mountainous area there was no incentive to establish major highways and these 'roads' remained narrow and unimproved for many centuries. The geography ensured that the chosen routes would use exactly the same **high passes** as are used today, some now having surfaced carriageways, some still being for foot traffic only. Zig-zags eased the most severe gradients for the packhorses, with bridges being constructed at important river and stream crossings. Many have survived, some being widened and strengthened for present day traffic.

Not dissimilar are the '**corpse roads**' along which coffin-bearers travelled from outlying communities to the parish church where burial would take place. Notable examples are the track from Wasdale Head by Burnmoor to Boot and that from Rydal to Grasmere. Coffin roads fell into disuse as more churches and chapels were built in the more remote places.

From 1739 the **first turnpike roads** were constructed around the outside of the district, including what later became the A6 trunk road over Shap, but it was not until 1762 that the road from Cockermouth to Keswick and Penrith and that from Keswick to Windermere and Kendal were made subject to the Turnpike Acts, as the first true 'modern' highways in Lakeland. With some realignment (especially of the A6), these have remained the only major roads in the district.

Although roads are the only means by which residents and visitors travel throughout the district, very few new roads have been constructed since the turnpikes. The difficult terrain and the need to protect the environment both militate against road construction. Widening and other improvements have been carried out, major in the case of a few selected roads such as the A66 and A591, both former turnpikes, and minor roads such as the Hard Knott Pass have been surfaced. With these exceptions, the prevailing philosophy is that the environmental damage of road construction and improvement is not acceptable in an area of such outstanding but fragile landscape beauty.

In recent years the M6 motorway has, of course, relieved the A6 of most of its long distance traffic and now provides access for the great majority of Lakeland visitors from both north and south, whilst the Kendal bypass has diverted visitor traffic away from the streets of that congested town.

Canals

The Ulverston and the Lancaster Canals served the Lake District fringe and, for a while, were of economic importance to Ulverston and Kendal respectively. For obvious reasons no canal penetrated into the Lake District proper.

Railways

The main line from London to Glasgow, now known as the West Coast Main Line, was opened in 1846, skirting the eastern fringe of the Lake District as it climbed laboriously over Shap summit. In the same decade, the **rich industrial wealth** of the coastal area attracted railways, linked first to Carlisle, and then to the Furness area in the south by 1850. In 1857, Furness was connected to the Scottish main line at Carnforth so that the railways virtually surrounded the district. In 1847 one important line penetrated the interior, when the Windermere branch, leaving the main line at Oxenholme, reached a terminus at Birthwaite, 2 kilometres (1.5 miles) from the lake, opening up the district to **mass tourism** for the first time. The hamlet grew spectacularly over the next few years, eventually merging with the much older village of Bowness on Windermere to form Lakeland's most comprehensive and busiest holiday resort. Violently opposed by William Wordsworth and, later, by John Ruskin, a proposed extension of this line to Ambleside and, possibly, to Keswick was abandoned.

The opening of the Coniston branch of the Furness Railway in 1859, was followed by the only through line in 1865, when Cockermouth, already linked to Workington, was connected to Keswick and Penrith. As with the Coniston branch the original motivation was industrial, bringing coke from Durham to the ironworks of West Cumberland, but the chosen route was also intended to maximise tourist traffic to the Keswick area. Yet another branch of the Furness Railway was opened from the Furness main line near Ulverston to Lakeside at the foot of Windermere in 1868–9. A station provided interchange facilities with the lake steamers, but the route by Backbarrow ensured that the line had commercial traffic in addition to the tourists.

The final railway into Lakeland was a line constructed to the curious gauge of 3 feet, running from Ravenglass to Boot in Eskdale, the primary purpose being to carry iron ore to the coast. After the failure of the mines the line was converted to 15-inch gauge as a tourist attraction, with the upper terminus moved to Dalegarth. In the latter part of the 19th century the mineral railways in the Workington–Whitehaven area proliferated as rival companies competed for the then lucrative iron and coal related trade.

The decline and closure of most of these railways has mirrored that of railways in Britain generally. The West Coast Main Line survives, as do the links across Furness to Barrow and along the coast north to Whitehaven, Workington and Carlisle, albeit with a mediocre service in the latter case. The Windermere branch still plays a considerable part in carrying visitors to and from the district and the Ravenglass and Eskdale is a very active and attractive little line. Part of the Lakeside branch has been restored as the Lakeside and Haverthwaite Railway, with a steam depot at Haverthwaite. But the rest is silent.

The multiplicity of lines between mountains and sea is now nothing more than a tangle of overgrown cuttings and embankments, sadly neglected bridges and former stations in a derelict industrial landscape. The terminus station at Coniston is a car park and, even on the operational Windermere branch, the fine old station has been incorporated into a supermarket. Perhaps saddest of all is the Cockermouth to Penrith line, now largely covered by asphalt in improvements to the A66 road, and with Keswick station standing forlorn, without apparent purpose. If the line had survived for just a few more years, a more enlightened attitude might well have prevailed and this line could then have continued to form a useful and attractive link across the northern part of the district.

ARCHITECTURE

With exceptions such as Sizergh and Muncaster Castles, the Lake District is not an area noted for stately homes. A greater interest for visitors lies in the evolution of the **vernacular buildings** which are, collectively, of great landscape importance. The rough terrain, the climate and proximity to raiders from across the Scottish border have, from early times, all played a part in shaping the siting, the layout and the construction of buildings.

Locally quarried stone is seen throughout the district as the

Above: Scafell. ***Below left***: Chapel Stile village in early evening.
Below right: Copper Mines Valley, Coniston, an area of good walks
north-west of the village.

natural material, skilfully sited farms and their outbuildings blending with the environment to achieve a satisfying sense of rightness. A few of the oldest farms, such as those at Burneside Hall and Kentmere Hall, are founded on a defensive pele tower of the 14th or 15th centuries. The area is famous for the **dry stone** construction whereby walls were built without mortar in the joints. Better quality buildings did, however, have clay mortar, internal wall plaster and several coats of limewash forming an external protective rendering against the weather. Early thatched roof coverings gave way to slate or thin cut stone late in the 18th century, some ridges being finished with interlocking 'wrestler' slates as a local substitute for properly shaped ridge tiles.

Most characteristic are the **chimney stacks**, massively cylindrical, at first limited to larger houses, but later being added to more modest dwellings. The chimney tops were initially without protection, but often had a pair of inclined slates added later; chimney pots are comparatively recent.

The variations of internal layout of traditional Lake District houses, often linking family accommodation with the housing of livestock are, in themselves, a fascinating study. As farming has changed and as living standards have risen over the centuries, modifications to

these layouts can often be traced by external observation, noting the positioning both of existing and of blocked-off doors and windows, changes to roof lines and other variations. Some of the older buildings are of cruck construction but this is usually impossible to detect from outside.

In the later part of the 17th century and the early part of the following century, the prosperity of the woollen trade resulted in a period of quite intensive new building and the improvement of older buildings. Fortunately, many buildings of this era are dated externally. A walk through Troutbeck (near Windermere), as set out in the author's *Town and Village Trails of Cumbria and the Lake District*, is highly recommended for the average visitor and Townend should certainly be visited.

Those with a much deeper interest in Lakeland architecture should read Brunskill's and Denyer's books which are a mine of information on all aspects of local vernacular architecture.

Among the many types of farm outbuilding, the **bank barns** are most characteristic, using the slope of the ground to give level access both to the lower floor housing livestock and to the upper floor normally used for threshing grain. Very common in Lakeland, Norway and the Black Forest of Germany, these barns are rare elsewhere in

Britain. Much admired by visitors are the **spinning galleries** provided in some farmhouses and outbuildings to give shelter from the elements, but with as good light as possible for the home-based woollen craft industry. However, use of these galleries was more likely to involve the drying and storage of the yarn than the actual siting of spinning wheels.

TRADITIONS

Not surprisingly in an isolated area like the Lake District, entertainments and sports developed on a very localised basis, the catchment area usually being the valley. These festivities have ebbed and flowed over the centuries but many, generally in a modified form, have survived.

First mention must go to **fox-hunting**; not the horse-riding, rather class-bound version common to the rest of England, but a hard grafting no-nonsense following of the hounds on foot, across mountains and valleys, doing what the sheep farmers believe is a vital job of work. Indeed, the farmers themselves make up a large proportion of the hunters, convinced that the fox is the prime predator of their flocks and that control by hunting is the best method of countering this threat. They do, of course, enjoy the chase and particularly successful huntsmen have long been celebrated locally. Who has not heard of **John Peel**, almost rivalling William Wordsworth in his worldwide fame and his instant identification with Lakeland? Active over a long period in the north of the district and buried at Caldbeck, ironically his enduring pre-eminence is due to a song of dubious merit. Equally celebrated locally are Tommy Dobson of Eskdale and Joe Bowman of Ullswater.

Fortunately, other once common animal related 'sports' such as cockfighting and bull baiting are long gone, although a few traces of former cockpits do remain.

During the late 18th and the 19th centuries, **lake regattas** were a popular pastime for the leisured classes. Eccentrics such as Joseph Pocklington, who then owned Derwent Island, staged elaborate mock naval battles, with cannons and muskets contributing to what must have been an incredible spectacle.

These regattas were the extravagances of 'offcomers', but the truly indigenous population held shepherds' 'meets', combining daytime business with evenings of simple rustic merry-making and fairs permitted by ancient charters, such as Egremont Crab Fair and, a little distant, Appleby Horse Fair. Both are still held although, in the case of Egremont, the nature of the fair has changed a good deal over the years. The twice-yearly hiring fair was another important local custom. At Kendal, Cockermouth, Keswick, Penrith and Ulverston, farm labourers and domestic servants were hired for a six-month period. The system lasted until the First World War and is well described in Melvyn Bragg's *The Hired Man*.

Local **annual sports meetings** have long been popular, with sports such as the skilful Cumberland/Westmorland wrestling, guides races and **hound trailing** providing the basis for a day of all-round entertainment. The hounds follow a laid trail of aniseed and oil along a route over rough mountain ground, including walls and other obstacles, starting and finishing in the sports arena. Competition is very keen and the dogs are carefully reared and trained by their proud owners. The best known Lakeland sports meeting is held at Grasmere, closely followed by Ambleside, Hawkshead and Eskdale. In recent years **sheepdog trials** have also become popular, both with competitors keen to show the abilities of their dogs which are, after all, an important part of the livelihood of the sheep farmer, and with spectators.

Quite different are the annual church ceremonies of **rush-bearing**, again best known at Grasmere and Ambleside.

The dates and places of the fairs, sports meetings and trials are listed in the relevant chapters of the main part of the guide, with a quick reference list in the FactFile

FLORA AND FAUNA

In an area with the rich diversity of the Lake District, flora and fauna are topics worthy of substantial books in their own right or of chapters in more general books such as Pearsall and Pennington's *The Lake District* .

The remaining semi-natural broad leaf woodlands are an important scenic and wild life asset but, at least in scenic terms, the same cannot be said of many of the conifer plantations, such as those planted by the former Manchester Corporation around Thirlmere and the much maligned Forestry Commission planting in Ennerdale. However, as felling takes place in these commercial woodlands, the opportunity is being taken to diversify the species, using native trees such as oak, ash and birch wherever appropriate. This must be an improvement. There are important **forest visitor centres** at Grizedale and Whinlatter. Although, historically, forest covered much of the mountain area, the present-day view is that the largely bare fellsides contribute greatly to the beauty of the landscape as we have known it for generations and attempts at re-afforestation will not be made.

There are distinct fauna associated with the different wood-lands: for example bird populations such as pied flycatchers, redstarts and wood warblers in the oak forest. The **red squirrel** is the most

Above: Not all the attractions are new; here is Castlerigg Stone Circle. *Middle*: Many hotels were built in Victorian times. This is the Windermere Hydro Hotel at Bowness. *Below*: The lakes and tarns are often very attractive. This is one of the largest – Ullswater.

characteristic Lakeland creature, Sadly, despite efforts at containment, the advance of the grey squirrel from the south seems to be inexorable and, as the two species never seem to co-exist for long, the demise of the red in the district is being forecast. Sightings of this lovely but shy creature are therefore to be treasured. Also associated with the woodland is the **roe deer**, plentiful, but elusive to the casual observer, its natural camouflage making it difficult to see when standing still. In the Martindale area there is a famous herd of the larger **red deer**.

Not surprisingly, the majority of the district is covered by grass, predominantly poor acid grass including much mat grass (*Nardus*) on most of the uplands, but with species richer grassland on the fringe limestone areas.

The lakes and tarns support an exceptional variety of plants and animals, including comparatively rare types of fish such as char, schelly and vendace. Many shores have important wetland habitats and, because of the large differences in altitude from the rushing headwaters of mountain streams to the placid flow in valley bottoms, the streams and rivers also feature a wide span of wildlife.

High on the eastern mountains the once common **eagle** has reappeared, under protected breeding conditions, joining the more common ravens, buzzards, and other birds of prey such as the peregrine in its soaring flight.

The delicate natural balance in the area has long been recognised and is protected by the creation of Nature Reserves and Sites of Special Scientific Interest, some very large and others tiny. These sites are listed in the FactFile; all can be visited, in one or two cases subject to first obtaining a permit.

THE LAKE DISTRICT TODAY

The Lake District as it exists today is a compact area of thrusting mountains, serene lakes, farms and woodlands, colourful and characterful at all seasons of the year, with an overall allure which brings back so many visitors time and time again throughout their lives. It is an area easy to think of as **timeless** but which, as we have already seen, has changed a great deal overall during the last few thousand years and, in some popular parts, even more during the present century; an area with the landscape largely determined by the **ebb and flow of farming**, yet in which the farming is, economically, entirely marginal and now dependent on constant subsidies; an area in which the **rough terrain and harsh climate** has bred tough, characterful people from the mixed Celtic, Anglo-Saxon and Viking stock, their farming and their industries having shaped what we now see; an area in which **major tourist centres** such as Bowness on Windermere, Ambleside and Keswick sometimes rub shoulders uneasily with **outstanding scenic beauty**.

So, how do we, as its temporary guardians for a few decades, keep this earthly paradise in a fit condition to hand on proudly to future generations?

Recognition of the need to protect the area came late in the 19th century, following the formation of the **National Trust** in 1895 by the great philanthropist Octavia Hill, the Reverend (later Canon) Rawnsley, and Robert Hunter. From its first Lakeland property at Brandlehow on the Derwentwater shore, the Trust, an independent charity, has gone from strength to strength in the district. It now owns, for the benefit of the nation, something of the order of 30 per cent of the land area, including many working farms and other properties. The Trust is much the largest landowner, with a high proportion of the land holdings in the central, most spectacular area. Rawnsley in particular was an extremely active Lake District enthusiast and was a close friend of Beatrix Potter and her brother. On her death in 1943, Beatrix Potter left her vast estate to the Trust.

Ownership of mountain land by the Trust is a guarantee of access in perpetuity by fell walkers. Likewise, Trust ownership of working farms is the best possible protection of rights of way across the farmland and of resistance to unsuitable alterations to the buildings or developments on the land.

THE NATIONAL PARK

In 1951, an area which includes the great majority of what is generally regarded as 'The Lake District' was designated as a National Park, as were several other outstanding areas of the country. They are not parks in the accepted sense, in that they contained towns and villages as working communities, and not national because they are not controlled centrally. The main purpose of the designation of these areas was to achieve strong, unified, planning control over proposed development of all kinds. Like other planning authorities, the National Park Authority publishes a structure or development plan setting out its aims and objectives for the area, against which individual planning applications will be judged. Overall, the Authority is charged by the constituting Act to 'preserve and enhance the natural beauty of the Lake District and to ensure that people can continue to enjoy the Lake District'. A tall order indeed!

Subsidiary duties include the securing of public access to open country, the provision of visitor accommodation, camping sites, car parks and toilets, the making of byelaws to control activities on the lakes and for better control of land owned by the Authority or over which it has access agreements, and the provision of information and warden services.

Considering the history and

Above: *Mrs Tiggywinkle hard at work at the World of Beatrix Potter Attraction.* **Below**: *The boat hire on Grasmere, just out of the village.*

the character of the area, and the commercial pressures, the Authority has an awesome responsibility; on the one hand to preserve the beauty of the landscape, including its flora and fauna, on the other to facilitate the public enjoyment of that beauty, accepting that more public presence, particularly in motor vehicles, puts pressure on limited road capacity and car parking facilities and also results in problems such as severe erosion of popular footpaths on the mountains. On the whole it is fair to say that the Authority has been successful, although the balance between environmental or ecological concerns and commercial interests is often uneasy, with occasional open warfare as in the case of the proposed speed limit on Windermere. Brockhole, 3km (2 miles) north of Windermere village, is the Authority's principal information and visitor centre.

The appearance of the unsightly 'draw down' areas (the parts of a reservoir exposed when the water level is particularly low) around the sides of Thirlmere and Haweswater serves as a useful reminder of the environmental damage caused by large-scale water abstraction by the then Manchester Corporation in the 1890s and 1930s respectively. More recent proposals for further abstraction have been opposed by the Park Authority and many other organisations including the Friends of the Lake District and local farmers, saving Ullswater, Wastwater, Ennerdale Water and even Windermere from similar official vandalism. Without this kind of vigilance and concerted action it is difficult to imagine how the Lake District would look, left to the pressure of commercial and economic forces. What is certain is that it would be a much less attractive place for the visitor seeking the 'quiet enjoyment', which must remain the fundamental characteristic of England's finest landscape and which is written into the constituting Act of Parliament.

One other official body which must be mentioned is the **Cumbria Tourist Board**. Visitors during peak season must surely doubt the need for an organisation with a strategic role of encouraging visitors to come to the district. Most people know about the Lake District and need no such encouragement. However, tourism is undoubtedly Lakeland's major industry and the Board plays a valuable role in overseeing the provision of the whole range of visitor accommodation and in assessing, grading and publicising that accommodation. The Board is also active in encouraging a wide range of improvements in visitor services generally, with public transport being an area of major concern.

BEATRIX POTTER AND THE NATIONAL TRUST

Peter Rabbit is undoubtedly one of the most famous characters in children's literature, along with favourites such as Jemima Puddleduck, Squirrel Nutkin and Mrs Tiggywinkle. Beatrix Potter, the creator of these delightful animals, wrote and illustrated the numerous small volumes which have been enjoyed all over the world throughout this century.

Contrary to popular belief, Beatrix Potter was not born in the Lake District but in London, in 1866. Typical of the Victorian era, she was educated at home, in Kensington, by a series of nannies and governesses. She and her young brother kept all kinds of small animals from caterpillars to rabbits and mice, which she drew and painted. She also did botanical studies, and often found inspiration for drawings in the nearby Natural History Museum.

She was 16 when she first visited the Lake District; her parents had rented **Wray Castle** near Ambleside for their annual holiday.

Some years passed before the Potter parents took over **Larkfield** (now Eeswyke Country House Hotel) for another of their long sojourns. Beatrix loved this house with its fine views of **Esthwaite Water**. She described Sawrey 'as near perfect a little place as I have ever lived in'. It was then, at the age of 30, that she decided that somehow, sometime, a small part of this area would belong to her.

In 1893, she illustrated a letter to the son of one of her governesses with pictures of a little rabbit. This was eventually to become *The Tale of Peter Rabbit,* published privately at her own expense in 1901. The next year saw *The Tailor of Gloucester* and by 1903 her work was being published by Frederick Warne, who continued to publish her work throughout her life.

In 1905 she purchased, mainly from the royalties earned from her by now immensely successful books, **Hill Top Farm** in Sawrey. Whilst her parents were tolerant about the enterprise, she was still expected to live for most of the time in London but she visited the farm as often as possible. To provide sufficient accommodation for the manager and his family, Beatrix had the farmhouse extended whilst retaining a sufficient living area for herself.

Throughout this period she wrote more of the little books, finding inspiration in the animals, buildings, and countryside of Sawrey and Hawkshead. In *The Pie and the Patty-pan* the cat Ribby and the small dog Duchess were owned by people in Sawrey, the story being set in cottages in the village. The tales of Tom Kitten, Jemima Puddleduck, and Tabitha Twitchet, are similarly set in Sawrey, Hawkshead, and the lakes, fields and lanes within a few miles of Hill Top Farm.

Increasing popularity and sales of the books enabled Beatrix to acquire more farms and land. Through these negotiations she met William Heelis, a local solicitor. From a business-based relationship a friendship developed and they married in 1913. The couple started their married life in another property owned by Beatrix in Sawrey. William would ride his motor-bike to and from his office in Hawkshead (the building is now The Beatrix Potter Gallery owned by the National Trust and open to the public). For Beatrix, life changed considerably following her marriage; she now lived permanently in the Lake District. Writing books became less important to her – perhaps because she was now surrounded by live animals she felt less need to fantasise about them. However, farming, rural life, and land management became more time absorbing and demanding.

Some years before her marriage Beatrix had been introduced by her father to **Canon Hardwick Rawnsley**, one of the three eminent people who founded the **National Trust**. Beatrix shared the Canon's ideals for preservation and conservation of the countryside. The friendship between Canon Rawnsley and Beatrix continued until his death shortly after the end of the First World War. His opinions were to bear on Beatrix for the remainder of her life and to have far-reaching influence in perpetuity.

Mrs Heelis was a shrewd business woman. With her husband's undoubted local knowledge and assistance, she purchased property and land in the locality; this helped to ensure that farms and estates were not broken down into units too small to remain viable. At the time of her death in 1943 she owned over 4,000 acres of land, 15 farms, large flocks of Herdwick sheep (a breed she particularly wished to conserve because of their hardiness in the severity of the fells), and numerous houses and cottages. This vast estate was bequeathed to the National Trust, showing that Beatrix Potter believed that the protection and conservation of parts of the Lake District could be safely left in the care of this relatively new organisation.

Many visitors ask where to find the grave of Beatrix Potter – it does not exist. She was cremated, her ashes scattered in an unknown place by Tom Storey, her faithful servant and farm manager at Hill Top.

This very brief biography of Beatrix Potter may tempt the visitor to explore the settings for her books and the land and farms she owned – but do remember that many are private residences – and the lovely villages of Sawrey and Hawkshead. Hill Top Farm is a justifiably popular place to visit (owned by the National Trust).

Place Names

The names of towns, villages, farmsteads, mountains, rocks and streams have long been a valuable resource, in some circumstances the only resource, in tracing the history of human occupation of the Lake District through the phases before documentary records began in the 12th and 13th centuries. Place names must, however, be treated with care. By no means all of today's names can be confidently interpreted, as spelling changes and other mutations have taken place over many centuries.

The first identified settlers in the area, well before Christian times, were **Celtic** people or Cymri, from whom the present name **Cumbria** is derived. The linguistic link with Celts in Wales is obvious. Relatively few names from this era have survived, but a few such as Blencathra, Glenderamackin and Penruddock have an authentic Celtic/British ring.

From the later period of Anglian domination, from the 6th to the 10th centuries, the typical place endings of 'tun' (ton), 'ham', and 'lea' are, overall, much less dominant in Lakeland than in the rest of the country. Their concentration around the Lake District fringe, on the better quality land, tends to indicate that the earlier Celts had been pushed inwards towards the core area of mountains and steep sided valleys. Examples of **Anglo-Saxon** names include Bampton, Workington and Clifton. There are more of the Celtic/British names remaining in the north of the area.

From the 10th century the invasion of **Viking** settlers superimposed Norse place names, particularly in the more mountainous part of the district, where they named lakes, tarns, rivers, mountains and rocks. Particularly important are those names which include, possibly in a modified form, one of the word endings indicating a summer pasture or shieling – 'ergh', 'side', 'saetr' – Ambleside, Sizergh. Even more commonly found are names ending in 'thwaite' – a clearing in woodland – Stonethwaite, Rosthwaite, Finsthwaite.

This list gives a selection of components of place names with their interpretations:

Band	ridge of hill	*Dodd*	rounded hill
Beck	stream	*Dub*	deep pool
Bield	shelter, animal's lair	*Earn*	eagle
Berg	hill, mountain	*Elter*	swan
Bothy	hut	*Esk*	water
Brant	steep	*Fell*	mountain
Byre	cowshed	*Force*	waterfall
Cald	cold	*Gate*	road, path
Cot	cottage	*Gill, gyll,*	
Derw	oak	*ghyll*	stream in narrow ravine

Grange	outlying farm (usually monastic)	*Mere*	lake or pool
		Mire	swamp or bog
Gimmer	yearling sheep	*Pike*	peak, sharp summit
Hause	narrow pass	*Rake*	path up hill
How	small hill	*Scar*	crag, precipice
Kirk	church	*Whin*	gorse
Lind	lime tree		

Place names, with their likely meanings

Ambleside	summer pastures by river sandbanks	**Keswick**	cheese farm
Askham	among ash trees	**Kirk Fell**	mountain above the church
Borrowdale	valley of the fort		
Bowness	bull's headland	**Langdale**	long valley
Brockhole	badger's hollow	**Ling Mell**	heather covered hill
Buttermere	lake by dairy pastures		
		Loweswater	leafy lake
River Caldew	cold river	**Patterdale**	St Patrick's valley
Cartmel	sandbank by rocky ground		
		Pike O'Stickle	peak with sharp summit
Coniston	the king's farm		
Dovedale	valley of the doves	**Rosthwaite**	clearing with heap of stones
River Derwent	many oak trees		
Dunmail Raise	the memorial cairn of King Dunmail	**River Rothay**	trout river
		Rydal Water	lake in valley where rye is grown
Elterwater	lake of the swans		
Esthwaite Water	lake by the eastern clearing	**Scales Tarn**	tarn (small lake) by shepherd's hut
Grasmere	lake with grassy shores	**Steel Fell**	mountain with steep path
River Greta	rocky river	**Styhead Tarn**	tarn at top of path
Grizedale, Grisedale	valley of the pigs		
		Troutbeck	trout stream
Hawkshead	shieling belonging to Hauk (family name)	**Ullswater**	Ulfr's (personal name) lake
Kendal	village with church in the valley of the River Kent (formerly Kirkby Kendal)	**Windermere**	Vinandr's (personal name) lake

At the Beatrix Potter Gallery in Hawkshead there is an exhibition of the original drawings and paintings. The display changes each year and the building is furnished as it was when used as the busy office of William Heelis and Co., Solicitors.

OUT AND ABOUT

Walking in the Lake District

In the Lake District walking is a prime activity. Ranging from the gentle amble around Bowness or Grasmere villages to the scaling of mountain tops by tough, demanding, routes, a high proportion of visitors will use their feet to a greater or lesser extent as an essential part of the enjoyment of the district.

Inevitably, there are many specialised books which will assist walkers, ranging from the author's *Town and Village Trails of Cumbria and the Lake District* and *Lakeland Walking on the Level* – in two volumes – to the late Alfred Wainwright's celebrated mountain guides. Whilst dealing more comprehensively with the features of towns and villages, a general guide can act only to whet the appetite in the case of the hundreds of country and mountain walks which are available. This book is not a primarily a walkers' guide, and it is stressed that even though the walks are described in detail, walkers should never attempt a walk without a relevant large scale map in addition (see Maps on page 44). However, all the highest and really famous mountain walks are included here, as are such unmissable easier walks as **Orrest Head, Tarn Hows** and the **Ullswater** lake shore.

But First a Word of Warning!

Although no Lake District mountain ('fell' in local parlance) reaches a height of 1,000m (3,282 feet) and by world or even European standards they are small, do not underestimate them, particularly in winter. Steep and dangerous cliffs abound, there are often wet, sometimes icy, conditions underfoot and the weather can change from benign to severe with great rapidity.

Always carry extra clothing and food and be well-shod. In Lakeland there is no substitute for strong waterproof boots with well formed semi-rigid soles. Cloud is often low, reaching well down the valley sides and in these conditions the mountain tops are confusing and potentially dangerous places, needing the correct use of a compass for safe descent.

There are Mountain Rescue Teams covering all parts of the area but the volunteer members are certainly not looking for extra work; for example the Ambleside and Langdale team answers about 100 distress calls each year; some of these are fatalities. You have been warned!

If you are not an experienced hill-walker but would like to

climb a mountain or two and feel sufficiently fit so to do, by all means go ahead. The rewards of Lakeland mountain views and the sense of achievement will make all the hard work worthwhile. But do choose a fine day and stick to the well used routes, not being tempted to cut across country. It is better not to walk alone and to allow more time than you really expect to take.

Guided walks organised by the National Park Authority are widely available. Those led by voluntary wardens are free; others carry a small charge. Details are available at all Tourist Information Centres, from which many of the walks start. South Lakeland District Council, which operates some of the Tourist Information Offices, has a programme of guided short walks, around towns and villages in the south of the district.

Most areas of Great Britain now have designated medium and/or long distance footpaths; the Lake District is no exception. For example, Wainwright's famous **Coast to Coast** has its start (or finish) at St Bees Head near Whitehaven, crossing the middle of the district on its way to Robin Hood's Bay in Yorkshire. More local to the district is the **Cumbria Way**, starting at Ulverston and crossing Lakeland in a south to north direction. The **Dales Way** is generally walked from east to west, starting at Ilkley in Yorkshire, crossing part of the Yorkshire Dales, keeping well to the north of Kendal and finishing at Bowness on the Windermere shore. Modest in length and without mountains is the **Cistercian Way** across the Furness district in the south of the county. From Grange-over-Sands to Roa Island, this 53-km (33-mile) ramble has a strong historic interest. Also without mountains and shorter is another coast to coast walk, from Askam on the Duddon Estuary to Rampside on Morecambe Bay, visiting Dalton and Furness Abbey en route, with a total distance of about 20–25km (12–15 miles).

Visitors considering tackling one of these footpaths will no doubt obtain detailed information from an appropriate Tourist Information Office, probably supplemented by one of the specialised books and maps available.

Cycle Rides

As it is assumed that keen visiting cyclists will have their own itineraries for substantial rides, the routes suggested in this guide are aimed at the more casual or occasional cyclist and are, on the whole, comparatively short. For obvious reasons many such cyclists will not enjoy climbing long, steep, hills, so the recommended routes tend to concentrate on the towns,

(cont'd on page 44)

Above: *The Langdale Valley with the Langdale Pikes in the background.*
Below: *Coniston Village.* **Opposite**: *Tarn Hows.*

villages and countryside of the attractive areas which surround the Lake District.

The places to be visited duplicate to some extent those included in the car tours but for cyclists, country lanes and other minor roads are always given preference over main roads. Apart from **Grizedale Forest**, no suggestions are given for off-road cross-country cycling using bridleways and other tracks; these are very much a matter of personal choice for the users of mountain bikes. These machines can be hired locally; refer to the FactFile.

Under the auspices of the Lake District National Park Authority there is a programme of guided bike rides, exploring the national park itself. Routes are graded 'easy', 'moderate' or 'hard', the latter two involving considerable amounts of rough track and open fell riding, and helmets are compulsory in all cases. Advance booking is essential and there is a charge.
☎ 015394 46601

Car Tours

Apart from the obvious drives to the Lake District towns and villages featured in this guide, visitors have a wealth of choice of destination in the very attractive areas which surround the district. Stately homes, wildlife centres, working restored mills, historic market towns and sea coast are only some of the features which will contribute to a rewarding excursion. Compared with the Lake District roads in high season, the comparative lack of traffic is an added bonus.

It is obvious that several of the suggested circuits have enough visitor attractions, such as stately homes and museums, to fill several days and the intention of the guide is to offer wide choices, with something to suit all the family or, perhaps, to encourage more than one visit to a particular area. The generally short distances in driving terms allow for viable half-day excursions. Conversely, with plenty of time available and no wish to spend hours at a particular property, two or more of the routes may be combined to provide a longer drive through good countryside.

Whilst road suggestions in each case are limited to the more major roads, giving the basic direction and shape of the tour, in virtually all cases there are permutations of minor roads which enterprising drivers with time to spare may wish to substitute.

Maps

For the great majority of visitors a suitable map is not only a great help in finding one's way around a district, but also considerably increases the appreciation and enjoyment of that district. Names can be given to lakes, tarns, mountains, woodlands and farms; places of historic interest can be identified with certainty.

For generations the Ordnance Survey has produced fine maps;

their Lake District Tourist 1-inch map was the mainstay for walkers and other visitors for many years after the Second World War. Subsequent metrication has brought diversity and, with it, the very fine Outdoor Leisure series, covering the Lake District in four sheets, nos. 4 - 7 inclusive, at a scale of 1:25,000 (roughly $2\frac{1}{2}$ inches to the mile). For those who want the ultimate in geographical features, with rights of way, bridleways and footpaths, and with other information useful for visitors, at a generous scale, these maps are wholeheartedly recommended. These maps have been reissued as part of the Explorer series, double sided to cover a great deal bigger area, with the numbers OL 4 to 7.

Mountain walkers will probably use these maps in conjunction with a mountain guide book. Mention must, therefore, be made of the series of eight books, covering the area geographically, written and illustrated by the legendary late Alfred Wainwright. Despite being up to 40 years old these books are still in print and are cherished as the most comprehensive guides to every route on every mountain. They include large scale maps and are widely regarded as minor works of art.

For visitors whose primary interest is to tour around the district by car, cycle or public transport, smaller scale maps are perfectly adequate. The Ordnance Survey Landranger series at a scale of 1:50,000 (roughly $1\frac{1}{4}$ inches to the mile) has superseded the old 1-inch maps. At this scale it might be expected that the district could be covered by a lesser number of sheets. Unfortunately, as this series is not tailored to the shape of the district, four maps are needed for full coverage – no. 89 – West Cumbria; 90 – Penrith and Keswick; 96 – Barrow in Furness and South Lakeland; 97 – Kendal to Morecambe. Possession of these four sheets does, however, have the advantage of including a great deal of the Lakeland fringe which features largely in the suggested cycle rides and car tours.

For economical coverage adequate for general tourism, the *Leisure Map of the Lake District* by Estate Publications highlights most of the visitor attractions in a clear format at a scale of 1:75,000 (a little less than 1 inch:1 mile). Another single map solution is Tourist Map no. 3, published by the Ordnance Survey, reverting to the old pre-metric 1 inch:1 mile scale.

1 THE SOUTH

KENDAL, BURNESIDE AND STAVELEY

Kendal

For the great majority of visitors, Kendal has long been the 'Gateway to the Lake District', although this is less apparent nowadays with the bypass whizzing motorists well away from the crowded streets of this bustling old town.

Standing astride the River Kent, Kendal is an ancient market town situated in a basin several kilometres south-east of the mountains of the Lake District proper, but with more gentle hills to the north, east and west. Immediately to the west, Scout Scar and Cunswick Scar, both facing away from the town, display some of the best surviving features of the limestone which once covered the whole district.

The strong north-south axis of the town, with the main street, named from the south, Kirkland, Highgate and Stricklandgate,

Above: Tilberthwaite, between Coniston and Little Langdale.

well over one kilometre (three-quarters of a mile) in length, is a reminder of the communications importance of the town from Roman times, when there was a fort at Watercrook, just to the south. The main road to Scotland, first a turnpike road, then becoming the A6, was along this main street. Later came the main railway line from London to Glasgow which passes a little way to the east, with a junction at Oxenholme. Last came the modern M6 motorway, again passing to the east of Kendal as it heads for the Lune Gorge and Shap as the easiest crossing of the high moorland.

The consistent use of local stone for the buildings gives Kendal a uniform, though at times rather dull, appearance - hence the nickname '**Old Grey Town**'. As would be expected in the centre of an ancient barony, there is a medieval castle (of about 1180), its ruins standing high on a knoll to the east of the town centre from which it is not visible. This is in fact Kendal's second castle. An earlier structure, probably of wood, stood on another elevated site, which can still be identified to the west of the main street. One owner of the present castle was the father of Catherine Parr, sixth of King Henry VIII's wives.

The town itself grew from two early settlements, one around the present Market Place and the other some distance to the south by the parish church. The two later coalesced. Very distinctive in the development were the many close-knit residential 'yards' reached through narrow openings off the main streets. Claims that the tight packing of these small dwellings was for defensive protection against Scottish raiders are unfounded, as construction was long after hostilities had ceased. As in northern industrial towns generally, it was advantageous to pack as many workers as possible close to the mills and factories, in Kendal's case largely along the banks of the adjacent river. Many numbered yard entrances can still be seen but the houses were demolished and cleared as having proper sanitation became obligatory.

As an industrial town, Kendal has long been famous for **woollens**, carpets and other textiles, (there is a reference in William Shakespeare's *King Henry IV part I* to knaves dressed in Kendal Green clothing), tobacco and snuff, leather goods (there is a present-day shoe industry) and water turbines.

Fortunately, many of the better old buildings have survived, at least in a modified form, largely along the main street where, above the mainly modern shop frontages, some fine old structures are apparent. There are several old inns. For those with an hour or two to spare, Kendal lends itself well to the 'town trail' approach; two admirable *Discover Kendal* leaflets published by the Civic Society are available at a small charge at the Tourist Information Centre.

The one-way traffic system in Kendal is notorious and is likely to be perplexing to visitors. Broadly, with clock-wise circulation, the system forms an elongated north-south oval, with a one-way cut across in the middle at Lowther Street, by the side of the town hall. Most of the car parks are towards the northern end of the town.

As befits a country centre with a considerable catchment area, the town is well provided with shops both traditional and modern. Unlike the smaller settlements in the Lake District proper, there are relatively few of the more gimmicky gift, Lakeland wool and so-called 'factory clothing' shops.

PLACES TO VISIT IN KENDAL

Kendal Museum
Station Road
A long established museum, administered in conjunction with the Abbot Hall complex (see below). Natural history, archaeology, and a special collection relating to the life and work of the celebrated local hill-walker and writer Alfred Wainwright. Admission charge; car park; opening hours - generally as Abbot Hall. ☎ 01539 721374. In winter, hours may be subject to variation. Enquire at museum or at Tourist Information Centre.

Castle Dairy
Wildman Street
The oldest occupied house in Kendal. The name may be a corruption of 'Castle Dowry' as it was believed to have been given by Sir Thomas Parr of Kendal Castle to his daughter Agnes as part of her dowry when she married his steward in about 1455. Originally a hall-house of the 14th century, it was extensively modified in the 16th century but many fine traditional structural features remain. Inside are the arms of both the Parr and the Strickland families. Now a restaurant, but inside viewing is permitted from Easter to September, Wednesdays, 14.00–16.00.
☎ 01539 721170

Quaker Tapestry

Friends Meeting House, Stramongate

An old Quaker site. Following a visit by George Fox in 1652, a first meeting house was opened here in 1688, followed by a school. The present building dates from 1815–16, designed for 850 people. The celebrated tapestry exhibition centre is open from spring to late autumn, Monday–Saturday, 10.00–17.00. Admission Charge.
☎ 01539 722975

Market Place

Small but attractively animated when the street market is held each Wednesday and Saturday. Adjacent is the Westmorland Centre, a modern shopping complex which includes a daily indoor market. Across the Market Place is the Shambles, an attractive little street, formerly the trading place of the town's butchers.

Tourist Information Centre

In the town hall building at about the mid point of the main street, by the traffic lights.
☎ 01539 725758

Kendal Castle

Easily reached from Aynam Road via Parr Street and Sunnyside and a short uphill walk, or from Castle Road and a longer walk. Unrestricted access as public footpaths cross the site. Fine views over the town. Street parking only.

Brewery Arts Centre

Highgate

By the side of the southern part of the main street, this former brewery has been tastefully converted into a multi-purpose centre, with theatrical productions, music, cinema and visiting exhibitions of various kinds. Café. Car Park (pay and display). ☎ 01539 725133

Abbot Hall

The Abbot Hall Art Gallery, situated in a Georgian mansion by the river, and the Museum of Lakeland Life and Industry on an adjacent site, are jointly administered. This highly regarded complex has first-class permanent collections, supplemented from time to time by visiting exhibitions. The Gallery is strong on Cumbrian painters, including locally born George Romney. Open 15 February–24 December, Monday–Friday 10.30–17.00, but with earlier closing time of 16.00 in February, March, November and December. Admission Charge. Car Park. Coffee Shop. ☎ 01539 722464; fax 01539 722494

(cont'd on page 52)

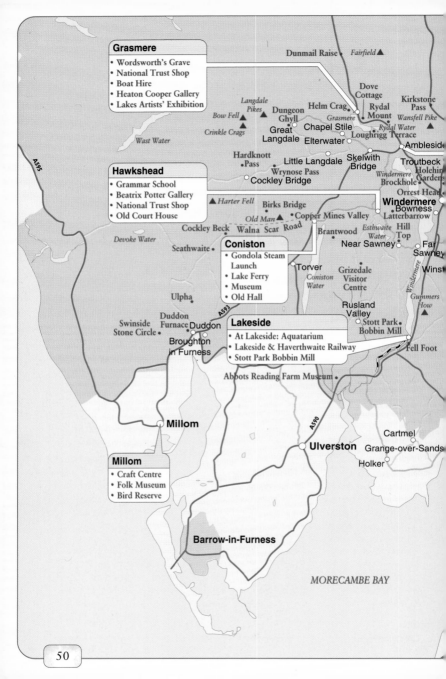

Grasmere
- Wordsworth's Grave
- National Trust Shop
- Boat Hire
- Heaton Cooper Gallery
- Lakes Artists' Exhibition

Hawkshead
- Grammar School
- Beatrix Potter Gallery
- National Trust Shop
- Old Court House

Coniston
- Gondola Steam Launch
- Lake Ferry
- Museum
- Old Hall

Lakeside
- At Lakeside: Aquatarium
- Lakeside & Haverthwaite Railway
- Stott Park Bobbin Mill

Millom
- Craft Centre
- Folk Museum
- Bird Reserve

Dunmail Raise • *Fairfield* ▲

Dove Cottage

Kirkstone Pass

Langdale Pikes

Helm Crag

Rydal Mount

Wansfell Pike ▲

Bow Fell ▲

Dungeon Ghyll

Grasmere

Chapel Stile

Rydal Water

Crinkle Crags ▲

Great Langdale

Elterwater

Loughrigg Terrace

Ambleside

Wast Water

Hardknott Pass

Little Langdale

Skelwith Bridge

Troutbeck

Wrynose Pass

Windermere

Holehird Gardens

Cockley Bridge

Brockhole

Orrest Head

▲ Harter Fell

Birks Bridge

Old Man ▲

Copper Mines Valley

Windermere

Bowness

Devoke Water

Cockley Beck

Walna Scar Road

Brantwood

Esthwaite Water

Latterbarrow

Hill Top

Seathwaite •

Torver

Grizedale Visitor Centre

Near Sawney

Far Sawney

Wins

Ulpha •

Coniston Water

Gummers How ▲

Swinside Stone Circle

Duddon Furnace

Duddon

Rusland Valley

Stott Park Bobbin Mill

Broughton in Furness

Fell Foot

Abbots Reading Farm Museum •

Millom

Cartmel

Ulverston

Grange-over-Sands

Holker •

Barrow-in-Furness

MORECAMBE BAY

50

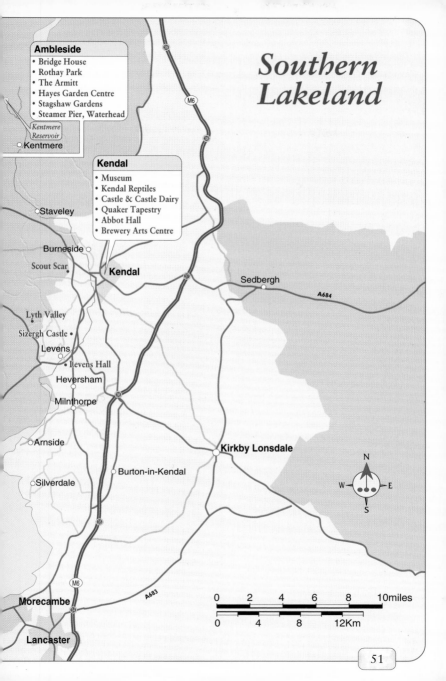

Southern Lakeland

Ambleside
- Bridge House
- Rothay Park
- The Armitt
- Hayes Garden Centre
- Stagshaw Gardens
- Steamer Pier, Waterhead

Kentmere Reservoir

Kentmere

Kendal
- Museum
- Kendal Reptiles
- Castle & Castle Dairy
- Quaker Tapestry
- Abbot Hall
- Brewery Arts Centre

Staveley

Burneside

Scout Scar

Kendal

Sedbergh

A684

Lyth Valley

Sizergh Castle

Levens

Levens Hall

Heversham

Milnthorpe

Arnside

Kirkby Lonsdale

Burton-in-Kendal

Silverdale

N
W — E
S

M6

Morecambe

A683

Lancaster

| 0 | 2 | 4 | 6 | 8 | 10miles |

| 0 | 4 | 8 | 12Km |

51

(Kendal cont'd)

Holy Trinity Parish Church

Mostly 18th century but standing on the site of an older church, this fine structure is found in Kirkland, close to the Abbot Hall. Reputed to be the largest parish church in the county, the width is particularly striking. Inside is the Parr Chapel, a memorial to Romney and the helmet and sword of 'Robert the Devil'. This character was Robert Phillipson of Belle Isle, Windermere who, during the Civil War, in pursuit of his Parliamentarian enemy Colonel Briggs, rode his horse into the church during a service, creating a fair amount of mayhem. Phillipson just about escaped with his life as the Parliamentarian congregation reacted violently, but lost his helmet, since displayed for all to see.

K Village

In recent years the ground floor of the K shoes factory in Lound Road has been converted into an assortment of tasteful shops specialising in factory 'seconds'. Included are Dartington glass, Laura Ashley and K shoes. Café. Car Park. ☎ 01539 732363

Kendal Leisure Centre

Burton Road

By the side of the main road from Kendal to Oxenholme, Endmoor and Burton in Kendal, this modern multi-purpose sport and leisure complex offers swimming, sauna/solarium, fitness room, squash, badminton and other indoor sports. Concerts and occasional theatre are held on some evenings. Café. Bar. Car Park. ☎ 01539 729777; fax 01539 731135

Kendal Golf Club

Situated on high ground to the west of the town, accessed by Allhallows Lane and Beast Banks. Turn right into High Tenterfell and follow the signposts up to the left. Established golfers welcome as visitors. ☎ 01539 723499 (professional's shop).

Carus Green Golf Course

In the valley of the River Kent, almost at Burneside.
Fork right from the A5284 Windermere road at the Methodist Chapel. The course is on the right in less than 2 km (1.25 miles) Pay and Play course. ☎ 01539 737277

Kendal Golf Driving Range

Along Oxenholme Road (B6252), close to Oxenholme station. Usual driving range facilities, including hire of clubs and tuition by appointment. Open all year except Christmas Day. Monday, Wednesday, Thursday, Friday 10.00–2100; Saturday and Sunday 10.00–18.00. Closed Tuesdays. ☎ 01539 733933

Lakekand Climbing Centre

Kendal. ☎ 01539 722975

Burneside

Situated to the north of Kendal is Burneside. It is an industrial settlement by the River Kent dominated by the large paper factory of James Cropper & Co.

Railway station on the Windermere branch line. **Carus Green Golf Course** is close by. **Burneside Old Hall** has more recent buildings grafted on to a 14th-century pele tower.

Staveley

Between Kendal and Windermere on the A591 lies Staveley, a large village well equipped with shops and inns and with a considerable industrial history. The River Kent and its tributary the River Gowan formerly powered several mills making bobbins and processing textiles. The village is much improved since the bypass was constructed a few years ago.

Woodcraft Workshop – Peter Hall and Son. Visitors can see craftsmen at work on a variety of new and antique furniture. Open throughout the year, Monday–Friday, 9.00–17.00; Saturday and Bank Holidays 10.00–16.00 (showroom only).

Railway station on the Windermere branch line.

Upstream of Staveley the valley of Kentmere becomes progressively hemmed in by the mountains of the two arms of the Kentmere Horseshoe, rising to High Street.

Kentmere

Kentmere hamlet north of Staveley has the 15th-century church of St Cuthbert and the Old Hall nearby, a 14th-century pele tower incorporated into more modern farm buildings.

WINDERMERE, BOWNESS AND TROUTBECK

Possibly the best known place name in the Lake District, **Windermere** can refer to either the lake or the large village which grew around the terminus of the railway line some 2km (1.25 miles) from the lake.

Windermere – the lake

The biggest lake in England, at nearly 17km (10.5 miles) in length, Windermere is a fine sheet of water with numerous, mostly small, wooded islands. The only inhabited island is the largest, **Belle Isle,** close to Bowness, which has a villa dating from 1774, the first truly circular residence in Britain. There is no public access to Belle Isle.

From its southern end in comparatively low-lying countryside the lake reaches close to high mountains at the north, the ring forming the **Fairfield Horseshoe** above Ambleside and Rydal providing a wonderful panorama. Along much of the west shore the well-wooded **Claiffe Heights** plunge steeply towards the water, whilst the gentler eastern shore has been more built up with individual residences and the settlements of **Bowness** and **Waterhead.** The lake is extremely popular

Above: Kendal is an important shopping centre for the Lakes. **Middle**: Sizergh Castle, south of Kendal. **Below**: The River Kent at Staveley.

Above: Ambleside Youth Hostel by the side of Windermere at Waterhead, perhaps the best in Europe, with lots of small family rooms. It used to be three separate hotels. *Middle*: Rydal Mount, the home of William Wordsworth. *Below*: Bowness on Windermere.

for boating, several thousand craft ranging from tiny dinghies to substantial cruisers being registered as users. Near the mid point is the **car ferry**, the modern vessel a successor to several more primitive ferries. Three hundred years ago a ferry sank with the loss of more than 30 lives. From the west side at **Ferry Nab** the road leads to **Far** and **Near Sawrey** and **Hawkshead**.

Timetabled boat services ply between Lakeside, Bowness and Waterhead (for Ambleside), with some calls at **Brockhole**, the Lake District National Park Visitor Centre. In season attractive large diesel powered 'steamers' are used, the late 19th-century *Tern* being particularly elegant. In winter much reduced services are operated by smaller motor launches. In addition to the scheduled services, during high season there are frequent and varied circular trips from Bowness and Waterhead. At **Lakeside** connections may be made with the steam-hauled trains of the Lakeside and Haverthwaite Railway, for which combined tickets may be purchased. A 'Freedom of the Lake' ticket allows unlimited cruising for a period of 24 hours, whilst a combined ticket for the boat and the Aquatarium at Lakeside is also discounted.

Rowing and small motor boats are available for individual hire at Bowness and Waterhead. Water-skiing and similar sports may be pursued at the Low Wood Hotel, by the side of the main road to the south of Waterhead and at Sport Aquatic at Windermere Quays, Glebe Road, Bowness. Hire of yachts, with a skipper, is possible at the Spinnaker Club, Windermere Marina Village, 1km (0.6 mile) south of Bowness on the A592 road to Newby Bridge. At Shepherd's Boat Yard, Glebe Road, Bowness, cruises on a modern luxury cruiser *Spirit of the Lake* are available. This boat may also be chartered by the hour.

Most important is the **Windermere Ferry**, which for centuries has crossed the lake at a narrow part between the landing stage just to the south of Bowness and Ferry Nab. The present vessel is fixed to a submerged chain, plying to and fro every 20 minutes from 07.00 until 22.00 in summer, but terminating at 21.00 in winter. Eighteen average size vehicles are carried each journey, together with foot passengers. Services are suspended in very windy weather. The ferry is operated on behalf of Cumbria County Council.

Bowness on Windermere

Although it is very much the holiday part of the Windermere/Bowness built-up area, with a good deal of modern development, ironically **Bowness** claims what is much the oldest portion of the settlement. The narrow streets clustered behind

PLACES TO VISIT IN WINDERMERE

Windermere village is basically a 19th-century settlement of rather austere solid stone buildings, with a small shopping centre and several inns and restaurants. There is a large car park for shoppers at Booth's supermarket. Pay and display public car park in Broad Street.

Lakeland Ltd
On former railway land beside the station, this trading enterprise (formerly Lakeland Plastics), with its comprehensive array of kitchen and other domestic equipment has developed into a substantial visitor attraction. Café. Open daily, including Sundays and Bank Holidays. ☎ 015394 88100

Tourist Information Office
Well situated between the railway station and the village, at the junction of the main A591 and High Street. ☎ 015394 46499

Baddeley Clock
By the roadside half way to Bowness is this monument erected in 1907 in memory of M.J.B. Baddeley, author of noted guide books.

Brockhole
The comprehensive visitor centre of the Lake District National Park Authority, 3.5 km (2 miles) along the A591 Ambleside road. Permanent exhibition; audio visual presentations; frequent events; large terraced garden; adventure playground; lake shore access; disabled access; gift and book shop; restaurant/tearoom. Free entry but charge for car parking. Open late March–end of October, 10.00–17.00 every day.
☎ 015394 46601; fax 015394 45555

Windermere Golf Club, Cleabarrow
Long established club with sporting upland course.
Established golfers welcome as visitors.
☎ 015394 43550 (professional)

Low Wood Hotel
By the A591 on the way to Waterhead.
Waterski-ing and other lake sports. ☎ 015394 33338

Events — The South

KENDAL, BURNESIDE AND STAVELEY
Westmorland County Show
Lane Farm, Crooklands, near Kendal. Comprehensive agricultural show with lots of events. Second week in September.
☎ 015395 67804

Lake District Sheepdog Trials
Ings near Staveley. Early August. ☎ 015394 33721

WINDERMERE, BOWNESS AND TROUTBECK
Lake District Summer Music
Occupying most of the first two weeks each August, this festival is held at several venues throughout South Lakeland, including the excellent hall at the school at Troutbeck Bridge, less than 2km (1.25 miles) along the main A591 Ambleside road.
☎ 01539 733411

Windermere Powerboat Record Attempts
Mid October. Low Wood Hotel.

AMBLESIDE
Ambleside Daffodil and Spring Flower Show
Mid March. Details from Tourist Information Centre.

Ambleside Rush-bearing
St Mary's Church. First Saturday in July. Ceremonial renewal of the rushes which covered the earth floor in medieval times.
☎ 015394 33205

Ambleside Sports
Rydal Park, by the A591 Grasmere and Keswick road, just north of the town centre. Includes traditional Lake District events. Late July/early August. ☎ 015394 45531

Ambleside Flower Show and Craft Fair
Rugby Club, Borrans Road. Early August. ☎ 015394 32252

RYDAL
Rydal Sheepdog Trials
Ambleside showground field. Early/mid August.

Opposite: Grasmere Church

GRASMERE
Grasmere Sports
On the large field adjacent to the main public car park/coach park. Largest and most popular of the traditional Lake District sports days, with a very comprehensive programme of events, including hound trailing and Cumberland and Westmorland wrestling. Held on the third Thursday after the first Monday in August.
☎ 015394 32127

Grasmere Rush-bearing
St Oswald's Church. Held on the Saturday nearest to St Oswald's Day (5 August). Rush-bearing goes back to the days when churches had earth floors, made more tolerable by a covering of rushes, which were ceremonially renewed each year.

Lakes Artists Exhibition
The Hall, Grasmere. Open daily late July–early September each year.

LANGDALE
Langdale Show
Traditional Lakeland country show held in mid August.

CONISTON
Coniston Water Festival
Late May and late July/early August.
☎ 015394 41707

HAWKSHEAD
Hawkshead Show
Hawkshead Hall Farm. Mid August.
☎ 015394 36609

LOWICK
Lowick Show
Early September. ☎ 015394 36364

BROUGHTON IN FURNESS
Millom and Broughton Show
West Park, Broughton in Furness.
Late August.
☎ 01229 772556

St Martin's parish church include buildings 300 years or more old; many houses were lived in by boatmen or fishermen.

The large number of shops includes a high proportion catering for visitors and there are inns and restaurants to suit virtually all tastes. Worth a special mention is the very old Hole in t'Wall, formerly the New Hall Inn, tucked away in the old part of the village.

By the lake shore, the promenade is a bustling place in high season, with all kinds of boating activity contributing to the holiday atmosphere. The characteristic boatmen's huts, replacements of 19th-century structures, are known locally as 'cushion huts'.

Sitting high above the promenade is the Belsfield Hotel, one

PLACES TO VISIT IN BOWNESS

Royalty Cinema
Crag Brow (the main road towards Windermere village). Three screens. Up-to-date films. ☎ 015394 43364

Blackwell – the Arts and Crafts House
1 1/2 miles south of Bowness, opens 7 days a week 10.00 to 17.00 (reduced hours in winter) ☎ 015394 46139

Beatrix Potter Experience
Crag Brow. A fairly recent conversion of a large old laundry building into two visitor attractions. The first is a small, versatile **theatre** offering occasional productions of high quality, exhibitions and some musical events. The autumn festival of theatre and music features artists of international repute.

The World of Beatrix Potter is a series of animated tableaux depicting the animals created by the great children's writer, supported by audio-visual displays and shop. Tearoom with light meals. Open every day apart from Christmas Day and the occasional shutdown for refurbishment of the exhibits. Easter to the end of September 10.00 to 1830, October to Easter 10.00 to 16.00.
☎ 015394 88444

St Martin's Church
Built in 1483. The east window includes glass believed to have been brought from Cartmel Priory following the Dissolution in 1539. Wooden statue of St Martin. Old font. 19th-century restoration has resulted in a light and bright interior. Not always open.

Windermere Steamboat Museum

About 1km (0.6 mile) from the centre of Bowness, along Rayrigg Road, this attractive modern museum, on the lake shore, displays the history of boating, including speedboat racing, on the lake. Pride of place goes to the collection of lovely old steam launches, evocative of the late 19th and early 20th centuries, when the families living in the recently built gracious houses nearby would steam around the lake either individually or as part of the frequent regattas, as a favourite leisure activity. Steam launch trips in season. Model boat rally (two-day event) during the second week in May. Annual steamboat association rally in late July.

Museum shop; disabled access; light refreshments; picnic area. Open daily from Easter to October, 10.00–17.00.
☎ 015394 45565

Tourist Information Centre

Centrally situated near the boat landings. Includes Countryside Theatre with talks and audio-visual displays. ☎ 015394 42895

Public Tennis Courts and Pitch and Put Golf Course

Glebe Road.
Booking at hut behind Tourist Information Centre.

Spirit of the Lake,

Shepherd's Boatyard, Glebe Road, Bowness.
Luxury cruises. Speedboat rides.
☎ /fax 015394 48322

Windermere Lake Cruises

Operating from Lakeside, Bowness and Waterhead.
☎ 015395 31188; fax 015395 31947

Windermere Outdoor Adventure Watersports Centre

Operated by South Lakeland District Council on the eastern shore of the lake about 1km (0.6 mile) north of Bowness village. Courses in dinghy sailing, canoeing, windsurfing etc. Open mid-March–end November, 09.00–17.00 daily.
☎ 015394 47183

of the early mansions built in a commanding position to provide fine views over the lake. The second owner, in the later part of the 19th century, was the industrialist H.W. Schneider, whose wealth was founded on iron, steel and armaments at Barrow in Furness. Each day Schneider walked down through the garden to his waiting steam launch, *Esperance*. His butler followed close behind with breakfast on a silver tray, for consumption during the sail down the lake to Lakeside. Here a private train (Schneider was a director of the Furness Railway Company) took the great man on to his business at Barrow.

Car parking – small – Crag Brow near the cinema. Large – Rayrigg Road (short and long stay sections). Largest – follow Glebe Road, passing a small car park, to reach Braithwaite Fold, near the caravan site. Some way from the village, but served in season by a 'road train'.

Troutbeck

North of Windermere lies Troutbeck. It is very much a linear village, a series of hamlets loosely strung together along the valley side well above the Trout Beck from which its name is derived. The best feature is the fine array of traditional vernacular Lakeland buildings, largely dating from the 17th century. Brunskill's *Vernacular architecture of the Lake Counties* sets out a fascinating trail from one end of the village to

the other, with detailed descriptions of more than 30 of these buildings. Included is one of the 'spinning galleries' in a building across the road from the post office stores. There are two inns, one of which – the Mortal Man – has a famous sign.

The views across the valley to the ridge which, from the right, includes Yoke, Ill Bell and Froswick, are very fine.

Townend

At the south end of the village, is a former 'statesman's (yeoman farmer) house of 1626 which was the home of the Browne family for more than 300 years. Since 1943 in the care of the National Trust, the interior has been kept as it was during occupation by the family. Admission charge. Open late March–end October, Tuesday–Friday, Sundays and Bank Holiday Mondays. ☎ 015394 32628.

Jesus Parish Church

On the site of an earlier church by the side of the main Windermere to Patterdale road (A592) in the valley bottom, the present structure dates from 1736, with restoration in the 19th and 20th centuries. The churchyard is noted for its daffodils. Inside, most notable is the large east window by the Pre-Raphaelite painter Edward Burne-Jones, allegedly assisted by his friends William Morris and Ford Maddox Brown who happened to be on a fishing holiday nearby at the time.

Holehird Gardens

To the right of the Windermere to Patterdale road (A592) about 1km (0.6 mile) north of the mini roundabout on the fringe of Windermere village. Entered by a drive past an obvious lodge, Holehird is a grand house of the mid-19th century, twice rented as a summer holiday home by Beatrix Potter's family and now in use as a Cheshire Home. A large area of the garden has been taken over by the Lakeland Horticultural Society and is beautifully maintained by the members. The national collections of hydrangeas and astilbes are housed here. Open to visitors. Car Park. No charge, but donation requested.

AMBLESIDE, RYDAL, GRASMERE AND LANGDALE

Ambleside

Situated close by the River Rothay 1.5km (1 mile) from the north end of Windermere, the stone-built market town of **Ambleside** has a fine scenic backdrop of mountains. Understandably popular with visitors, but still a thriving community in winter, the town seems large by Lake District standards; its truly compact size can best be appreciated by climbing a little way up one of the surrounding hillsides.

The oldest part of the town rises steeply to the east of the main street, from North Road by the Salutation, an old coaching inn, up to Smithy Brow and Chapel Hill, with narrow streets and old stonework making an attractive combination. How Head, close to the converted chapel, dates in part from the 15th century, and is almost certainly the oldest building in town.

Stock Ghyll, a tributary of the River Rothay, tumbles down a famous waterfall, **Stock Ghyll Force**, signposted along the road behind the Salutation. The fall is just a few minutes walk away. Between the foot of the fall and the town centre was an impressive array of water-powered mills, which produced bobbins, processed fabrics and ground corn. Although the mills are long closed and most have been demolished or converted, the view from the main street bridge upstream along the beck still gives some impression of those industrial days.

The modern town has many shops, both for basic needs and for visitor requirements. Particularly plentiful are those selling climbing, mountain walking and general outdoor activity clothing and gear. Similarly, there is no shortage of inns, cafés and restaurants. The combination of cinema, vegetarian restaurant and mini-shopping arcade at Zeffirelli's in Compston Road is unique in Lakeland.

All in all, Ambleside is a pleasant place in which to wander. Many will continue, either on

PLACES TO VISIT IN AMBLESIDE

Bridge House
A curious little structure which has graced a million post cards, bestriding Stock Beck by the side of the main road. Formerly the apple store to Ambleside Hall.

National Trust information centre and small shop.

Old Stamp House,
Church Street
Where William Wordsworth worked as Distributor of Stamps.

St Mary's Church
At the bottom end of Compston Road 19th-century with spire, very unusual in Lakeland. Colourful mural of rush bearing and also sculpture by the celebrated Josefina de Vasconcellos, a local resident.

Rothay Park
Large grassed areas behind the church, fine for picnics and children's play. Footpaths to the river.

The Armitt
Just beyond Bridge House Esteemed local history library and collection, recently expanded into an interactive exhibition of Lakeland life and times. Natural history watercolours by Beatrix Potter. Gift shop. Admission charge. Open all year, daily 10.00–17.00.
☎ 015394 311212

Adrian Sankey
Glass-blowing workshop close to Bridge House. Café/restaurant. Open daily 09.00–17.30.
☎ 015394 31139

Bowls, Tennis, Putting Public facilities beside the church.

Market Very small. On car park in Kelsick Road, opposite the library. Wednesday.

Hayes Garden Centre
Lake Road. A considerable all-weather visitor attraction.
☎ 01539433434

Steamer Pier, Waterhead
☎ 015394 32225

Stagshaw Gardens
National Trust.
Situated along the A591 Windermere road, 500m beyond the Waterhead traffic lights. Narrow turning to left, easily missed. Very much a spring garden, open to visitors 1 April–end June, daily 10.00–18.30. No visitor facilities.

Galava
1st-century Roman fort on low-lying land by the head of the lake, beyond the lakeside gardens. National Trust. Foundations only.

Sail 'n' Dine
Jetty at Langdale Chase Hotel, on A591 1.5km (1 mile) south of Waterhead. Sailing with meals provided on board. End of March to end of October. Sailing tuition also available.
☎ 015242 74255; Yacht mobile: 0421 836 470

Tourist Information Centres:
Ambleside, Central Buildings, opposite the new Market Cross development.
☎ 015394 32582

Waterhead, Public car park.
☎ 015394 32729

PLACES TO VISIT IN RYDAL

Rydal Hall

A large building mostly of the 18th and 19th centuries, but with older portions. The home of the Le Fleming family for about 300 years, now used as a conference and retreat centre by the Diocese of Carlisle. The house is not open to the public. The formal gardens were laid out by Thomas Mawson in 1909 and the parkland extends almost to Ambleside. There are large camping areas and a youth centre used by organisations such as Boy Scouts and Girl Guides.

Rydal Beck cascades through the grounds, with two good waterfalls; the oldest 'viewing house' in the country (1669) is carefully sited below the lower fall, but is not open to the public. This fall has been painted by many artists, including Joseph Wright of Derby (see special feature on painters, page 182).

A right of way runs behind the house and on through the park land and there is limited access to the gardens. Sculpture by Josefina de Vasconcellos of Ambleside. Teashop behind the house.

Rydal Mount

At the top of the no through road, a substantially extended old farmhouse rented and occupied by William Wordsworth and family from 1813 to 1850, the last 37 years of his life. Pleasant gardens and lake views. The house belongs to descendants of Wordsworth and contains some of his furniture and belongings.

Car Park. Admission charge (reciprocal discounted tickets with Dove Cottage and Wordsworth House are available). Open March–October 09.30–17.00; November–February 10.00–16.00 (closed Tuesdays in winter). ☎ 015394 33002; fax 015394 31738.

St Mary's Church

Built by Lady LeFleming of Rydal Hall in 1823, originally as a chapel – Wordsworth was a chapel warden. His family pew is at the front on the north side. Dr. Arnold and family, who lived nearby, had the opposite pew. The church was considered to be rather cramped and was enlarged in 1884.

Dora's Field

National Trust. Just behind the church, this piece of land was purchased by Wordsworth in 1826, when he was at risk of eviction from Rydal Mount His intention was to build a house on the land. However, he stayed at Rydal Mount and later gave the land to his daughter Dora. The fine display of daffodils to be seen in spring was not the subject of the famous poem!

Above left: Angle Tarn near Bowfell. *Above right*: Dungeon Ghyll Waterfall in Langdale. *Below*: The Langdale Pikes from High Close.

Above: The Bridge House, Ambleside. **Below left**: Elterwater.
Below right: Slater's Bridge, Little Langdale.

foot or by car along Lake Road or Borrans Road to Waterhead at the lakeside, an outpost where hotels and boat landings contribute to the holiday atmosphere. The steamer pier is the northern terminus of the scheduled services. Close by are lakeside gardens and the 1st-century Roman fort of Galava.

The largest car park is by the side of the main A591 road to Grasmere and Keswick, just north of the town centre, opposite the attractive Charlotte Mason College, now part of St Martin's College, Lancaster. Smaller car parks are found in Kelsick Road, opposite the library, and off Lake Road just south of the Kelsick Road junction. Further out of town along Lake Road, there is usually space at Low Fold car park. Waterhead has its own large car park.

Rydal

With a picturesque setting between the steep face of Nab Scar and the placid Rydal Water, the scattered village of **Rydal** is by the side of the A591 Ambleside to Grasmere and Keswick road. Were it not for **Rydal Mount** and **Rydal Hall** the village would scarcely warrant a mention.

However, the small lake is very beautiful and there are attractive walks linking it with the better known Grasmere. The start (or finish!) of the Fairfield Horseshoe mountain walk is at Rydal and a very good, but more modest, ramble is

along the former 'coffin track', starting near Rydal Mount. (see Walks at the end of the chapter).

Grasmere

A major and readily accessible visitor attraction, **Grasmere** village sits by the head of the lake in a broad vale at the foot of Dunmail Raise, where the main A591 road climbs over a low pass to Keswick. The village is overlooked by mountains. Silver Howe, the sharply pointed Helm Crag and Stone Arthur are most prominent, but the greater heights of Helvellyn and Fairfield are also close by.

Until comparatively recent times the vale was a centre of farming, mainly sheep, with a rural tranquillity which was highly acclaimed by the distinguished tourists of the 18th century. Thomas Gray, one of the earliest of these literary visitors, waxed eloquent – 'Not a single red tile, no flaring gentleman's house, or garden walls, break in upon the repose of this little unsuspected paradise; but all is peace, rusticity, and happy poverty in its neatest, most becoming attire'. Whether Gray had any evidence of the happiness or otherwise of those suffering the poverty is not recorded. Anyway, whilst the vale is still beautiful, Grasmere itself is now a much more sophisticated place, with tourism replacing farming as the main local occupation.

The village is large, with separate hamlets at Town End

and Town Head, and is well served with shops, hotels and a small number of cafés/teashops. The lake is almost 1.5km (1 mile) in length, with a wooded island adding to its charm. Rowing boats may be hired from a site close to the village. Fittingly for a place which has so excited literary figures over the years, this is very much Wordsworth country, with three residences, a dedicated museum and his family grave all to be seen.

Likewise, it is hardly surprising that painters have also long had an interest in this rather special place. Two galleries now offer original works and, in one case, a large choice of prints for purchase.

A car and coach park is prominent by the southern entrance to the village. There are more car parks a little way along the road which turns off to the left, opposite the church, and at the far end of the village, beside the village hall.

Langdale

Easily reached from the M6 motorway and the railway station at Windermere, for the great majority of visitors **Great Langdale** provides the readiest access to the heart of Lake District mountain country. The

---

PLACES TO VISIT IN GRASMERE

Dove Cottage

A former inn, the Dove and Olive Branch, at Town End hamlet on the east side of the A591 main road. The home of William, Mary and Dorothy Wordsworth from 1799 to 1808, when the increasing size of the family necessitated a move to larger accommodation.

Much of William's best and most youthful work was done at Dove Cottage. Many of the great literary figures of the day, including Samuel Taylor Coleridge, Thomas De Quincey, Sir Walter Scott and Robert Southey, were hosted here. The cottage is still much the same as it was in Wordsworth's time. An agricultural building at the rear has been converted into a museum housing the William Wordsworth Trust's collection of manuscripts, books and paintings. Special exhibitions each year.

Cottage and museum open to visitors daily 9.30–17.30, but some winter closing, usually mid January to mid February.

Small car park. Shop. Admission charge, but reciprocal tickets with Rydal Mount and Wordsworth House. ☎ 015394 35544

Tearoom open daily 10.00–17.00. Restaurant open Fridays, Saturdays and most evenings in season 18.30 to 21.30 (last orders). ☎ 015394 35268; fax 015394 35748

(cont'd...)

St Oswald's Parish Church
In the village centre. Largely 13th and 14th century with later extensions. The rendered exterior is unprepossessing, but the interior is full of interest, not least the curious lop-sided effect brought about by enlargement, a memorial to William Wordsworth and a *Madonna and Child* by Ophelia Gordon Bell, of the Heaton Cooper family. The Wordsworth family grave and that of Hartley Coleridge are at the rear of the churchyard.

Old Rectory
Opposite the church. Home of the Wordsworths from 1811 to 1813, a very unhappy time as two of their children died during this period, and the house itself was not very satisfactory, being cold and damp. Not open to the public.

Sara Nelson's
A tiny shop close to the church, formerly the village school room. Gingerbread made to a secret recipe has been sold here since the middle of the 19th century.

National Trust Shop
Across the road from the gingerbread shop.

Heaton Cooper
Overlooking the central village green, a prominent gallery displaying and selling the work of several members of the Heaton Cooper family. Some original works but mainly prints of favourite Lakeland scenes, of various sizes and with choices of frame available.
☎ 015394 35280

Tourist Information Office
Tucked in behind Grasmere Garden Centre, opposite the church.
☎ 015394 35245

Allan Bank
Prominent white house on high ground to north-west of village centre. Occupied by the Wordsworths from 1808 to 1811, although William had earlier expressed disapproval of its white colour and its impact on the landscape. He planted some screening trees. Not open to public.

Rowing Boats
Small boat hire premises a short distance along the road past the garden centre.

head of the valley is dominated by the great bulk of the Crinkle Crags and Bowfell, while the ice-scraped sides embrace a fine example of a textbook U-shaped valley. Most characteristic, and visible from far away on the approach to Lakeland, are the Langdale Pikes, by no means the highest of the mountains but unmistakable in their uncompromisingly rocky outline. Rock climbers have long practised their skills on buttresses such as Gimmer Crag.

The lower reaches of the valley are altogether more gentle, with woodland and the rather elusive small lake of Elterwater. Below Skelwith Bridge the Great Langdale Beck becomes the River Brathay for its short remaining journey to the head of Windermere.

The whole of this area is prime walking country, ranging from a gentle stroll between **Skelwith Bridge** and **Elterwater** village to the hard day's march to **Scafell Pikes** and back.

The two villages in Great Langdale are Elterwater and **Chapel Stile**. Elterwater sits attractively at the foot of a great common, surely on a fine day one of the best picnic sites imaginable, with the immensely popular Brittania Inn providing snug comfort in less clement weather. South of the village an immense quarry provides the fine, highly esteemed, green Lakeland slate.

Chapel Stile is also well situated below the wide bulk of Silver Howe, with the solidly built parish church prominent. By the side of the main road, a little way short of the village, is Wainwright's Inn, a hotel and bar managed by the Langdale timeshare group.

Skelwith Bridge is merely a hamlet at an important road junction, with hotel and bar and the Kirkstone Gallery. Each village has a general store.

Car parks are to be found:
1. in a former quarry on the right, a little way past Skelwith Bridge
2. opposite the Brittania Inn, Elterwater village
3. on the lower part of Elterwater Common
4. opposite the New Dungeon Ghyll Hotel
5. on the right just beyond the New Dungeon Ghyll Hotel
6. at the Old Dungeon Ghyll Hotel.

As the valley road in Great Langdale seems to be heading for a dead end by the Old Dungeon Ghyll, a sudden twist takes it past Wall End Farm and then steeply (25 per cent) uphill to Blea Tarn, where there is another car park and wonderful views back to the Langdale Pikes.

The subsequent descent is into **Little Langdale**, another fine valley, less dramatic than its bigger neighbour but with its own little tarn and with mountains such as Wetherlam, Pike of Blisco and the Crinkle Crags all close in view. From the junction at the foot of the hill, the road to the right climbs over one of the great passes, Wrynose, to the Duddon valley. The beck from Little Langdale Tarn tumbles down Colwith Force (waterfall) on its way to Elterwater. The valley has no villages but the Three Shires Inn, with a hamlet including a part-time post office, is a focal point.

PLACES TO VISIT IN LANGDALE

Holy Trinity Church, Brathay
Italianate structure of 1836 on an open site above the River Brathay, a little way beyond Clappersgate. Fine wood carving and brass memorials inside.

Kirkstone Gallery, Skelwith Bridge
Extensive gallery/shop, with Lake District slate for sale, both natural and manufactured into a variety of fireplaces, ornaments, etc. Good teashop with light meals. ☎ 015394 34002

Holy Trinity Church, Chapel Stile
On the site of an earlier chapel, this sturdy, no-nonsense, structure is of the mid 19th century. Inside there is good wood carving and a window with brightly coloured glass in the south wall. Before 1821 burials were not allowed here and the coffins had to be carried up the valley side and over the top to Grasmere.

Dungeon Ghyll
A ravine descending precipitously from the Langdale Pikes behind the New Dungeon Ghyll Hotel. There are three waterfalls in the ravine, of which the lowest may be safely visited by those prepared to climb up the path from the hotel. The two upper falls form part of a sporting route to the top of Harrison Stickle or Pike of Stickle.

New Dungeon Ghyll Hotel, Old Dungeon Ghyll Hotel
Two old, traditional, hostelries, which have long been landmarks in Great Langdale and the starting points for important walkers' routes. Now serving a wide variety of food and drink to suit all tastes.

Gig House Gallery
Elterwater
Original paintings by artists in all media, both local and from further afield.

CONISTON, HAWKSHEAD, GRIZEDALE, NEAR AND FAR SAWREY

Coniston

Beautifully situated between mountains and lake, the former mining and quarrying village of **Coniston** has transformed itself into a popular destination for visitors, full of bustling activity at most times of year. Shops and inns, such as the 16th-century Black Bull, patronised by Coleridge and De Quincey, offer plenty of choice in the compact village centre.

Best known of the shapely group of mountains overlooking Coniston is **Coniston Old Man,** most southerly of the great Lakeland peaks and a particular favourite locally.

Coniston Water is very attractive; several of the locations used by Arthur Ransome in his *Swallows and Amazons* children's stories are based on actual places on and around this lake and Windermere. In the 1950s and 60s it became well known nationally and internationally when the Campbells, Sir Malcolm and Donald, father and son, made several attempts, successful and otherwise, on the world water speed record here. The attempts ended in tragedy in 1967 when *Bluebird* somersaulted at about 483km (300 miles) per hour. Donald's body was eventually found more than 30 years later. There is a simple memorial at the junction of Tilberthwaite Avenue and Ruskin Avenue.

Across the lake the impressive house with the fine situation overlooking both lake and mountains is **Brantwood,** home of John Ruskin, philosopher, poet, painter and social reformer, from 1872 until his death in 1900. In many ways, Ruskin was to Coniston what Wordsworth was to Grasmere and Rydal. A foot ferry service links Brantwood to Coniston during the season, with limited Sunday sailings in winter. Ruskin's grave is at the back of the churchyard in the middle of Coniston; the memorial is of local stone, carved to designs by the celebrated local historian W.G. Collingwood, for many years Ruskin's secretary. The designs depict Ruskin's principal interests – The Guild of St George craft organisation, poetry, music, nature, science and some of his principal writings such as *The Stones of Venice* and *Seven Lamps of Architecture.*

The main car park, with Tourist Information Office and public conveniences is close to the centre, accessed from Tilberthwaite Avenue. A smaller car park is on the site of the former railway station, steeply uphill along Station Road. There is also car parking by the lake shore.

Hawkshead

East of Coniston is the popular village of Hawkshead. Once a remote, off the beaten track, self-sufficient little market

PLACES TO VISIT IN CONISTON

Coniston Old Hall
1.5km (1 mile) from the village centre, close to the lake shore. The oldest surviving building in the area, claimed to be based on an ancient defensive pele tower. Now used for farming and as reception for a camping site. Not open to the public but a right of way passes close by.

Copper Mines Valley
1.5km (1 mile) above Coniston. Heart of the formerly great mining industry with remains and shafts scattered over a wide area. Attempts are being made to provide limited visitor facilities, including museum and interpretation displays.

St Andrew's Parish Church
On the site of an older chapel, the present building is of the 19th century, including a general renovation in 1891. Ruskin memorial in graveyard.

Lake Ferry
The *Coniston Launch*, accommodating more than 50 passengers, plies between Coniston, Monk Coniston (Waterhead), Brantwood and Torver several times a day in season – late March to the end of October. A restricted timetable operates during the winter. A very useful link to Brantwood, with a small discount on combined ticket. Also special interest cruises in high season. Free car parking at Waterhead. ☎ /fax 015394 36216

Gondola
A beautiful steam launch of 1859, abandoned and derelict for many years. Restored and operated by the National Trust. Operates to a scheduled daily timetable from late March to the end of October, weather permitting. Sailings from the Coniston jetty, at the end of the cul-de-sac Lake Road (less than 1km – 0.6 mile) start at 11.00, except on Saturdays, when commencement is about an hour later. Calling points at Brantwood and at Park-a-Moor at the south-east end of the lake. ☎ 015394 41288

Coniston Boating Centre
Sheltered bay with gravel beach close to the Coniston jetty (see above). Operated by the National Park Authority. Electric launches, rowing boats, sailing dinghies and Canadian canoes for hire. Firm slipway, car parking, picnic area and café. ☎ 015394 41366

Brantwood

Elegant 18th-century house purchased, extended and renovated by John Ruskin in 1872, and his home until his death in 1900. Became one of the greatest literary and artistic centres in Europe. Displays of Ruskin's drawings and watercolours; video programme; bookshop; special exhibitions; tearoom with light meals; nature trails; lake shore and woodland gardens. Open to visitors daily mid March–mid November 11.00–17.30; Wednesday–Sunday 11.00–16.00 in winter. Closed Christmas Day and Boxing Day. ☎ 015394 41396

Ruskin Museum

Small museum in Yewdale Road, renovated in 1997. Specialises in Ruskin memorabilia. ☎ 015394 41132

Summitreks Ltd

14, Yewdale Road, Coniston   Adventure activities on lake and mountains. Equipment for hire. ☎ 015394 41212

Tourist Information Office

By the main car park. ☎ 015394 41533

Above: Coniston Water from Bank Ground Farm with the village and Coniston Old Man in the background.
Right: The Coniston Boating Centre where boats may be hired.

town, set in the gentle countryside of south Lakeland, **Hawkshead** is now readily accessible to visitors and has become a very popular place indeed. With white-painted buildings, many of considerable antiquity, clustered around small squares and narrow alleyways, it is quite unlike any other Lake District town or village.

Partial pedestrianisation has been a great advantage, making Hawkshead one of the best places to wander on foot. The mixture of shops, including a National Trust shop, caters well for both residents and visitors, whilst four inns, tea and coffee shops all compete to provide varied refreshments. The associations with William Wordsworth and Beatrix Potter add considerably to visitor interest (see below).

Car parking is close to the village centre, approached from the main by-passing road.

PLACES TO VISIT IN HAWKSHEAD

Hawkshead Grammar School

Across the village street from the car park. Founded in 1585 by locally born Edward Sandys who became Archbishop of York. The present building dates from 1675 and the school continued in use until 1909. Wordsworth was a pupil here from 1779 to 1787. A desk on which he carved his initials can still be seen. Upstairs is a famous old bible and initials carved on a windowsill by Wordsworth's brother John. Open to the public Easter–October, daily 10.00–12.30, 13.30–17.00; Sundays 13.00–17.00. Closes 16.30 in October. Admission charge.

St Michael and All Angels Church

Part of the structure, including the tower, is more than 700 years old, side aisles being added in about 1500. Wordsworth's 'snow white church upon her hill'. The white-painted rough cast was removed in 1875/76. Sandys family private chapel. Primitive dug-out chest about 400 years old. Season of summer evening concerts.

Ann Tyson's Cottage

Reached through a narrow passage by the Methodist church. Boys from the Grammar School, including William Wordsworth, lodged here with Ann Tyson for some years. Not open to the public.

Red Lion Inn

Main Street

Claimed to be a 15th-century coaching Inn. Two interesting carved figures high on the front wall, one depicting a farmer taking his pig to market and the other of a man holding the whistle which was blown at market opening time.

Grizedale

A substantial area of land to the south of Hawkshead, between Coniston Water and Windermere has long been covered by the commercial forestry of the former Forestry Commission, now Forest Enterprises.

In recent years there has been a more enlightened and visitor friendly approach to the operation of these vast woodlands than was previously the case. More regard is paid to the conservation of natural life and the environment generally; planting in this area is quite diverse in species and there are substantial clear areas.

A particular feature of this forest is that visitors are positively encouraged by the provision of a comprehensive visitor centre, the creation of numerous trails for walkers and cyclists and, by no means least, a great number of diverse and ingenious **sculptures in wood** along

---

Beatrix Potter Gallery
Main Street
National Trust
The former office of Beatrix's solicitor husband, William Heelis, now open as a gallery displaying a selection of the 500 or so watercolours and drawings which provided the wonderful illustrations for the famous books. The selection on display is changed each year; enthusiasts will be able to recognise some of the buildings of Hawkshead and district which provide the background to the characters in the books. Open from April to the end of October.
☎ 015394 36355

Old Courthouse
A gatehouse which is the only surviving portion of the former Hawkshead Hall, used by the monks of Furness Abbey as an outpost from which they administered the estates in this area. Later used as a courthouse, hence the name. 0.6km (0.3 mile) along the B5286 towards Ambleside. Nothing to see inside but key is available from either the National Trust shop or the Beatrix Potter Gallery in Hawkshead

Trout Fishing, Esthwaite Water
The Boathouse, on the west side of the lake.
Brown and rainbow trout may be fished from hire boats and from the shoreline. Rods available for hire. Fly-fishing tuition can be given (minimum two days' notice). ☎ 015394 36541

Tourist Information Centre
Main car park. ☎ 015394 36525

most of the trails, adding interest and a touch of whimsicality.

Grizedale Visitor Centre

Forestry interpretation exhibits of many kinds. Shop. Tearoom, with light meals available. Art/craft gallery. Children's play area. Cycle hire. Theatre in the Forest – plays, talks and musical concerts. Car parks at the centre and further afield for walks or rides on the forest trails. Trail maps available at visitor centre. Forest trails of varying length as indicated by the map at the visitor centre. One of the best walks is along the designated **Silurian Way**, which has about 80 of the famous sculptures.

☎ 01229 860010

Near Sawrey

An attractive village along the B5285 road from Hawkshead to the Windermere ferry, close to Esthwaite Water. The prime attraction is Beatrix Potter's house, **Hill Top**, which has became a Mecca for Beatrix Potter enthusiasts from all over the world. Owned by the National Trust, it is kept almost exactly as it was in her day. Many of the scenes which provide the background to the characters in the illustrations of the famous children's books can be found in and around Near Sawrey.

Also of interest is the Tower Bank Arms, with its clock, a traditional village inn which is in National Trust ownership, a very rare situation indeed.

The National Trust car park is not very easy to find. From the Windermere approach it is about 100m past the Tower Bank Arms, on the left.

Hill Top was purchased by Beatrix Potter with the earnings from her first book, *The Tale of Peter Rabbit*, and a small legacy. For some years she spent as much time as she could at Hill Top, furnishing it very much to her own taste. During this time she wrote the other children's books. After her marriage in 1913 she moved to nearby Castle Cottage, not open to the public, keeping Hill Top as a studio, study and private place of relaxation. Open to the public late March–end of October, Saturdays–Wednesdays and Good Friday, 10.30–16.30. Shop open every day 10.00–17.00. Admission charge.

☎ 015394 36269

Far Sawrey

Further along the road towards the Windermere ferry, another quite substantial village with a hotel, a general store and the parish church.

Newby Bridge, Lakeside, Haverthwaite and the Rusland Valley

In this area there are no towns or large villages, no mountains and no lake other than the southern tip of Windermere, so not surprisingly, this is one of the less busy parts of the district. In spite of that, there is a great deal here for visitors, and the

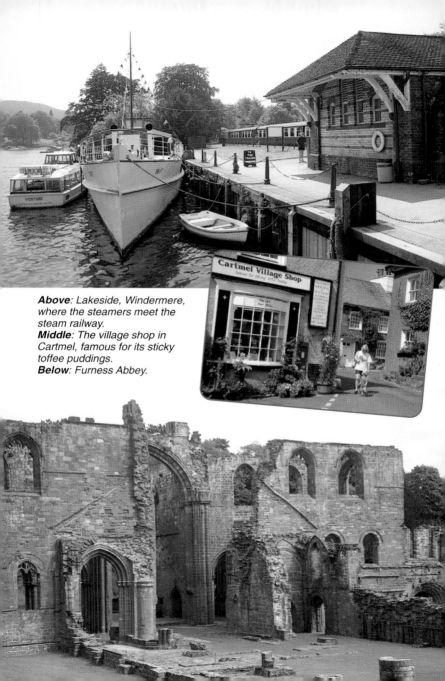

Above: Lakeside, Windermere, where the steamers meet the steam railway.
Middle: The village shop in Cartmel, famous for its sticky toffee puddings.
Below: Furness Abbey.

PLACES TO VISIT IN THE FAR SOUTH

Fell Foot Country Park

7 hectares (17 acres) of gardens and park at the foot of Windermere, accessed from the A 592 Newby Bridge to Bowness road. Owned by the National Trust. Formerly the garden of a grand house, long demolished, Fell Foot now offers car parks, formal garden, children's adventure playground, picnic areas, informal lake swimming – with care! – rowing-boat hire, slipway, toilets, shop and tearoom serving light lunches. There is a passenger ferry across the lake to Lakeside (see below). Occasional theatre productions. Charge per car. Open all year daily, park and garden: 09.00–19.00 (or dusk if earlier). Shop and tearoom - late March–end October, 11.00–17.00. ☎ 015395 31273

Newby Bridge

A large, impressive, stone-arched structure across the River Leven a short distance below the outfall from Windermere. A small settlement has grown around this important river crossing, including two sizeable hotels. Downstream of the bridge is the weir which regulates the water level in Windermere.

Lakeside

At the foot of Windermere, on the west side. The southern terminus of the scheduled 'steamer' service on the lake and the northern terminus of the Lakeside and Haverthwaite railway line. Interchange facility and combined tickets available.

Aquarium of the Lakes, Lakeside.

Opened in 1997, this major attraction displays the water, animal, bird and plant life of a typical Lakeland river from mountain top to the final outfall into Morecambe Bay. Multimedia presentation. Water laboratory. 'Underwater' walk. Shop. Restaurant/café. Wheelchair access to all areas. Admission charge. Open daily from 09.00 throughout year except Christmas Day. ☎ 015395 30153

Lakeside and Haverthwaite Railway

A branch line of the former Furness Railway, leaving the main line near Ulverston and terminating at Lakeside. Closed by British Railways in 1967. The length from Haverthwaite to Lakeside has been subsequently taken over by a preservation group and reopened as a visitor attraction, using steam locomotives for haulage. Depot with static railway exhibits and visitor facilities including car parking, shop, cafe, toilets, at Haverthwaite, 4km (2.5 miles) south-west of Newby Bridge on the A590 main road. Steam-hauled trains operate during the Easter period, weekends in April, and daily from early May to the end of October. ☎ 015395 31594

Artcrystal Clock Tower Buildings, Low Wood, Haverthwaite. Crystal glass engraving studio. Visitors welcome. Shop. Free admission. ☎ 015395 31796

Stott Park Bobbin Mill

1km (0.6 mile) north of Lakeside on the road to Hawkshead. Built in 1835, this was one of a large number of similar mills which combined the coppiced woodland and abundant water power of south Lakeland to produce vast quantities of wooden bobbins for the Lancashire cotton industry. The mill also used its lathes to make a variety of other wooden articles.

The introduction of plastic bobbins and the shrinkage of the cotton trade rapidly killed off the bobbin mills. Stott Park was one of the last to close, in 1971. The machinery was originally powered by a waterwheel, later a combination of water turbine and steam engine, and latterly by electricity.

Minimal restoration has been carried out by English Heritage and the mill is now a wonderful working museum with 19th-century machinery, powered by the steam engine on Tuesdays, Wednesdays and Thursdays and electrically on other days. Admission charge. Wheelchair access to ground floor. Toilets. Car park. Open late March–end October, daily 10.00–18.00 (last tour 17.00). ☎ 015395 31087

Abbots Reading Farm Museum and Rare Breeds Centre, Haverthwaite. Accessed from the main A590, Newby Bridge to Barrow road, turning north at Haverthwaite cross roads (signpost – Grizedale Forest), then right at Causeway End. 1km (0.6 mile) from the main road. Rare breeds of farm animals. Collection of agricultural machinery and bygones. Picnic area and children's play area. ☎ 015395 31203

OTHER PLACES TO VISIT

Duddon Furnace

Situated in woodland along the minor road which leaves the A595 immediately to the west of Duddon Bridge, Duddon Furnace was at the forefront of modern technology when constructed in 1736, close to the abundant supplies of iron ore, charcoal and water power required at the time for the production of iron.

Taken over by the National Park Authority, this is one of the best preserved furnaces in Britain. Ore store, charcoal barn and remains of the water system which powered the bellows are all evident.

Swinside Stone Circle

From Duddon Bridge, 3km (2 miles) along the A595 towards Hallthwaites take a right turn into a minor road to Broadgate. Continue uphill for just over 2km (1.25 miles), forking left before Cragg Hall. The circle is at the end of a long track. After Castlerigg, near Keswick, this is the finest stone circle in the Lake District.

Tourist Information Centre The Square, Broughton in Furness. ☎ 01229 716115

comparatively gentle, quiet, countryside is unfailingly attractive.

The Rusland Valley is a charming backwater served only by minor roads. From Grizedale head south through Satterthwaite and the tiny former industrial settlements of Force Mills and Force Forge. Even more minor is the direct road from Hawkshead, via the western shore of Esthwaite Water. From the south the road is from Haverthwaite, through Bouth. Rusland church has a commanding position in the valley with lovely views from the churchyard, which is the resting place of the children's author Arthur Ransome.

The Duddon Valley and Broughton in Furness

The **Duddon** is a long and beautiful valley which divides roughly into three recognisably different parts. The higher Duddon is wild and desolate, with the little road climbing high over the **Wrynose Pass** to Little Langdale. At the top 393m (1,290 feet) is the **Three Shires Stone** marking the pre-1974 meeting place of the former counties of Cumberland, Westmorland and Lancashire (Furness). From the junction at Cockley Bridge the road to Eskdale over the **Hard Knott Pass** rises even more steeply (30 per cent gradient in several places) to its summit at the same height as the Wrynose Pass.

Below Cockley Bridge the

hard landscape is much softened by trees and by farming. The trees are mostly the work of Forest Enterprise who have substantially clothed all but the higher slopes of Harter Fell, a shapely peak which dominates the west side of the middle Duddon. This part of the valley has a rich mixture of bare rock, rushing green waters and dense forest. Across the valley from Harter Fell the less spectacular side of the Coniston group of fells provides a continuous high wall along both upper and middle Duddon, unbreached by any road pass to Coniston or Torver.

The lower Duddon, below **Ulpha,** is softer in its landscape, but Caw and the Dunnerdale Fells to the east are still sufficiently high and rugged to permit only one steep minor road to pass over to Broughton Mills. From Ulpha a road crosses high moorland to reach Eskdale. With a final sharp little drop the valley road joins the main A595 road from Barrow in Furness to the Cumbrian coast, close to Duddon Bridge. Two kilometres (1.25 miles) further south the river broadens into the huge sandy expanse of the Duddon estuary, across which there are traditional (and possibly dangerous) rights of way on foot.

The River Duddon is highly regarded as arguably the most attractive river in Lakeland, a bold claim indeed which would be hotly disputed in Borrowdale and other places. It entranced William Wordsworth and inspired the great series of 'Duddon Sonnets'. The middle section, from a little way above Birks Bridge to Ulpha, is particularly fine. Much of this part of the river can be seen only from the riverside path.

There is no lake in the valley, no town and no significant village. **Seathwaite**, which has an inn, and Ulpha come closest to the latter status. Consequently, even in high season the valley remains comparatively quiet. Both Seathwaite and Ulpha do have small, simple, churches. That at Ulpha has fragments of 18th-century wall decorations, including the arms of Queen Anne.

Broughton in Furness

Broughton in Furness is a small former market town on the very edge of the National Park, 1.5km (1 mile) east of Duddon Bridge. The main road now bypasses the town, which has lost its market and its former importance. Broughton now has more of the character of a large village but remains well provided with shops, inns, restaurants and cafés.

The Georgian **Market Square** is quietly attractive and has changed little in 200 years or so. The obelisk was erected to commemorate the jubilee of King George III in 1810. Fish caught in the River Duddon were sold from the traditional slabs still *in situ* in the Market Place. Nearby are the old stocks. The former **Town Hall** building of 1766, now used for tourist information, at one time contained a number of small lock-up shops.

The large parish church has the predecessor Norman church as its south aisle.

To the north of the village centre the 14th-century defensive pele tower, **Broughton Tower**, is now incorporated into a school, closed to the public.

KENDAL, BURNESIDE AND STAVELEY

Kentmere Reservoir

Almost level walk on good tracks. 8km (5 miles).

From the small car park at Kentmere hamlet continue along the surfaced road and keep right at a junction in 400m or so. Where the road ends, bypass Hartrigg Farm and continue along a good track beneath the steep slopes of Rainsborrow Crag to the reservoir at the head of the valley, a very pleasant spot ideal for family picnics.

Cross to the other side of the valley, either at the dam or about 400m downstream. The return path passes through the ruins of Tongue House; there is the site of an ancient settlement at the rear. At Overend Farm keep right to pass below Hallow Bank hamlet, continuing along a walled lane (Low Lane) which angles up to join a surfaced roadway (High Lane).

At the first road junction turn right, downhill, then right again to return to the car park.

WINDERMERE, BOWNESS AND TROUTBECK

1 ⋀ Orrest Head

2.25km (1.5 miles). A very short but quite steep little walk, often a revelation for first time visitors as the views from the top, at 239m (784 feet), include much of the glory of southern Lakeland.

Cross the main A591 road close to the NatWest bank in Windermere. A signboard points the way along a broad, surfaced roadway, rising steeply as it weaves around substantial properties. There is soon a view of the lake. With more open country on the right, the surfaced road ends at Ellerey Wood Cottage. Continue along a broad, stony track, straight across at a junction of paths, now more level and possibly muddy.

Bend right along the side of a wall to rise again towards the summit, now visible to the left, above. Go left through a kissing-gate to reach the summit, where identification of the mountains is helped by a view board.

Return to the kissing-gate and down by the wall. Return either by the same route or make a circular walk as follows. By an arrowed post leave the outward route by continuing down by the wall to meet another track. Turn left, then right at another yellow arrow, along a broad, unsurfaced track, descending more gently.

Masses of wild rhododendron cover this hillside. Go right as the track forks, bear left at a junction by a high stone wall, and rejoin the surfaced road, turning right to go back to the village.

2 ⋀ Windermere shore and Rayrigg Wood 6km (3.75 miles)

A very varied short walk combining woodland with a very attractive section of lake shore. Views across the lake to Claiffe Heights.

From Crag Brow in Bowness, set off down Longlands Road, close to the cinema. Bear right to pass the rugby club and continue along the broad track into and through the woods, ignoring any side tracks. Emerge at Beemire Road, soon reaching Birthwaite Road. Turn left, then right at a signposted footpath. Follow this path to the main A59, reached close to St Mary's Church.

Turn left, then left again at once into another signposted path. Stay with this path as it descends steadily to Rayrigg Road. Cross the road to a gate and continue down by the side of an attractively rushing stream to the lake shore at Low Millerground, the site of a ferry many years ago. The housing for the call bell can still be seen. Turn left and take the delightful lake shore path, soon passing the landing stages and barbecue/picnic area at Rayrigg.

As the path ends, turn left to cross a meadow, back to Rayrigg Road. The ancient Rayrigg Hall is to the right. Turn right at the road, and walk by the roadside towards Bowness. Close to the Steamboat Museum turn left up a broad roadway to rejoin Longlands Road. Turn right to return to Crag Brow.

AMBLESIDE, RYDAL, GRASMERE AND LANGDALE

1 Wansfell Pike

484m (1,588 feet) Circular walk of 8km (5 miles) with a steep climb but no real difficulty underfoot. Ambleside's own mountain, with good views over the town and surrounding countryside.

Start up the road behind the Salutation, towards the waterfall, Stock Ghyll Force. After passing the fall, turn right at a junction of paths to head uphill towards the top of Wansfell Pike, visible ahead. The path is well used and has been much repaired to counter erosion. The way is never in doubt.

Continue over the top, along a path heading towards Troutbeck. Reach a cross wall in less than 1km (0.6 mile) and turn right on the far side. For about the same distance this path is a little vague but there is intermittent way marking. By an attractive little stream bear left to follow a rough roadway (Hundreds Road).

At a junction by the foot of this roadway, turn sharp right through a gate and descend to High Skelghyll Farm, continuing into Skelghyll Wood, where the celebrated Jenkin Crag viewpoint is passed. On reaching a major junction of paths, turn left, downhill to Waterhead or carry straight on to reach the main A591 road close to Hayes Garden Centre in Ambleside.

Above left: The Bluebird Cafe at Coniston. Here Donald Campbell tried fatally to break the world water speed record. *Above right*: Ivy Crag from Skelwith Bridge. *Below*: The Gondola steam boat on Coniston Water.

2▲ Fairfield Horseshoe
•••• A classic circular mountain walk of 17km (10.5 miles) over the peak of Fairfield – 873m (2,865 feet) – and several lesser heights. Broad ridges all the way without any scrambling. May be walked either way round; a start and finish at Rydal allows the steepest ground to be part of the ascent. Superb views, including Ullswater. The top of Fairfield is a confusing place in low cloud or mist and a compass is a great advantage.

Cars may be parked along one side of the cul-de-sac leading to Rydal Mount. Start up the roadway, passing Rydal Mount, soon climbing steeply up the side of Nab Scar, heading for the first peak, Heron Pike. The way along the ridge, over Great Rigg, to Fairfield is unmistakable.

After enjoying the views, turn right from Fairfield summit, almost due east and then south-east, towards the next summit, Hart Crag. Ignore any paths going to the left and continue to Dove Crag. Fork right to head due south towards Ambleside. The ridge descends over High Pike and Low Pike, with the path close to a wall most of the way down. The well-known High Sweden Bridge is below to the left, soon after the path wriggles among Brock Crags, and may be visited by making a small diversion along a connecting path.

The direct path continues to Low Sweden Bridge and a roadway behind Charlotte Mason College. Turn right and right again in Ambleside and walk beside the main road to the gate leading into Rydal Park. Finish the circuit along the broad trackway, passing behind Rydal Hall to regain the cul-de-sac road.

3▲ Loughrigg Terrace and the 'Coffin Road'
•••• A circuit of 8 km (5 miles) (*shorter version available*), which embraces all the best of Rydal and the Vale of Grasmere. A fair amount of comparatively gentle up and down, but no hills or mountains.

From the cul de sac road at Rydal, cross the main road, turning right for a short distance. Turn left to cross the River Rothay on a footbridge. Turn right after the bridge to follow a good path rising gently above Rydal Water.

After passing the far end of the lake there is a major junction of paths. *For the shorter version, turn right here, to descend through woodland to a bridge across the River Rothay. Cross the river and turn right to reach part of the White Moss car parking area, with public conveniences. Go up to the main road, cross, turn right for a few metres, and ascend a stony track to the left. At the top, join another track and turn right. This is the 'Coffin Road', clear on the ground all the way back to Rydal.*

For the full circuit go straight on at the junction. This is now the famous **Loughrigg Terrace**, giving wonderful views over the Vale of Grasmere. *At the far end of the Terrace a path to the left gives direct access to the summit of Loughrigg Fell 335m (1,099 feet).*

87

Bend slightly right to go through woodland, angling towards the road which comes over Red Bank from Elterwater. Join the road and descend to Grasmere.

Turn right by the church, walk to the main road, and take the minor road opposite. Pass Dove Cottage as this minor road climbs towards a tiny tarn. Leave the through road to keep uphill, then bend right by a seat. This is the 'Coffin Road' which loses its surface to become a rough trackway and then a bridleway as it keeps close under Nab Scar on its return to Rydal.

4A Helm Crag
●●●●

A challenging and well-shaped little peak of 398m (1,306 feet) overlooking Grasmere village and dominating all the views over the Vale from the south. The ascent is steep but is not too prolonged, and the circuit is barely 5km (3 miles) in distance.

There is a small car park in Easedale Road, the minor road which leaves Grasmere opposite the bookshop on the Green.

From this car park continue along Easedale Road, keeping straight on at the junction by Goody Bridge. At the end of the road go across a field towards a small hamlet, bending right, uphill, to a gate to start the ascent proper. The well-used path is initially to the left but then zig-zags a little as it gains height rapidly. The top is soon reached. Here, there are two great rocky outcrops on which many feel impelled to test their rock climbing skills.

Continue over the top and descend to the saddle between Helm Crag and Gibson Knott. Turn left to take a fairly vague path which goes steeply down the hillside until it joins the main Far Easedale path at the bottom. Turn left to return to the hamlet and Grasmere. *If you don't like the look of this path you can always return by the outward route. Alternatively, if you want a longer walk, continue over Gibson Knott and along the rather vague ridge. There is a path all the way. At the far end, bend left until the Far Easedale path is met. Turn left to descend the long valley back to the hamlet and Grasmere.*

LANGDALE

1A Scafell Pikes
●●●

At 978m (3,210 feet), the highest mountain in England, Scafell Pikes has an obvious attraction for those with the necessary strength and determination. Often climbed from Great Langdale by a quite long – 17.5km (11 miles) – return walk, but is more easily reached from Wasdale (see Chapter 9). No particular difficulty, but the ability to walk safely on rough rocks of all shapes and sizes is required.

Set off from the Old Dungeon Ghyll Hotel along the broad track up Mickleden, now part of the Cumbria Way. At a junction of paths by a footbridge keep left and tackle the prolonged and rugged ascent of Rosset Gill. There are path variations here, but all emerge at the same place at the top, just above Angle Tarn.

Drop a little, pass the tarn, and climb again, with Great End impressive ahead. Turn left at a cross paths and rise to Esk Hause, another junction of routes. Turn right here to climb up Calf Cove and gain the Scafell Pikes summit ridge, a broad, stony wilderness. Bear left along the ridge, passing Broad Crag on the way to the summit.

After due admiration of the extensive view, the easiest return by far is by retracing the outward route.

2 Langdale Pikes

Harrison Stickle – 736m (2,416 feet) – and Pike of Stickle – 709m (2,327 feet) – are fine mountains rising abruptly from the Great Langdale valley floor. A circuit of only 6km (3.75 miles) takes in both peaks but this is a prime example of the horizontal distance greatly underestimating the time and effort required. Despite the formidable appearance, there are no problems other than the prevailing steepness.

Park in either of the car parks close to the New Dungeon Ghyll Hotel and start up the engineered footpath beside the rushing waters of Stickle Ghyll, climbing remorselessly up to Stickle Tarn, a former reservoir which provided the abundant water power needed by the gunpowder mills at Elterwater. Bear left here and take the obvious path up the flank of Harrison Stickle. Across the tarn the great cliffs of Pavey Ark tower dramatically above the water. The cleft of Jack's Rake rises diagonally from right to left and has long been a challenge to walker/scramblers with steady nerves and heads. Occasional fatalities emphasise that this is no place for the casual and unprepared walker.

The top of Harrison Stickle is reached by turning up left. Return to the path behind the summit, turn left and descend to a wide, boggy area, aiming for the peak of Pike of Stickle, which is nothing like as impressive when seen from behind. This peak is reached by a little gentle scrambling up to the left.

Retrace steps from the peak and bear right along a path which joins the path descending from Harrison Stickle, between the two peaks. Turn right to follow this well-used route all the way back to the New Dungeon Ghyll.

To shorten the walk, Pike of Stickle can be omitted.

3↑ Skelwith Bridge and Elterwater

A truly gentle valley bottom ramble of 2.5km (1.5 miles), with a waterfall and Elterwater as prime attractions. This route offers the only opportunity of being close to the lake. The views up the valley, dominated by the Langdale Pikes, are superb.

Parking at Skelwith Bridge is limited; a disused quarry on the right a little further along the Langdale road provides a good alternative. If this car park is used, cross the road to find the path to Elterwater, which is joined after Skelwith Force. A left turn is then needed to view the waterfall.

From Skelwith Bridge take the path beside the Kirkstone Galleries and through the slate dressing works behind the galleries. Sandwiched between the River Brathay and the road, the path soon reaches the famous waterfall, not high, but with impressively surging power. Keep hold of small children!

Continue along the unmistakable path, across fields and through the bog woodland by the side of the lake, all too soon reaching Elterwater village opposite the Brittania Inn. To return, retrace the route or catch the bus.

With time and energy to spare continue along the valley; for the most part the road can be avoided. From Elterwater village, use the quarry approach road to access a signposted footpath reaching the road by Wainwright's Hotel, then another road-avoiding path on the left for a short distance, then along the road before reaching the near end of the former valley road. This road was replaced by the present road due to persistent flooding and now makes a good route for walkers as far as the New Dungeon Ghyll Hotel. From the back of the hotel a rougher but still acceptable path stays parallel with the road all the way to the Old Dungeon Ghyll Hotel, terminus of the valley bus service.

From Elterwater village to the Old Dungeon Ghyll Hotel is a very level walk of 8km (5 miles).

1↑ CONISTON AND TARN HOWS
Coniston Old Man

At 803m (2,635 feet), the highest point of the Coniston group of fells, the Old Man is the obvious first choice for a mountain walk. There are several routes from the Coniston area to the top, but the one below is the most straightforward. An out and back ascent is a total of 9km (5.5 miles); the full recommended circuit is 13km (8 miles). There are no difficulties involved.

Go past the Sun Inn and through Dixon Ground Farm, soon rising by the side of the turbulent Church Beck. Don't cross Miners' Bridge with its

waterfall, but keep left to ascend the hillside by a well-marked path.

The route goes through extensive old quarry workings before reaching Levers Water. From here the ascent is steep, with twists and turns before reaching the fine summit. The extensive views include the Isle of Man on a clear day.

Return routes are many and varied as more of the adjacent peaks can readily be included in a day's walk. The broad ridges of this group of fells are exceptionally kind underfoot. A good circuit is as follows:

Head north from the Old Man, dropping to Levers Hause before rising again to Swirl How (801m – 2,630 feet). A right turn here gives a descent along the Prison Band ridge, with a final rise to Wetherlam (762m – 2,501feet). From this last peak there are two footpaths to the right, both heading roughly south towards Coniston. The more westerly path drops quickly into the Red Dell valley, whilst the well-used more easterly path keeps its height for some distance along the broad south ridge of Wetherlam.

2 ∧ Tarn Hows
●●●● 3km (2 miles). One of Lakeland's finest jewels, a beautiful little lake in a partially wooded setting, with the Coniston fells providing the perfect backdrop. There is a National Trust car park adjacent to the tarn, reached from Coniston by the B5285 Hawkshead road making two left turns in the Hawkshead Hill area (signposted). From Hawkshead, turn right at Hawkshead Hill. A limited access for wheelchair users has been created by the Trust.

Walk down from the car park and continue around the tarn in either a clockwise or anti-clockwise direction; either is delightful and needs no route guidance.

WINDERMERE (SOUTH END)

1 ∧ Gummers How
●●● Only 321m (1,054 feet) in height, but a fine viewpoint at the south end of Windermere. Easily climbed from a nearby car park by a short walk of 2km (1.3 miles) there and back. Total ascent about 110m (361 feet).

Opposite Fell Foot Country Park leave the A592 to take a minor road rising steeply towards Bowland Bridge in the Winster valley. Near the summit of the road there is a car park on the right.

Cross the road and take the obvious footpath which heads straight to the summit of the shapely little peak. Return by the same route.

THE DUDDON DISTRICT

1⋀ Harter Fell
●●●
A steep uphill walk to the rocky summit of this shapely peak, at 653m (2,143 feet) the highest on the ridge separating the Duddon valley and Eskdale. Only 9km (5.5 miles) in length but quite demanding.

Use the Forest Enterprise car park by roadside above Birks Bridge.

Cross the river by the bridge and turn left at once on a footpath, soon rising, initially in woodland, to the farmstead of Birks, standing at the top of its open area. Turn right here. Above Birks, turn left for a short distance on a forest roadway, then turn right to find the start of what becomes a steep minor path heading straight for the summit of the mountain. The true top is the middle of the three rocky tors.

To return, first take the path towards Eskdale. When below the upper crags fork left to follow a distinct path descending to the pass linking the Duddon and Eskdale. Turn left to descend towards Grassguards Farm, forking right at a junction on the way down. By the farm, cross Grassguards Gill at a ford, then turn right immediately to continue through beech woodland down to the river. Don't cross the stepping stones but turn left again along the delightful but rough and often muddy riverside path back to the car park. The muddiest sections have been improved by the installation of boarded walkways. Apart from one section opposite Troutal the path stays close to the water.

2⋀ High level route to Coniston
●●●●
9.5km (6 miles), with suggested return over the mountain tops – 15km (9.25 miles) in total. No difficulty underfoot, but considerable ascent in total if done as a circuit.

From Seathwaite walk up the valley road towards the Wrynose Pass for more than 500m. Turn right at a footpath leading to a lane which is the access road to Seathwaite Tarn (reservoir). Turn right again. Shortly leave the lane to the right to continue along the unsurfaced Walna Scar Road, which crosses the ridge at a height of just over 600m (1,969 feet), close to the summit of Brown Pike, before descending obliquely below the slopes of Coniston Old Man to Coniston village.

For the energetic, a good return may be made by climbing Coniston Old Man (see Chapter 4), descending to Goat's Hawse between the Old Man and Dow Crag, and thence to Seathwaite Tarn. From the tarn start along the access roadway. After 500m. there is a choice of roadway or footpath back to Seathwaite.

SOUTH OF WINDERMERE

1A **Lyth and Winster Valleys**
● ● ● 39km (24 miles). A ride through lovely, undulating countryside, with the two traverses of Scout Scar as the only significant hill climbing. **Levens Hall** and/or **Sizergh Castle** can be visited.

From the traffic lights opposite the town hall in Kendal, ride up Allhallows Lane, then Beast Banks. At the junction fork right, go over the main A591, and continue to Underbarrow then, broadly straight on in an area of many lanes, to Crosthwaite.

Bear left, reach the main A5074 in 1km (0.6 mile), turn right and in less than 500m turn left on a minor road to Bowland Bridge.

The well-known Mason's Arms is a little further, on the right at Strawberry Bank. From Strawberry Bank head south for 2km (1.25 miles) along a little lane then turn sharp left to Cartmel Fell where there is a fine little church. After the church, rake back again, this time to the right, to continue south along the foot of Newton Fell for almost 5km (3 miles).

Turn left to head for Witherslack. Turn right in Witherslack to Town End, then turn right again, then left to ride along a minor road parallel with the main A590. Join the A590 briefly then, just after the junction with A5074, turn left into a lane leading to Levens village. Head north to Brigsteer, then turn sharp right to climb back over Scout Scar to Kendal.

The entrance to **Levens Hall** is from the A6, about 1km (0.6 mile) south-east of Levens village.
Sizergh Castle can be reached by turning right in Levens village. The distance is almost 2km (1.25 miles). From Sizergh Castle the direct (and lower level) route back to Kendal is by Sedgewick and Natland.

WINDERMERE, BOWNESS AND TROUTBECK

1A **Fell Foot, Lakeside and tour of the lake**
● ● ● 25km (15.5 miles) or 48km (30 miles). No real hills, pleasant countryside, lake views and plenty of interest.

Leave the promenade at Bowness by the road towards Newby Bridge (A592), continuing by the lakeside almost to the foot of the lake. At Fell Foot the National Trust has recently reorganised the country park which now includes a formal garden, adventure playground, picnic areas, rowing-boat hire, tearoom, toilets and shop. A foot ferry crosses to Lakeside.

Carry on along the A592. Turn right at the A591, then right again to cross the River Leven by the Swan Hotel
From this point the Haverthwaite terminus of the Lakeside and Haverthwaite Railway is just 3km (2 miles) further along the A590. Visitor facilities include engine sheds, café and shop.

Keep right towards Lakeside to reach the other terminus of the steam railway, boat landings and aquarium .

From Lakeside continue north. **Stott Park Bobbin Mill** is 1km (0.6 mile) further. The road stays roughly parallel with the lake. Fork right after passing Graythwaite Hall, quite steeply downhill, to Low Cunsey and High Cunsey, forking right again to join the B5285 approx. 1km (0.6 mile) from the Windermere ferry. Turn right to descend and return to Bowness using the ferry, with its superb views along the lake.

For an extended ride completely circumnavigating the lake, keep left at High Cunsey, into Near Sawrey (Hill Top, Tower Bank Arms) and keep left to Hawkshead. Continue north to Outgate and join the A593 at Clappersgate, turning right, then right again at Borrans Road, to reach Waterhead (Roman fort). Turn right at the traffic lights to return to Bowness along A591. The shortest route is to turn right at the mini roundabout into Rayrigg Road.

FROM AMBLESIDE

1 A Kirkstone Pass, Ullswater and Askham
••• A longer than average ride of 93km (57 miles), including crossing the Kirkstone Pass, high and steep.

From Ambleside start up the 'Struggle', rising up a 25 per cent gradient direct from the main street and continue climbing all the way to the top of the Kirkstone Pass at about 455m (1,493 feet). Join the main A592 opposite the Kirkstone Inn, turning left towards Patterdale.

Descend past Brotherswater and its inn, soon reaching **Patterdale** and then **Glenridding,** both with shops, catering and public conveniences. After a minor climb the road continues along the side of Ullswater with plenty of places to pull off for idyllic lakeside views and picnics. Keep right at a junction, for **Pooley Bridge.**

Leave Pooley Bridge, for a short distance along the B5320. Turn right for Askham, a lovely village with large greens and fine old cottages. Nearby is Lowther Castle and Wildlife Park. From Askham continue south via Halton, Bampton and Bampton Grange, the latter after two left turns and crossing the River Lowther. Head gradually uphill to **Shap**, where the A6 Kendal to Penrith road is joined.

Turn right towards Kendal. This formerly extremely busy road is now comparatively quiet and is very scenic as it crosses the high moors to the south of Shap village, descending steadily towards Kendal. Look out for a turning on the right signposted to Burneside, and take the minor road. At Burneside turn right to Bowston, gradually angling towards the main A591 Kendal to Windermere road, joined at Plantation Bridge.

Turn right to return to Ambleside, bypassing the centre of Windermere village.

2▲ Langdale and Little Langdale

•••• A circuit of 26km (16 miles), visiting two fine mountain valleys, with a short but hard climb between the two.

Leave Ambleside by the road to the west, over the tight little bridge by the Rothay Manor Hotel and continue towards Coniston. Close to the top of the climb, turn right at a road junction to descend steeply towards Elterwater and Colwith. At Colwith hamlet turn left to climb towards Little Langdale, passing the Three Shires Inn and Little Langdale Tarn.

At the next road junction the road ahead climbs towards the high **Wrynose Pass.** Ignore this and turn right for a lesser climb to Blea Tarn, prettily set with views of the Langdale Pikes to the north. Descend into Great Langdale, reached close to the Old Dungeon Ghyll Hotel.

Follow the valley road back towards Ambleside, passing the New Dungeon Ghyll Hotel, Chapel Stile, Elterwater and Skelwith Bridge on the way. The mountain scenery with the Langdale Pikes and at the valley head, Crinkle Crags and Bowfell, is very fine indeed.

Below left: Brantwood, the home of Ruskin, above Coniston Water.
Below right: Barrow in Furness, outside Dock Museum.

car tours — the south

The four itineraries set out below offer attractions of great diversity, in sufficient quantity to provide many happy days for the visitor. All are naturally much enhanced by the attractive countryside, ranging from the sandy estuary of the River Kent to the high, wind-swept, moorland above the Lune Valley.

1 KENDAL-SEDBERGH-KIRBY LONSDALE-KENDAL

From Kendal take the A684, heading east to **Sedbergh**, a fine little market (Wednesday) town just inside the boundary of the Yorkshire Dales National Park. Historic main street; cannons left by Bonnie Prince Charlie in 1745; well-known public school; Tourist Information Office ☎ 015396 20125.

From Sedbergh head south along the Lune Valley, A683, to **Kirkby Lonsdale**, another historic market (Thursday) town, with a good square, old inns and narrow lanes with intriguing names. Don't miss **'Ruskin's View'** behind the churchyard, a fine panorama of the Lune Valley and Pennine Hills. St.Andrew's Church has a Norman base to the tower, with well-carved doorway. **Devil's Bridge** is a few minutes' walk to the south of the town, a high stone bridge over the river, with rocky scenery around, painted by J.M.W. Turner. Tourist Information Office ☎ 015242 71437.

Leave Kirkby Lonsdale along the main road back to Kendal, A65, joining the A591 near Levens. To the left about 1km (0.6 mile) after the junction is **Sizergh Castle**, home of the Strickland family for more than 750 years and now in the care of the National Trust. Not uncommonly in this area the house is founded on a defensive pele tower. This was extended in Tudor times. English and French furniture. Limestone rock garden. Tearoom. Most of garden, lower hall and tearoom accessible to wheelchair users. Wheelchair and powered mobility vehicle available. Admission charge. Car park. Open late March–end of October, Sunday–Thursday, 13.30–17.30 (last admission 17.00) Shop and garden are open on the same days from 12.30–17.30. Admission to garden only at reduced charge. ☎ 01539 60070

Return to Kendal by A591/A6.

2 KENDAL-LEVENS BRIDGE-BEETHAM-ARNSIDE-KENDAL

Take the A6 to the south from Kendal, then A591, A590, A6. to Levens Bridge. From Windermere/Bowness take the A5074 Lyth Valley road and turn left on to A590, then right to A6. On the right is the entrance to **Levens Hall**, an Elizabethan mansion built around yet another

13th-century pele tower. The hall is the home of the Bagot family. Jacobean furniture, paintings, early English patchwork. The splendid gardens are particularly noted for the intricate topiary. Collection of working steam engines, operational 14.00–17.00. Wheelchair access to all areas except the house. Café serving lunches and teas; gift shop; plant centre; children's play area. Admission charge. House open 12.00–16.30 (last admission) Sunday–Thursday from end March to end September. Gardens also open Sundays and Monday–Friday during October.

Continue along the A6, through Milnthorpe, to Beetham for the **Heron Corn Mill and Museum of Paper Making.** On the banks of the River Bela, this is one of the few working mills in the area, having been restored in 1975. Powered by a 14ft (4m) waterwheel, traditional machinery is still in place. In 1988 a barn on the site was refurbished to house the Museum of Paper Making. Entered via Mill Lane, a sharp turn off A6. Admission charge. Open 11.00–17.00 daily except Mondays, from Easter (or 1 April if before Easter) until 30 September. Open Bank Holiday Mondays. ☎ 015395 63363; fax 015395 63869

From Beetham a minor road leads through Storth to **Arnside**, a pleasant village on the south side of the Kent estuary. The railway viaduct was finished, after a great deal of difficulty, by the engineer Brunlees in 1857. Turn left in Arnside and drive between Arnside Knott and Arnside Tower, to **Silverdale**. Along a minor road to the south of the village is **Wolf House Gallery,** housed in restored farm buildings. Here traditional and contemporary British crafts and paintings are displayed and may be purchased. Adventure play area; tearoom. Open daily except Mondays from 1 April–24 December, 10.30–13.00 and 14.00–17.30. From January to Easter open Saturdays and Sundays only, 10.30–17.30. Closed Christmas Day and Boxing Day. ☎ 01524 701405

From Silverdale head east, over the railway, towards Yealand Conyers. Just after Silverdale station is the entrance to **Leighton Moss Nature Reserve,** a large and important reserve of the Royal Society for the Protection of Birds with a wonderful variety of waterfowl and other birds. Also deer, and at least 532 species of plants. Wheelchair access to several hides. Visitor centre and tearoom. No dogs allowed on the reserve. Open all year 09.00–21.00 (or sunset, if earlier). ☎ 01524 701601

Continue through Yealand Redmayne to Yealand Conyers and the entrance drive to **Leighton Hall**, a fine house built in grey limestone, with 19th-century garden and woodland walks in the extensive grounds. Very much a 'lived-in' house. Collection of birds of prey. Tearooms. Admission charge. Programme of special events each year, including antiques fairs, concert and fireworks and Shakespeare in the garden.

Open daily May–September, 14.00–17.00 (11.00–17.00 in August). Closed Saturdays and Mondays, except Bank Holiday Mondays. ☎ 01524 734474; fax 01524 720357

From Leighton Hall return to Yealand Conyers and turn right. Go through Warton and on to Carnforth. On entering the town look out for **Steamtown** signs before the railway station. Steamtown comprises a large collection of steam locomotives and other rolling stock on the site of the former locomotive depot and yard, with a short length of operating track. Visitor facilities including tearoom, shop and toilets. ☎ 01524 732100

Head up A6 back towards Kendal. A short diversion at the second roundabout (2.5 km – 1.5 miles) towards Burton in Kendal reaches Tewitfield, just after the bridge over M6, on the long disused **Lancaster Canal**. For a few years this canal, one of the most scenic in the country, provided an important link between Kendal, Lancaster and Preston, with a branch to the sea at Glasson Dock. The arrival of the railway killed off the trade but the canal lingered on. Construction of the M6 motorway severed the waterway in several places but some lengths still have water navigable by shallow draft boats. At Tewitfield there is a small flight of locks.

Return to A6 and turn right. In 6km (3.75 miles) on the left is the **Lakeland Wildlife Oasis,** half zoo and half museum with interactive hands-on exhibits and exotic wildlife, including butterfly house and tropical halls. Coffee/snack bar; gift shop; picnic facilities. Wheelchair access throughout. Admission charge. Car park. Open daily, except Christmas, from 10.00–18.00 (last admission 17.00) in summer 10.00–17.00 (last admission 16.00) in winter. ☎ 015395 63027

3 ▲ GRANGE-OVER-SANDS-HUMPHREY HEAD-CARTMEL

From Kendal take A6, A591/A590. From Windermere, Bowness, Ambleside and places north take A592 (Newby Bridge)/A590. From Coniston take A593/A5084/A5092/A590. In each case drive to **Grange over Sands**, a dignified little Victorian seaside town on the shore of Morecambe Bay, with tastefully laid out gardens and arcaded shops. Continue along B 5277 to Kent's Bank, one end of the famous route, still a public right of way, which crosses Morecambe Bay from Hest's Bank near Morecambe. Once crossed by coaches, this potentially hazardous route should never be attempted without the assistance of the Queen's Guide. Next is **Flookborough,** once a town with an ancient market charter but now comparatively sleepy, but still with some Morecambe Bay fishing industry. Turn left here, then left again to the limestone hump of **Humphrey Head**, jutting well into the Bay, and supposedly the place where the last wolf in England was killed. Cars may be parked on the beach and the headland makes a fine little stroll with views over the

Bay. There is a cave and the 'holy well of St Agnes Water', said to be good for rheumatism, gout and bilious complaints.

Return to Flookborough and drive through Cark. In 1km (0.6 mile) after Cark is **Holker Hall**, an early 16th-century mansion, now home of the Cavendish family and a major visitor attraction. In addition to the hall itself, there is a noted motor museum, birds of prey centre and award winning gardens. Picnic area; adventure playground; café; gift shop. Special exhibitions and events such as a Garden and Countryside Festival. Basic charge for gardens and deer park; extra charges for hall, motor museum and birds of prey centre. Open daily, except Saturdays, from late March–end October, 10.00–18.00 (last admissions 16.30). House closes 16.30.
☎ 015395 58328

Return to Cark and turn left, shortly reaching **Cartmel**, a delightful small town or big village centred on a compact square, with old inns, cafés and bookshops tightly clustered. Pride of place goes to **Cartmel Priory**, more than 800 years old. When the former priory was dissolved by King Henry VIII after 1537, the villagers managed to retain the nave as their parish church, very grand indeed for such a modest sized place. Look out for the bullet holes in an external door, dating from the civil war (1643). Inside this light and lofty church there are many interesting features, notably the Cavendish family memorial and a Holy Family by Josefina de Vasconcellos of Ambleside. In the Square, dominated by the former Priory gate house (National Trust – exhibitions), look out for the old fish dressing slabs and the remains of the old market cross. Car parking is at the edge of the **racecourse**, one of the smallest in the country, with meetings in late May and late August each year. ☎ 015395 33434. Cartmel Show is held on the Wednesday after the first Monday in August. ☎ 01539 722777

A minor road to the north from Cartmel leads to A590 1.5km (1 mile) south-east of Newby Bridge.

4 ▲ ULVERSTON-PIEL ISLAND-BARROW-IN-FURNESS

From Kendal take A6/A591/A590 to Newby Bridge and on to **Ulverston.** Connect from Windermere, Bowness, Ambleside, Coniston, as in tour 3 above, but turning right at Newby Bridge or Greenodd as appropriate. Ulverston is a good sized market (Thursday and Saturday – largest in the area) town, about halfway along the main road to Barrow in Furness. Much of the town has a pleasantly old-fashioned character and the adjacent hill with a two-thirds size replica of the Eddystone lighthouse (1850) is a viewpoint well worth the short ascent. Features of the town follow:

PLACES TO VISIT IN ULVERSTON

Cumbria Crystal Glass Factory, Lightburn Road, open to visitors. Factory: Monday–Thursday 09.00–16.00, Friday 09.00–15.00. Shop: Monday–Friday 09.00–17.00, Saturday 10.00–16.00. Open all Bank Holidays except Christmas and New Year. ☎ 01229 584400.

Ulverston Heritage Centre, through a gift shop in Lower Brook Street. Local history. Open all year, Monday–Saturday 09.30–16.30. Closed Wednesdays, Christmas–Easter. ☎ 01229 580820

Market Hall, indoor market daily.

Classic Bikes Working Museum, Victoria Road. Collection of motorcycles and associated memorabilia. Restoration workshop. Shop. Open Tuesday–Saturday 10.00–16.30. Open all Bank Holidays except Christmas and New Year. ☎ 01229 586099; fax 01229 586399

Heron Glass, The Gill. Craft industry, with glassblowing on premises. Goods for sale. Admission charge refundable on purchases in shop.

Laurel and Hardy Museum, King Street. Stanley Laurel, one half of what was, arguably, the world's greatest comedy duo, was born in Ulverston. Small museum, an individual enterprise. ☎ 01229 582292

Festivals Carnival Week, early July, Charter (1280) Festival Fortnight, beginning of September. ☎ 01229 582183

From Ulverston take the A5087 road along the coast towards Barrow, pass Conishead Priory (not open to the public), the attractive village of **Bardsea,** then take a narrow road on the right up to the **Sunbrick stone circles** on the edge of Birkrigg Common. Return to the coast road, pass **Baycliff**, then divert left to **Aldingham**, a tiny settlement on the shore, with picnic places and a beautifully situated little church, of 12th-century origin, with later additions. There is a stature of St Cuthbert, to whom the church is dedicated. After Aldingham, a short inland diversion to Gleaston allows a visit to **Gleaston Water Mill,** a restored water-powered mill of 1774, on a site in use from even earlier times. 18th-century machinery, operational most days. Some rare breeds of pigs and cattle. Licensed café/restaurant; gift shop. Admission charge. Open Easter–end of October, 11.00–17.00. Closed Mondays except Bank Holidays. Winter 11.00–16.00, closed Mondays and Tuesdays. Nearby is the ruin of Gleaston Castle, incorporated into a farm.

Continue to **Rampside,** with its curious tower on the beach, and **Roa Island,** which is not an island at all. From Roa a foot ferry crosses to **Piel Island,** which has an inn and the remains of Piel Castle, used by the monks of Furness Abbey as a depot and staging post for their trade across the Irish Sea.

Drive back to Rampside, then turn left to **Barrow-in-Furness**, not usually regarded as a visitor attraction, but now having a sizeable new town centre development. The **Dock Museum** has been constructed on a Victorian dock, with a landscaped site, exhibition gallery; adventure playground; shop; café; wheelchair access. lift to all floors; ample car parking; film show. Free admission. Open Easter–October: Tuesday–Friday, 10.00–17.00, Saturday and Sunday 11.00–17.00 (last admission 16.15. November–March: Wednesday–Friday 10.30–16.00, Saturday and Sunday, 12.00 to 16.00 (last admission 15.15). ☎ 01229 870871. **Walney Island,** reached across a bridge, is largely a residential suburb, but there is a nature reserve in the north and nature trails at the south end.

Leave Barrow on the main A590, soon forking right to follow signposts to **Furness Abbey,** one of the greatest of the northern abbey ruins, the massive red sandstone buildings still conveying something of the wealth and power once possessed by the Abbot and monks of this remarkable institution. Maintained and managed by English Heritage. Exhibition; free audio tape. Admission charge. Open daily from beginning of April–end of September, 10.00–18.00; October daily 10.00–18.00 (or dusk if earlier); November–March, Wednesday–Sunday, 10.00–16.00. ☎ 01229 823420. Also in Barrow is the **Park House Animal Farm,** Park House Road, not far from the abbey, with farm animals, birds of prey, playground, indoor play area, disabled facilities, including lift, home-made meals. Car park. Admission charge. Open April–October, 10.00–17.00; November–March 10.00–16.00. ☎ 01229 827300

Continue towards **Dalton in Furness**, where Dalton Castle, built about 1340 as the manorial courthouse of Furness Abbey, is now in the care of the National Trust. Display of armour. Admission free, but donations welcome. Open Easter to the end of September, Saturday only, 14.00–17.00. ☎ 01524 701178

Just north of Dalton, at Crossgates, the **South Lakes Animal Park** is fast becoming an important conservation zoo, with daily events to entertain visitors. Safari railway, children's farm, café, gift shop, picnic areas. Admission charge. Open daily April–September, 10.00–18.00, October–March, 10.00 to dusk. Closed Christmas Day. ☎ 01229 466086.

A short diversion to the right from the A590, on the way back to Ulverston, is **Lindal in Furness**. Here, at **Colony Country Store** is a candle-making workshop with visitor facilities; gift shop; café. Open all year except Christmas Day, Boxing Day and New Year's Day, Monday–Saturday 9.00–17.00, Sunday 12.00–17.00. The café closes 15 minutes earlier than the shop. ☎ 01229 461100

Return via Ulverston to Kendal or other place of departure.

2 THE WEST

ESKDALE

Eskdale is a long and very attractive valley. Its upper reaches are ringed by Scafell, Scafell Pikes at 978m (3,210 feet) the highest mountain in England, Esk Pike, Bowfell and the Crinkle Crags, whilst the foot of the valley reaches the sea at Ravenglass. The wild upper part of the valley is accessible only on foot, a great boggy waste quite devoid of farm or other human habitation.

From the point where the little road over the **Hard Knott Pass** (with 30 per cent gradients) drops precipitously into Eskdale, the landscape is quite different. Close to the foot of the pass are the two highest farmsteads in the valley, Brotherikeld and Taw House.

Below these farms, the River Esk meanders a little as the valley floor levels out and, although the valley is never wide, there are fields providing reasonable grazing for farm animals.

Like the nearby Duddon, Eskdale is without lake, town or

Above: *Yewbarrow, Kirk Fell, Great Gable and Lingmell (left to right) create a backcloth to this view of Wastwater.*

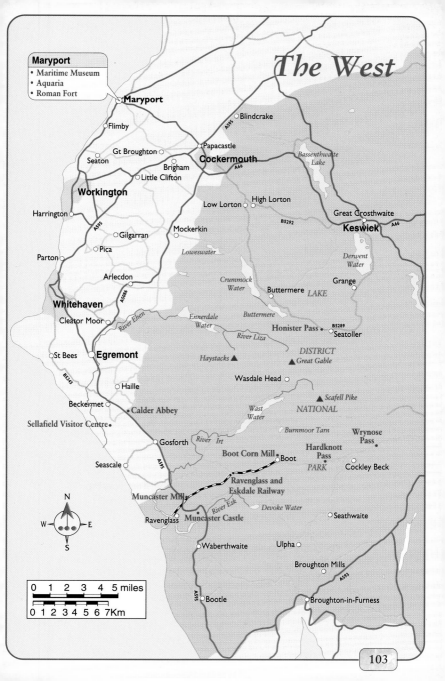

The West

Maryport
- Maritime Museum
- Aquaria
- Roman Fort

Maryport

Flimby

Gt Broughton

Seaton

Brigham

Little Clifton

Workington

Harrington

A595

Gilgarran

Pica

Parton

Arlecdon

A5086

Whitehaven

Cleator Moor

River Ehen

St Bees

Egremont

B5345

Haille

Beckermet

Calder Abbey

Sellafield Visitor Centre

Gosforth

River Irt

Seascale

A595

Boot Corn Mill

Boot

Muncaster Mill

Ravenglass and
Eskdale Railway

River Esk

Ravenglass

Muncaster Castle

Waberthwaite

Ulpha

Broughton Mills

A593

A595

Bootle

Broughton-in-Furness

Blindcrake

A595

Papacastle

Cockermouth

A66

Bassenthwaite
Lake

Low Lorton

High Lorton

Mockerkin

B5292

Great Crosthwaite

A66

Keswick

Loweswater

Derwent
Water

Crummock
Water

Buttermere

LAKE

Grange

Ennerdale
Water

Buttermere

River Liza

Honister Pass

B5289

Seatoller

DISTRICT

Haystacks ▲

Great Gable ▲

Wasdale Head

Scafell Pike ▲

Wast
Water

NATIONAL

Burnmoor Tarn

Wrynose
Pass

Hardknott
Pass

PARK

Cockley Beck

Devoke Water

Seathwaite

N
W E
S

0 1 2 3 4 5 miles

0 1 2 3 4 5 6 7Km

103

Places to Visit In Eskdale

Hard Knott Fort

Perched high above the valley by the side of the pass of the same name, the remains of this remarkable Roman fort are well worth a visit, not least for the spectacular views down the valley. Its commanding position secured the safety of the road which crossed the mountains at this point, leading from the port of Ravenglass to Galava fort at Waterhead, Ambleside.

Boot Corn Mill

Small restored water-powered mill, with small shop, exhibition and picnic area. Admission charge. Open late March to end of September, 11.00–17.00, daily except Mondays.

Ravenglass and Eskdale Railway

This much-loved narrow gauge (15-inch) railway ('La'al Ratty' in local dialect) was originally opened in 1875, to a broader gauge (3 feet), primarily to carry iron ore down to the sea at Ravenglass. Passenger services were added and there was also traffic in stone from Eskdale quarries. However, a few years later the line was struggling financially, and it closed in 1913. Its conversion to the narrower gauge and re-opening as a tourist attraction in 1914 has, in recent years, proved to be one of Lakeland's most popular features. The line runs for nearly 11km (7 miles) from its base at Ravenglass, where it connects with the coastal railway service, to Dalegarth, close to Boot. There are intermediate stations at Muncaster Mill, Irton Road, The Green and Beckfoot. The full journey lasts for 40 minutes. Although there are diesel locomotives, it is predominantly a steam railway, with a collection of beautifully maintained little engines.

There are services for all but a few winter weeks, although those in winter are minimal and likely to be diesel-hauled other than at weekends. Museum, Ratty Arms Inn and other facilities at Ravenglass. ☎ 01229 717171; fax 01229 717011

Muncaster Castle

Standing on land granted to the Pennington family in 1208, the castle is founded on an ancient defensive pele tower. Still the home of the same family, the castle has a fine site, surrounded by formal and woodland gardens. A replica of the 'Luck of Muncaster', a glass drinking bowl given to the family in 1464 by King Henry VI in gratitude for shelter and hospitality after defeat in battle, is on display. The King declared that as long as the bowl remained intact the Penningtons would live and thrive at Muncaster.

The church of St Michael, with 12th-century nave and fragments of Saxon crosses, is within the castle grounds. Audio tour of castle.

Paintings by Gainsborough and Sir Joshua Reynolds. Fine furniture. Owl Centre ('meet the birds' daily at 14.30 mid March to end of October). Children's play area; plant centre; nature trail; café/restaurant. Gift shops. Facilities for the disabled. Programme of special events each season.

Admission charges. Castle open from Sunday–Friday, 12.30–16.00 (last entry) from mid March to end of October; the gardens and Owl Centre daily throughout the year from 11.00–17.00.

☎ 01229 717614: fax 01229 717010

Muncaster Mill

1.5km (1 mile) north east of Ravenglass on A595 road to Workington. Water-powered corn mill, with 19th-century machinery restored and producing organic flour (available for sale) daily. Ravenglass and Eskdale railway station adjacent. Picnic area. Admission charge. Open daily, Easter–end of October, 10.00–1700. Weekends, November–March 11.00–16.00. ☎ 01229 717232

Ravenglass

An interesting village with hotel, teashop and many former fishermen's cottages, straggling along one street to the shore of the estuary. Former Roman port. Home of the Ravenglass and Eskdale Railway. Walls Castle, the bath-house of a former Roman fort, is less than 1km (0.6 mile) along a track to the south of the village. The surviving stonework is claimed to be the highest genuinely above ground Roman building in England. The railway along the coast was opened by the Whitehaven and Furness Junction Railway in 1849, later becoming part of the Furness Railway. There are still passenger services south to Barrow and north to Whitehaven, Workington and Carlisle.

significant village. Tiny **Boot** is the highest hamlet. It does have a restored corn mill, the parish church of St Catherine, an inn and the terminus of the **Ravenglass and Eskdale Railway** close by at Dalegarth. The church structure is largely of 1881, when extensive restoration and rebuilding was carried out. Inside, the font and the stained glass windows are of interest. In the churchyard are memorials to two legendary Lakeland huntsmen. One of these, Tommy Dobson, rivalled John Peel in his local fame. His tomb carries a portrait and appropriate carvings. A little further down the valley, by the George IV inn, the road towards the coast separates and the

Events

ESKDALE
Eskdale Show
Late September.
☎ 01946 852939,
(Whitehaven TIC)

ENNERDALE
Ennerdale Show
Late August. ☎ Tourist
Information Office as above.

LOWESWATER
Loweswater Show
Mid September.
☎ 01900 822634,
(Cockermouth TIC)

countryside becomes altogether more gently pastoral, although the long, narrow, bulk of Muncaster Fell 231m (758 feet) is between the two routes. From close to this junction, a road goes over to Ulpha in the Duddon valley, to the south. The River Esk runs to the south of Muncaster Fell, together with the more minor of the two roads.

To the north of the Fell, **Eskdale Green** is a rather scattered community, but with inns, shops and two stations on the little railway.

On the desolate high ground above Boot, between Eskdale and Miterdale, there is a noted Bronze Age occupation area, with extensive small stone circles and cairns as evidence, accessible only on foot.

As the River Esk reaches the sea, it is joined by the River Irt and the River Mite to form the great sandy estuary at Ravenglass, part of which is a Nature Reserve, although the southern section has Ministry of Defence danger areas. The Barrow in Furness to Carlisle railway line, with a station at Ravenglass, hugs this part of the coast.

WASDALE AND ENNERDALE

Wasdale

With the grandest valley head in the whole country and the uniformly steep slopes of The Screes plunging fjord-like below the surface of **Wastwater**, the deepest lake in England, **Wasdale** is a valley of great character, with a severe beauty all of its own.

The ring of mountains which contributes so much to this character includes Yewbarrow, Kirkfell, Great Gable, Scafell Pikes and Scafell. Despite the general severity of the landscape, the precious flat land between the head of the lake and the mountains has been painstakingly farmed since at least Viking times. The immensely thick field walls and the great piles of stones bear evidence to the efforts of generations of farmers in clearing their meagre fields.

Ancient yew trees all but hide one of **England's smallest churches**, dwarfed in this mighty landscape. The tiny building, dedicated to St Olaf, is of uncertain age, but the roof timbers are believed to have come from Viking ships. The church was largely restored in 1892. The south window has a stained glass depiction of Napes Needle, a climbers' pinnacle on nearby Great Gable, as a memorial to members of the Fell and Rock Climbing Club killed in World War I. The churchyard has the gravestones of climbers who have perished over the years in following their sport in the Wasdale area. The nearby Wasdale Head Hotel is widely regarded as the birthplace of rock climbing in Britain.

Behind the hotel the lovely packhorse bridge is a reminder that important trade routes used the **Styhead** and **Black Sail** passes.

Below the lake, the broad valley drained by the River Irt and its principal tributary the River Bleng is gently pastoral, with farms and hamlets such as Nether Wasdale and Santon Bridge connected by delightful little lanes. The major village is **Gosforth**, just off the A595, an attractive place with shops and refreshments. Here, pride of place goes to St Mary's Church and its churchyard. This very early Christian site probably had a pre-Norman church, then a Norman building in about 1100, in turn replaced by the present Early English church. Ancient relics include pieces of Norse (Viking) crosses. Inside the church are 'hogback' tombstones of the 10th century,

which were originally erected over the graves of Viking chieftains, with a roof to represent a house for each man. Of more recent times are a Chinese bell captured in a 19th-century skirmish on the Canton River, and cannon balls from the Crimean War.

Finally, and greatest of all, is the **Gosforth Cross,** at 4.5 m (14 foot 6 inches) high the tallest ancient cross in England, a remarkable survival from the late 10th or early 11th centuries. Carved by Viking craftsmen, the cross shows acceptance of the Christian religion by a people who still to some extent embraced traditional Scandinavian mythology. The carving is explained in a leaflet available in the church.

The **Gosforth Pottery** and shop offers instruction in pot throwing. Open, summer, 10.00–17.30 every day. Winter from 10.00–17.00, Sunday, 12.30–17.00, closed Mondays. January and February, closed Mondays, Tuesdays and Wednesdays. ☎ 019467 25296

Ennerdale

In common with the western dales generally, **Ennerdale** is remote of access and is probably the quietest of all the major Lakeland valleys. There are fine mountains at the head of the valley, notably the dominant **Pillar**, with its famous climbers' Pillar Rock standing out below the summit. The northern side is bounded by the less spectacular side of the high ridge comprising Red Pike, High Stile and High Crag. The latter is separated by the Scarth Gap Pass (footpath only) from the lower Haystacks, beloved of the late Alfred Wainwright and resting place of his ashes.

Ennerdale Water is a large, attractive lake, fed by the River Liza, but the valley is probably best known for its forestry plantations, originally dating from the 1930s, when the regular outlines and limited variety of conifer species were severely criticised. In more recent years the Forestry Commission, now Forest Enterprises, has greatly improved the appearance of the commercial forestry and has also become much more visitor friendly, with waymarked forest trails and information boards.

Within the National Park, the only settlement is the small village of **Ennerdale Bridge,** with an inn. Below Ennerdale Bridge the River Ehen wends its short course to the sea at Sellafield, passing through much of the former mining and general industrial area of West Cumberland.

Close to the main A595, about 1km (0.6 mile) along a minor road to the east from Calder Bridge is Calder Abbey. Founded more than 800 years ago, the abbey had a chequered early history, including pillaging by the Scots and a subsequent period of disuse. Later reoccupied, a new church was constructed by 1180, in turn superseded by the construction of a more comprehensive abbey, including a new church, in the 13th century. Most of the substantial ruins seen today are of this structure. The site is privately owned and public access is possible only on an occasional basis, although a right of way footpath starting near the church at Calder Bridge does pass quite close to the ruins. Prior enquiry at a tourist information office is recommended.

Tourist Information Office (Egremont) ☎ 01946 820693 (Whitehaven) ☎ 01946 695678

BUTTERMERE, CRUMMOCK WATER, LOWESWATER AND BORROWDALE

The Buttermere Valley

Generously endowed with no less than three lakes, the fine valley containing Buttermere, Crummock Water and Loweswater has long been a great favourite among the western dales, not least because of its comparative accessibility by road. Although for visitor purposes it is convenient to call this area the Buttermere Valley, in strict geographical terms there is one very large valley, the **Vale of Lorton,** drained by the River Cocker, and a small tributary valley containing Loweswater.

At the main valley head Fleetwith Pike, a comparatively modest mountain, is seen at its best, with the formidable Honister Crag guarding the high 356m (1,168 ft) pass of the same

PLACES TO VISIT IN BUTTERMERE

St James' Church
Buttermere

Constructed in 1846, this small building is entirely appropriate for its surroundings and purpose. Of particular interest is the wrought iron gate depicting shepherd and sheep and, inside, a tablet by the south window. This tablet is a memorial to the late Alfred Wainwright, Lakeland walker and writer supreme. Through the window the resting place of his ashes, the summit of Haystacks, is visible.

Fish Hotel

Formerly the Fish Inn and home of Mary Robinson, a celebrated local beauty later immortalised as the Maid of Buttermere. Mary was deceived, seduced and 'married' in 1802 by Joseph Hatfield, a remarkable swindler and bigamist posing as the Hon. Alexander Augustus Hope. Following his return from the honeymoon, Hatfield was apprehended and hanged at Carlisle in 1803 for forgery. The romantic story caught the mood of the nation at the time; even Wordsworth and De Quincey were intrigued and became involved. Melvyn Bragg's novel *The Maid of Buttermere* is firmly based on the story. Happily, Mary was apparently none the worse for this experience, later marrying a farmer and bringing up a family in Caldbeck, where her grave may be seen in the churchyard.

Tourist Information Centre
Town Hall, Cockermouth. ☎ 01900 822634

---

name over into **Borrow-dale**. The mountains on the south-west side are the isolated Melbreak, by Crummock Water, then the more spectacular side of the continuous ridge of Red Pike, High Stile and High Crag. After the dip through which the Scarth Gap Pass (foot only) climbs over to Ennerdale, Haystacks makes the most of its small stature.

The north-east side of the valley has Whiteside, then the huge bulk of Grasmoor. After the interruption of the valley of Mill Beck, which allows the little road to pass on its steep route to the **Vale of Newlands**, the relatively bland sides of Robinson, Hindscarth and Dale Head form a long wall above Buttermere and the Honister Pass.

Forested areas are by no means dominant, the most substantial being Burtness Wood by Buttermere, Lanthwaite Wood at the foot of Crummock Water and Holme Wood by Loweswater. All add to, rather than detract from, the overall beauty of the valley.

Buttermere village is situated

Above: The interior of Muncaster Mill.
Middle: Great Gable and Kirk Fell from near Blackbeck Tarn with Scafell in the distance.
Below: Muncaster Station and mill.

Above: Wastwater.
Middle: Eggs of the Black
Headed Gull, Wastwater.
Ensure you don't tread on them
or touch them.
Below: The Vale of Newlands
looking towards Cat Bells.

in magnificent surroundings between Buttermere and Crummock Water, where the flat land is the alluvial accumulation now dividing what was formerly one lake. The village is a popular little place, with two hotels, café, car park and toilets. The small church of St James must rank highly in any contest for the most beautifully situated church in Lakeland.

The easiest road access to the valley is from **Cockermouth**, along the lower part of the Vale of Lorton, comparatively rich agriculturally, with small villages or hamlets such as High and Low Lorton and Loweswater. High Lorton and Loweswater have inns and churches. St Cuthbert's at High Lorton and St Bartholomew's at Loweswater are both early 19th century, although the former does occupy an old religious site.

From the Keswick area the **Whinlatter Pass,** B5292, provides a lower and easier route to Buttermere than either the Honister or Newlands Passes and may be combined with one or other as a circular drive. The final easy way to reach Buttermere is from the coastal plain via Mockerkin and the road along the side of Loweswater.

LITERATURE AND THE LAKE DISTRICT

The Lake District has long had a reputation for inspiring great poetry, as the separate feature devoted to **William Wordsworth** emphasises. Despite the enormous success of both **Beatrix Potter** and **Arthur Ransome** in their very different writing for children, prose of comparable stature is less in evidence. Here is a selection of those writers whose poetry or prose has been significantly influenced by the special qualities of the district or whose lives were linked with the region.

Eighteenth Century

The pioneers of Lakeland travel must be considered first – the first 'tourists', who 'discovered' the beauty of the landscape, analysing and writing in great detail. Notable among these intrepid travellers was **Daniel Defoe** (1724/7) who found the district to be 'barren and wild, of no use or advantage to man or beast'. To Defoe the hills were filled with 'inhospitable terror'. **Thomas Gray**, who in 1769 exclaimed on the mixture of horror and beauty, was particularly overwhelmed by the scenery in the Jaws of Borrowdale. **William Gilpin** was brought up in the district and was very concerned to analyse and to lay down ground rules for the translation of landscape features into good pictures.

The first guide book was **Thomas West's** *Guide to the Lakes* of 1778. The recommendation of 'viewing stations', from which the discerning tourist might obtain the best views of any particular scene, was a significant feature of this popular guide.

Lakes Poets and After

The firm establishment of the Lake District as the most picturesque part of the country set the scene for the arrival of the **Lakes Poets**. Now a term applied with some acclaim, it was originally coined in 1801 by a critical newspaper editor who was by no means enamoured of the work of Wordsworth, Southey and Coleridge, the three originals.

Samuel Taylor Coleridge was born in Devon in 1772 and toured the district in 1799 with his great friend Wordsworth. Coleridge was enchanted with the scenery. From 1800 to 1803 he lived at Greta Hall in Keswick with his family, and then from 1808 to 1810 he shared the occupation of Allan Bank, Grasmere with William and Dorothy Wordsworth. After leaving the district he never really settled until his death in London in 1834. Coleridge's son **Hartley**, born in 1796, was a child prodigy doomed to lead an unfulfilled life largely due to the effects of alcohol and opium. He died at Nab Cottage, Rydal, in 1849 and is buried at Grasmere, beside Wordsworth.

Robert Southey was born in Bristol in 1774. He married Coleridge's sister-in-law and joined Coleridge at Greta Hall in 1803, spending the rest of his life in the Lake District, exchanging visits with the Wordsworths. Southey became Poet Laureate in 1813. He died in 1843 and is buried at Great Crosthwaite, Keswick.

Alfred Lord Tennyson hardly qualifies as a Lakeland resident, but his *Idylls of the King*, including the death of Arthur, was largely conceived by the Bassenthwaite Lake shore whilst he stayed with his friends at Mirehouse.

Prose

Thomas De Quincey was born in Manchester in 1785. He took over the tenancy of Dove Cottage from Wordsworth in 1808, staying until 1830. For some years he was the editor of the *Westmorland Gazette*. Like Coleridge he was an opium addict, his best known work being *Confessions of an Opium Eater* of 1821. Another well known work is his *Recollections of the Lakes and the Lake Poets*, in which he denied the existence of a 'school' of Lake Poets. De Quincey died in Edinburgh in 1859.

John Ruskin was much more than a writer. The interests of this extraordinary man also embraced philosophy, social reform, the establishment of craft guilds, botany and painting. From 1871 until his death in 1900 he lived at Brantwood, Coniston and is buried at Coniston church.

Harriet Martineau lived at Ambleside from 1844 to 1876. Best known as an advocate of social reform, she also wrote the *Complete Guide to the Lakes* in 1855.

Among prose writers, the most prominent was probably **Sir Hugh Walpole**, once immensely

113

Above: Crummock Water.
Middle: Exploring Eskdale on the steam railway.
Below: Cockley Beck Bridge, between the Wrynose and Hard Knott passes.

popular but now rather out of fashion. Walpole settled in the Lake District in 1924, producing the four *Herries* novels, including *Rogue Herries* and *Judith Paris*, with settings in the Borrowdale area. Walpole died in 1941 and is buried at St John's, Keswick.

Quite different from anything published before or since are **A. (Alfred) Wainwright's** *Pictorial Guides to the Lakeland Fells* produced in seven volumes between 1955 and 1963. An eighth volume covering the outlying fells was added in 1974. These books, arguably the most important contribution to Lakeland literature this century, are a fascinating blend of the painstaking research of every route on every mountain, with hand-drawn maps, sketches and hand-written homespun comment, much of it of a philosophical nature. Although now in some respects outdated as route guides, the books remain in print and are still revered, at least by the older generation, as minor works of art.

Many other books followed, including sketch books and lavishly illustrated coffee table volumes. More significant are the Pennine Way guide and the 'Coast to Coast' walk. Wainwright came to the Lake District from his home town, Blackburn, in 1941 on gaining an appointment in the Borough Treasurer's office in Kendal. He was promoted to Borough Treasurer in 1948, staying in Kendal until his death in 1991, when his ashes were scattered on the top of Haystacks, a favourite place selected by the author many years previously. A recent biography (see Bibliography) has revealed important facets of Wainwright's character which had not featured in the publicly perceived personality established by his own writing.

Arthur Ransome has a secure place in children's literature. Born in Leeds in 1884, he had an adventurous early career as a journalist, travelling all over the world, often in areas of conflict. He moved to the Lake District in 1925 for the first of four residential spells, changing house each time. The work by which he is best remembered is the series of twelve children's novels beginning with *Swallows and Amazons* in 1930. His enthusiasm for boating and his fine sense of place combined to give these novels a lasting authenticity. Ransome died in 1967 and is buried at Rusland church.

Among other 20th-century writers the most significant are the poet **Norman Nicholson,** born in Millom in 1914; novelist and broadcaster **Melvyn Bragg,** born at Wigton in 1939, (*Maid of Buttermere*; *Credo*); **Hunter Davies** (*A Walk around the Lakes*), journalist and biographer of A. Wainwright; and **Martyn Hanks,** cartographer and guide.

ESKDALE AND SCAFELL

1 An easy, almost level walk of 6 km (3.75 miles) around the **middle section of the valley.** Cars may be parked at the foot of the steep descent of the Hard Knott Pass.

Start down the road, soon turning right along a track to Brotherikeld Farm. Bear left past the farm, cross a small stream on a sleeper bridge and follow a sign pointing to, *inter alia*, Taw House. At Taw House Farm turn left to follow the farm access roadway as far as the public road.

Turn right to walk along the road, passing the Woolpack Inn and the youth hostel. About 200 metres after the Woolpack turn left towards Penny Hill Farm. Cross the River Esk by Doctor Bridge, a fine picnic spot. Fork left to Penny Hill Farm. After the farm, bend right into a walled lane.

A good path returns along the valley side. Keep left at a waymarked post and follow further waymarks. Cross a stream and reach a signpost by a wall. Go straight on to take a route signposted 'footpath, Hard Knott' Rise a little through bracken before a left fork and a plank bridge over Dodknott Gill and a gate in the wall ahead.

Traverse woodland, then open hillside, go through a kissing-gate and join a wider path

After two more kissing-gates descend to cross Hard Knott Gill by the tiny Jubilee Bridge. Climb the far side to return to the parking area.

2 Scafell

15km (9.25 miles). A circuit over the summit of one of the great Lakeland peaks, 964m (3,162 feet) high. Hard ascent, rough in places.

The car parking at the foot of the Hard Knott Pass is closest to Scafell.

As in 1) above, go past Brotherikeld to Taw House, but turn right here, cross Scale Bridge, then turn sharp left for a climb to the Eskdale upper basin. In about 5km (3 miles), turn left at a junction of paths. The rough, stony, Cam Spout path now heads steeply uphill for Mickledore, the col linking Scafell and Scafell Pikes at a high level.

Before reaching Mickledore, turn left to take a path leading below East Buttress to Foxes Tarn, a small pool below the summit. From the tarn climb a long scree slope to the saddle above. The top is a further 250m of easy going.

To return, set off in a southerly direction along a broad ridge, going over Slight Side. The way is straightforward in clear weather, after Slight Side descending steeply for some distance, still generally to the south. This is the Terrace Route, much of it an attractive path, which goes all the way down to join the Eskdale valley road opposite Wha House Farm.

Turn left to walk along the valley road back to the car park.

If so desired, the walk can be adapted to climb Scafell Pikes – 978m (3,207 feet) instead of Scafell. Continue up Cam Spout to Mickledore, then turn right to cross the boulder-strewn waste to the highest of the three Scafell Pike summits. Continue along the top for a further 500m, then turn right to return to Eskdale down Little Narrowcove. Turn right at the junction at the bottom or go straight across. Either path leads back to the parking area.

FROM WASDALE HEAD

1 Around Wasdale Head
An easy, level, walk of 5km (3 miles), close to the great mountains. Car park close to the head of the lake, a right turn from the valley road, then past the National Trust camping site.

Set off along the lane. Turn left before the bridge over Lingmell Gill. Turn left at a gate into the camp site and follow the camp roadway to a gate/stile at the far end.

The path crosses a stony floodwater bed and is then easily followed to the valley road.

Head for the inn, but fork right by a car parking area towards the church. Continue past the church to Burnthwaite Farm. Turn sharp left at the farm to follow a path which crosses and recrosses a small beck.

Join the major track which descends from the Black Sail Pass and turn left to reach the packhorse bridge behind the Wasdale Head Hotel. The route continues along a path on the far side of the bridge, keeping close to Mosedale Beck. Join the road at a kissing gate by Down in the Dale Bridge. Turn right to return to the car park.

2 Great Gable
The shortest ascent of this most shapely mountain of 899m (2,950 feet) is from Wasdale. There are several possible routes; the following keeps to well-used paths. There is no difficulty but, inevitably, there is a fair amount of steep, hard, ascent. The full circuit is 9.5km (5.75 miles).

Walk to Burnthwaite Farm, as in 1) above, but keep right here to commence the great walkers' highway to Styhead. The path forks in 1km (0.6 mile). Either route leads to Styhead. At the top of the pass many paths come together.

Turn left to take the well-cairned route which goes directly to the top. Close by the summit cairn is the bronze war memorial tablet dedicated to members of the Fell and Rock Climbing Club; remembrance services are held here and this has long been a very special place for generations of climbers and fell walkers.

The most direct return to Wasdale Head is by the path over Gavel

Neese ('Gable Nose'); but with very steep uncomfortable sections. A better circuit is made by descending north-east to Wind Gap, between Great Gable and Green Gable. Turn left here, to descend, then left again to head due west to Beck Head Tarn. Turn left here to follow the Moses Trod path back to Wasdale.

3▲ Scafell/Scafell Pikes
•••• The previous chapter (Eskdale) includes a route for the ascent of England's highest mountain and its close companion. Wasdale offers the shortest routes to both these superb mountains, with circuits of 9km (5.5miles) in either case.

From Wasdale Head set off down the valley road. Where the road bends to the right, turn left to take a path which soon crosses Lingmell Beck on a footbridge, before angling up the hillside. *From the car park suggested in route 1) above, a connecting path follows close to Lingmell Gill, rising steeply to meet the path from Wasdale Head.* After crossing Lingmell Gill, the path continues by Brown Tongue and a right fork to head for Mickledore, the high col connecting the two mountains.

Before reaching Mickledore, cross the scree to the right to reach the foot of Lord's Rake, a wide gully which is a classic route of ascent for Scafell. The Rake is steep and a bit awkward, but not sensational or dangerous. The surrounding rock scenery is magnificent. From the top of the Rake, the path to the nearby summit is obvious.

For a straightforward descent, return along the same path but ignore the right turn into Lord's Rake. Carry on down over Green How to join the Eskdale to Wasdale track close to Groove Gill. Turn right to return to Wasdale, reaching the valley bottom near the camping site. See route 1) above for the best route to Wasdale Head.

For **Scafell Pikes**, start as above, but continue all the way to Mickledore. Turn left to cross the stony waste to the main Scafell Pikes summit. After savouring the experience of being on the highest ground in England, turn left along a path a little west of north, descending over rough ground. Keep left at a junction of paths and bear round to the left again to descend over Hollow Stones and rejoin the outward route.

Strong walkers may well wish to combine these two summits, which seems from the map to be straightforward and quite obvious. But the straight route is out of bounds to walkers, the step over Broad Stand being for rock climbers only. A detour via Lord's Rake or, alternatively, Foxes Tarn is required (see routes above). In either case there is a considerable loss of height and commensurate extra effort. Allow about one hour from peak to peak.

IN ENNERDALE

1▲ Circuit of Ennerdale Water

●●●
A ramble of 13km (8 miles) for the most part very level, but with one short section including a few short, sharp rises and falls and two mini scrambles, entirely without danger.

The car park which is easiest to reach is 1.5km (1 mile) from Ennerdale Bridge, on a no through road passing through part of a forested area. It is close to Bleach Green Cottage.

Leave the car park through a high kissing-gate and walk down to the lake outfall, with weir. Turn left to cross the River Ehen on a footbridge. The path along the shore is easy to follow, passing through National Trust land and the occasional muddy section. White-painted Beckfoot Farm is in view ahead before a right turn is made to descend a stony lane leading back to the lake shore. The track now heads for Bowness Farm.

Just before the farm there is a choice of route – left to reach a Forest Enterprise car park, with picnic area and toilets (closed in winter) or right to stay close to the lake shore and bypass the car park.

The tracks rejoin as a roadway, part surfaced, along the lower edge of the extensive Bowness Plantations. The view ahead includes a good profile of Pillar and its rock. As the wetland at the head of the lake is approached, a gravel path on the right provides an alternative to the roadway.

Turn right at a wide junction and cross the River Liza on a rather utilitarian bridge. Cross the valley bottom and turn right over a ladder stile, signposted 'lakeside path', and follow the grassy path back towards the lake. Continue along the lake shore path, now largely stony underfoot and to some extent artificially improved. Towards the end of the walk, the side of Anglers' Crag, falling steeply into the lake, is crossed: a little more exciting but not in any way dangerous.

After the Crag, the path goes obviously to the weir and back to the car park.

2▲

●●●●
Drive to the Forest Enterprises car park mentioned above and select a **forest trail** from the map on the information board. The various trails are waymarked. Best known is the Nine Becks Walk.

3▲ Ascent of Pillar

●●●●
At 892m (2,928 feet) one of the Lakeland giants and very much Ennerdale's mountain. No particular difficulty with the route set out below, but the usual amount of hard climbing to reach this elevation. 13km (8 miles) from Gillerthwaite.

Pillar is remote from public roads and the nearest car park is the Forest Enterprise car park already mentioned.

119

From the access roadway 1km (0.6 mile) below the youth hostel at Gillerthwaite head across the valley bottom, crossing various waterways. Enter the forest, turning left then right at junctions to rise steadily. Leave the woodland on a path rising straight towards the summit of Tewit How.

Continue beyond the summit in the same direction until a cross-paths is reached, close to Haycock. Turn left here to walk over Scoat Fell and Little Scoat Fell to Pillar, in almost 3km (2 miles), ignoring all diversionary paths along the way.

From Pillar take the path descending to the north-west, over White Pike. As Ennerdale Forest is reached the path continues. Bear right at a junction, still downhill, to reach the valley bottom.

Turn left here to return to the crossing place and retrace the outward route.

BUTTERMERE AREA

1 A circuit of Buttermere

A great favourite for walkers and ramblers of all ages. An easy 6.5km. (4 miles) without significant gradient.

From the public car park in Buttermere village, start along the road towards the Honister Pass. Take the public bridleway through Syke and Willinsyke Farms and follow the broad track which descends gently towards the lake shore.

The path traverses through light woodland and a tunnel where a steep rocky slope leaves no space at the edge of the water. At any junction keep as close to the lake shore as possible. On reaching the Honister road, turn right and continue to Gatesgarth Farm, with the fine ridge of Fleetwith Pike ahead. The prominent white cross is a memorial to a Fanny Mercer, accidentally killed in 1887.

Turn right and carefully follow the signed bridleway through the farm, heading for the lake shore. Turn right at the far corner of the lake to follow the bridleway back towards the village, largely through the National Trust owned Burtness Wood. For one section there is a choice between lake shore path and a broad track a little way further up the hillside.

At the foot of the lake cross Sourmilk Gill on a small bridge, then Buttermere Dubs on a longer bridge. The route back is now entirely straightforward.

2 Circuit of Crummock Water

In character quite similar to the previous walk, but at 13km (8 miles) about twice the length.

In addition to the public car park in Buttermere village, there are small car parks by the roadside which can be used as start/finish for this walk.

From the village walk along the road towards Cockermouth. In 700m a track on the right may be used to avoid one length of road. Rejoin the road. As it reaches the edge of the lake, a path rises diagonally to the right. At the expense of a modest ascent this path avoids more of the road and gives enhanced views both up and down the valley.

Back on the road continue past Rannerdale Farm and Cinderdale Common. Turn left to leave the road at a kissing-gate 120m beyond the second of the car parks on the Common, signposted Fletcher Fields. Turn right. All apparent paths lead eventually to a well-defined route by the lake shore, with abundant picnic spots and a shingle beach.

Woodland is entered, firstly High Wood, followed by Lanthwaite Wood. Fork left at a junction to descend towards the lake. Bear left to cross the footbridges at the outfall, where the waterworks structures, including a double fish ladder, are reasonably discreet.

Bear left again to keep to the lake shore. Cross another footbridge to pass the octagonal pump house with its *Workington Corporation* plaque of 1903. Go over the stile on the right and turn left to keep close to the shore soon reaching a bay with shingle beach. The continuation along the shore is without complication.

After the inviting little promontory of Low Ling Crag, a diversion by a path on the right leads to **Scales Force**, highest waterfall in Lakeland. An ascent of about 90m (295 ft) is required.

Before the head of the lake is reached, there are pretty little islands. By this time the path has left the shoreline and has been joined by the major track linking Buttermere village and Scale Force. Turn left to cross Scale Bridge over Buttermere Dubs and return to the village.

3∧ Red Pike and Scale Force
•••• Red Pike is the mountain directly facing Buttermere village across the valley, the name resulting from the pinkish colour of much of the rock, geologically a granitic intrusion into the predominant Borrowdale Series volcanics of this area. Its height of 755m (2,478 feet), reached in a comparatively short horizontal distance, ensures a steep ascent, with little respite. The recommended return is by Scale Force, highest waterfall in Lakeland, giving a distance of 9km (5.5 miles). *For a longer walk of 11km. (6.75 miles), turn left at the summit and follow the broad ridge over High Stile and High Crag. After the latter turn left along an indistinct path to join the Scarth Gap Pass track, turning left again to descend to the valley. Return to the village may be along either side of Buttermere. (see 1 above)*

From the village head across the flat land towards the foot of Sourmilk Gill, a fine sight after rain as it tumbles down the steep hillside. Cross the footbridges and commence the ascent, initially through woodland on a

Above: The Buttermere Valley from the top of Warnscale Beck.
Below: Wasdale Head.
Opposite: Buttermere, with Haystacks beyond.

track which has been extensively engineered to combat erosion.

This track first goes left across the hillside, then turns back right to join Sourmilk Gill below its outfall from Bleaberry Tarn, sitting prettily in its fine text book corrie. From the tarn the path is steep and scrambly up to the Saddle, on the right, separating Dodd from the Red Pike summit. Turn left at the Saddle for the final ascent to the top.

Turn right to follow the broad descending ridge into the valley containing Scale Force, ignoring a path which goes left to Little Dodd and Starling Dodd. From the waterfall a very well-used path heads back to the village. (see 2 above)

4 ∧ Fleetwith Pike and Haystacks
●●●●

From the valley floor Fleetwith Pike is a fine mountain, its dominance belying its modest height of 648m (2,127 feet). Another lesser height at 597m (1,959 feet), Haystacks is noted for the interest and beauty of its summit and as a viewpoint. Most of all, it is a special place for the legions of admirers of the late Alfred Wainwright, legendary walker and writer, whose ashes were scattered here after his death in 1991. From a start/finish at the privately-owned car park (charge made) by Gatesgarth Farm, the distance is approximately 8km (5 miles).

Walk a little way up the road and take the footpath on the right which heads unmistakably for the well-defined ridge climbing steeply up to the summit of Fleetwith Pike. As height is gained, the views back down the valley are superb.

From the summit the way is basically to the right to join a path which runs from the top of the Honister Pass to Warnscale Bottom or Haystacks. However, there is no continuous path across the rough intervening ground and many walkers might prefer to follow the good path from Fleetwith summit towards the Honister Pass, turning right on meeting the first mentioned path. The extra distance is about 1km (0.6 mile).

By whichever route, Warnscale Beck is crossed and the path rises to cross broken ground towards Blackbeck Tarn before bearing right to the top of Haystacks. Avoid any track which descends, right, towards Warnscale Bottom. Innominate Tarn is passed before the summit.

From Haystacks there are two paths descending to the top of the Scarth Gap Pass. Use either, then turn right to follow the well-worn route down to Gatesgarth.

Alternatively walkers can overnight in the Black Sail Youth Hostel which is situated below Haystacks in the upper reaches of Ennerdale. This former bothy has not a lot in the way of comfort, but is tremendously popular. It serves meals and has a shower, so allowing a stay high in the mountains, especially on warm summer evenings!

WEST OF ESKDALE

1 **Coast and mountain circuit** of 57km (35 miles). Hard climbing but wonderful views.

From any base in Eskdale ride down towards the coast, forking left by the George IV Inn and then right a little further on, to keep Muncaster Fell on the right. Turn left at the main A595 for 3km (2 miles). At Waberthwaite the Woodall family have produced Cumberland sausage and traditional dry-cured bacon for several generations. The Royal Warrant is held in respect of the sausage. Turn right at Lane End to head for Newbiggin.

The road goes under the railway before bending left to follow the coast, passing the M.O.D. 'danger area'. Cross the railway again at Bootle Station and carry on to join the main road at Bootle. Turn right and stay with the main road for 13km (8 miles).

Turn left to take a minor road close to Broadgate and climb back over Thwaites Fell, passing close to the fine **Swinside stone circle**. The top of the road reaches a height of 400m (1,313 feet), from which point there is a long downhill to rejoin the main road at Broad Oak, north of Waberthwaite, and return to the start.

The above return route is best for Ravenglass and the lower part of Eskdale.

To return to a base further up the valley than the George IV Inn, stay with the main A595 road as far as Duddon Bridge, turn left up the Duddon valley as far as Ulpha, then turn left again to return to Eskdale over Birker Fell.

2 **Circumnavigation of Muncaster Fell**

A shorter, altogether easier, ride of 22km (14 miles).

From a start above The George IV Inn, fork right by the inn and continue through Eskdale Green to the main A595 road. Turn left, passing by Muncaster Mill on the way to Ravenglass (for the railway and Muncaster Castle).

Leave Ravenglass by the same road but turn right along the A595. After crossing the River Esk, turn left at a minor road which stays with the river until it joins the road which goes over Birker Fell. Turn left to return to the George IV Inn.

From a start at Ravenglass the same circuit is completed, turning left by the George IV Inn unless, of course, exploration higher up Eskdale is desired.

WESTERN LAKELAND

1 Gosforth, Seascale and Lower Wasdale countryside

An easy ride of 28km (17.5 miles).

From the foot of Wastwater, where there is a youth hostel at Wasdale Hall, set off towards the coast, shortly turning right to pass through Nether Wasdale. This minor road leads directly to Gosforth (see above for features of this interesting village).

Cross the main road to head for Seascale along the B5344. Victorian Seascale had ambitions as an off the beaten track seaside resort, particularly after the construction of the railway in the 1850s. Never really succeeding, Seascale is now a quiet backwater with a few shops and the occasional hotel and inn.

From Seascale follow the **Cumbria Cycleway** south-east to Drigg and Holmrook. Turn right at the main road, then shortly left to head for Santon Bridge. Go left then right here for a return to Wasdale Hall, passing Nether Wasdale on the way.

2 Cumberland coast and Sellafield.

A more strenuous ride of 38km (23.5 miles).

From Ennerdale Bridge follow the minor road along the south side of the River Ehen to **Egremont**. Go through the town to take the road to the north-west to **St Bees**. Turn left to climb the hill and then fork right along the minor road closest to the sea, leading to Nethertown, despite the name just a village, with inn.

Continue to the attractive village of Braystones, bearing left to Beckermet. Turn right here to take the Cumbria Cycleway direct to the **Sellafield Visitor Centre**.

Return to Ennerdale by leaving the centre by heading to the main road at Calder Bridge. Turn left into the minor road by the church, turning left then right just before the ruins of Calder Abbey (see above). A very minor hill road now goes via Cold Fell and Blakeley Moss all the way back to Ennerdale Bridge.

From a Wasdale base a ride to the Sellafield Visitor Centre means initially heading for Gosforth, turning right at the main road, then left at Calder Bridge. Reverse the directions above to use the coastal road as far as St Bees. A return via Egremont, Haile and Calder Abbey to Calder Bridge keeps use of the main road to a minimum.

3 Whitehaven to Ennerdale Cycle path

This recently created 16km (10 miles) path uses the trackbed of a long disused mineral railway line to create a link from Ennerdale to the sea. Sculpture trail and other features along the way. This is the first leg of a sea to sea route from Whitehaven to Sunderland. Map and

information from Groundwork West Cumbria, 48, High
Street, Cleator Moor. ☎ 01946 813677

FROM BUTTERMERE

1 ⋏ **Buttermere, Newlands, Whinlatter**
●●● Circuit of 50km (31 miles). Includes strenuous climbs.
Leave Buttermere along the minor road past the
church, soon climbing steadily to the 333m (1,093 feet) summit at
Newlands Hause. Apart from the views, the reward is a long downhill
through the beautiful Newlands Valley, virtually all the way to
Braithwaite.

Turn left in Braithwaite, well before reaching the main A66 road, to
start the ascent of the Whinlatter Pass, B5292, largely in woodland. Well
before the 253m (830 feet) summit of the Pass is the **Forest Enterprises
Whinlatter Visitor Centre**, well worth a visit.

The road descends to join B5289, Buttermere to Cockermouth road,
but a left turn to High Lorton provides a short cut to B5289, which
provides a straightforward return to Buttermere village. *From close to
High Lorton a minor road via Hopebeck provides an alternative to B5289
for part of the distance along Lorton Vale.*

2 ⋏ **Lorton Vale, Cockermouth and Mockerkin.**
●●●● A fairly level ride of 39km (24 miles).
From Buttermere ride down the Vale of Lorton along B5289
to Cockermouth.

Return by leaving Cockermouth on the road connecting to the bypass.
This starts as Station Road in the town centre. Go straight across at the
large roundabout, towards Egremont on the A5086. If this road is busy,
which is unusual, there are minor roads between villages to right and left.
In 7km (4 .25 miles) turn left for Mockerkin and climb a little before
descending to the shore of Loweswater. Continue to the junction with
B5289. Turn right to return to Buttermere.

*For a more adventurous return leave A5086 on a left turn 2km (1.25
miles) from Cockermouth. Turn right in 1km (0.6 mile) to follow a very
minor road through farming hamlets and over Mosser Fell, rejoining the
basic route by the Loweswater shore.*

To extend this short ride to 65km (40 miles), cross the River Derwent
in Cockermouth, soon turning left to go through Papcastle, site of a
Roman fort. Continue through Great Broughton and Broughton Moor to
Maryport. Leave Maryport by the A596 towards Carlisle. Turn right at Moor
Park, cross the River Ellen, and go through Dearham bearing left towards
Gilcrux. Well before Gilcrux turn right to Tallentire. After Tallentire fork left to
Bridekirk and continue to the main A595 road. Turn right to return to
Cockermouth and then back to Buttermere as above.

3 ▲ Keswick

Only 37km (23 miles) in length, but a tough circuit using two high passes. Set off along the B5289 on the northern side of Buttermere, pass Gatesgarth, and climb to the top of the Honister Pass. at 332m (1,090 feet). Descend carefully into **Borrowdale,** reached at **Seatoller** (refreshments and tourist information).

Continue along the delightful valley road through **Rosthwaite**, bypassing **Grange in Borrowdale** before reaching **Derwentwater** and Keswick. *Should the Borrowdale road be busy, a good diversion would be to turn left through Grange on the little road which goes attractively above the lake and on through Portinscale to the A66, turning right then right again to Keswick.*

From Keswick take the main A66 to Braithwaite. Turn right at the bridge over the Coledale Beck and start the long but generally gradual ascent to Newlands Hause at 333m (1,093 feet), followed by the shorter, steeper, descent to Buttermere.

For a longer but lower return the Whinlatter Pass (see above) may be used instead of Newlands Hause.

c a r   t o u r s   —   t h e   w e s t

Tours from bases in the western section of the Lake District must, of necessity, heavily involve the coastal towns and villages, with visitor attractions such as the Sellafield nuclear establishment adding variety. Because the mountains are close to the sea, these tours are generally short in distance. Although each tour has a notional starting place based in one or other of the valleys, obviously the various places of interest can be reached from any of the western valleys, generally by using the A595 as a link. For a longer drive, two or more of the routes may be linked together and many places listed for tours in the south and north sections of the book can also readily be reached.

1 ▲ ESKDALE-HAVERRIG-MILLOM-ULPHA-ESKDALE

From **Eskdale** drive down the valley to **Ravenglass** and **Muncaster Castle**. Continue along the A595 through Bootle, with the great bulk of Black Combe above to the left. Keep right to follow A5093 to **Millom** as

the A595 turns left. A small diversion right to **Silecroft** reaches a sand and shingle beach in 1.5km (1 mile). Formerly a hive of industry as a bustling 19th-century iron town, Millom has had to come to terms with being a quiet backwater. The site of the former iron ore mining at **Hodbarrow** is now a major Royal Society for the Protection of Birds nature reserve. At nearby **Haverigg** there are children's adventure play features and safe beaches, with a waterski centre at an artificial lake. In Millom itself there is still a fair range of shops and a park with bowling green, putting green, tennis courts and children's facilities.

The **Folk Museum** has a reconstruction of a drift mine and a permanent exhibition of the life and work of the late Norman Nicholson, the celebrated 20th-century local writer and poet. ☎ 01229 772555. There is still a railway service on the Barrow to Whitehaven (and Carlisle) coastal line.

To return to Eskdale, head north along the A5093. Just out of Millom, close to the road, are the remains of Millom Castle and a 12th-century church with a 'fish' window. Join the A595 and continue to Duddon Bridge and take either left turn to Ulpha. The second turning is the more direct route. Turn left again at Ulpha to return to Eskdale over Birker Fell. The distance is 85km (53 miles) from Eskdale Green.

2 WASDALE-SEASCALE-SELLAFIELD

From **Wasdale** drive via Nether Wasdale to **Gosforth**. Go across the A595 and take the B5344 to **Seascale,** once a minor Victorian seaside resort, now very quiet with just a few shops and the odd inn. Go back to the A595, turn left, then left again at Calder Bridge to visit **Sellafield,** the major centre of British Nuclear Fuels Ltd. The comprehensive visitor centre has hands-on interactive scientific experiments, shows and a welter of technology designed to inform and entertain the whole family. Admission is free. Open every day except Christmas Day, April–October 10.00–18.00, November–March 10.00–16.00. ☎ 019467 27027; fax 019467 27021

From Sellafield return to the A595 at Calder Bridge. Turn right, then left by the church into a minor road which passes close to the ruins of **Calder Abbey,** which are occasionally open to the public. Back again to the A595 and a left turn to return to Gosforth and Wasdale. The distance is 36km (22.5 miles) from Wasdale Hall.

Above left: The Whitehaven Beacon Centre.
Above right: Black Sail Hut Youth Hostel in Ennerdale .
Below: The Sellafield Visitor Centre, where there is a fantastic attraction for visitors.

Above: The sculpture of an iron ore worker at Egremont.
Below left: Buttermere Church gate, displaying a shepherd and sheep.
Below right: The Norman monastery at St Bees.

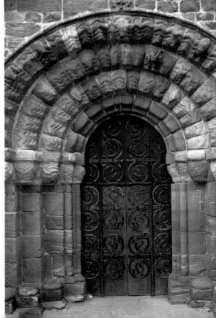

3A ENNERDALE-WHITEHAVEN-ST BEES-EGREMONT-ENNERDALE

From **Ennerdale** the most interesting drive is through part of the former Cumberland iron ore mining area to Whitehaven, returning via St Bees and Egremont, a distance of only about 35km (22 miles) from Ennerdale Bridge, but packed with features.

From Ennerdale Bridge take the minor road to **Cleator Moor,** a former iron ore mining town. Before the town centre is **St Mary's Roman Catholic Church,** designed by Pugin. The church has a grotto similar to that at Lourdes, built by local people during the depression of the 1930s. Each September there are pilgrimages to the grotto. There is a street market in the square at Cleator Moor every Friday.

Continue along B5295 to **Whitehaven**, a largely Georgian town with the town centre streets set out on a·regular rectangular pattern. During the 18th century Whitehaven ranked, after London and Bristol, as the third largest port in England. The main export was coal from the highly productive local mines, matched by imports of tobacco and rum from America and the West Indies. George Washington's grandmother was a local resident; she is buried in **St Nicholas Gardens** and a memorial plaque can be seen in **St Nicholas Chapel.**

The notorious American sea captain and privateer, John Paul Jones, raided the town in 1778 during the American War of Independence. The raid was of little consequence but a spiked cannon can still be seen near the old fort. This was the last occasion on which England was 'invaded' from the sea. Today the port activity is much reduced, but the fine **west pier**, built by the great engineer Sir John Rennie can still be admired. The entire harbour has been declared a conservation area and the **Beacon Centre** has been opened as a modern museum telling the story of Whitehaven's social, industrial and maritime heritage. All areas are accessible by wheelchair. Shop. Exhibitions and events. Admission charge. Open Tuesday–Sunday all the year round, plus Bank Holiday Mondays, 10.00–17.30 Easter–October, 10.00–16.30 November–March (last tickets 45 minutes before closing). Closed Christmas Day. ☎ 01946 592302; fax 01946 599025

Beyond the harbour a notable landmark is the **'candlestick' chimney**, actually a ventilation shaft for one of the mines. Nearby are other mining relics: the last mine closed as recently as 1986.

As would be expected in a substantial town, there are parks and recreation facilities to suit most tastes. In Roper Street, **Michael Moon's Bookshop** has long been a mecca for book collectors and browsers; there is also a small gallery. Street markets are held on Thursdays and Saturdays. **Tourist Information Centre** – the Old Market Hall, ☎ 01946

695678. Of the various churches, the most unusual is **St James,** in High Street opposite the top end of Queen Street. This 18th-century Georgian structure has a beautiful altar piece by a pupil of Correggio, a decorated ceiling and interesting windows. Railway service north to Carlisle and south to Barrow in Furness.

From Whitehaven head south along the B5345 St Bees road (Newtown, then Preston Street in the town centre). Most of the village of **St Bees** rises along one street, with shops, inns and the occasional restaurant. There is, however, a sizeable detached area right by the sea, with some visitor facilities including a café. The **priory church of St Bega** has a fine 12th-century Norman doorway and a wealth of stone relics from the 10th century onwards. St Bega was the daughter of a minor Irish chieftain. In the 7th century she was believed to have crossed the Irish Sea, landed here, become a nun and, after a period at Whitby, founded her own small convent by the shore of Bassenthwaite, on the site of the present St Bega's church. Railway station.

Immediately to the north of the village a path climbs to the top of **St Bees Head**, site of an RSPB nature reserve. Wainwright's Coast to Coast long-distance footpath to Robin Hood's Bay starts (or finishes) at St Bees.

From part way up the main street in St Bees there is a left turn direct to **Egremont**, a small but historic market town with a ruined **Norman castle** on a hill overlooking the River Ehen. **Lowes Court Gallery** on Main Street combines the functions of a gallery, local craft shop and **Tourist Information Centre**, ☎ 01946 820693 Opposite are two attractive sculptures commemorating the former iron ore mining of the area. On the third Saturday in September each year the **Crab Fair** is celebrated. First held in 1267, the fair is based on the free distribution of crab apples to the public, originally by the Lord of Egremont. The apples are still given away but the fair now includes a variety of events. Most unusual is the **World Gurning Championship**, in which contestants pull ugly faces through a horse collar. Street market each Friday.

Of the mining industry which, not so long ago, covered this area there is just one working mine remaining. This is the **Florence Mine**, found on a minor road to the east at the south end of the A595 Egremont bypass. There is a Heritage Centre at the mine, with facilities for the disabled, souvenir shop, coffee shop. Open to visitors every day from the beginning of April to the end of October, 10.00–16.00. Underground tours at 10.30 and 13.30 each Saturday, Sunday and Bank Holiday. ☎/fax 01946 820683

From Egremont a minor road leaves the bypass near its northern end, crosses the River Ehen, joins another road just east of Cleator Moor and stays south-east of the river all the way back to Ennerdale Bridge.

4 ▲ BUTTERMERE-COCKERMOUTH-MARYPORT

From **Buttermere** a drive via Cockermouth to
Maryport is recommended; a suitable circuit gives
a distance of about 65km (40 miles).

Drive by the side of Crummock Water, then the Vale of
Lorton, on the B5289 to **Cockermouth**. Leave
Cockermouth by the A594, cross the River Derwent and rise to a large
roundabout. Go straight across to drive to **Maryport,** a small town which
has grown from mid 18th-century origins. The development was started
by Humphrey Senhouse II, Lord of the Manor at the time. The town
which he built was named after his wife, Mary. Once a busy little port,
Maryport has shared in the general industrial decline of the area. How-
ever, successful efforts are being made in redeveloping parts of the
harbour for leisure and tourism. The **Maritime Museum**, at the foot of
Senhouse Street, has objects, models and paintings illustrating
Maryport's proud maritime tradition. Free admission. Open from Easter
to the end of October, Monday–Thursday 10.00–17.00, Friday and
Saturday 10.00–13.00 and 14.00–17.00, Sunday 14.00–17.00. From 1
November to Easter, Monday–Saturday 10.00–13.00 and 14.00–16.30.
The Museum is also a **Tourist Information Centre**. ☎ 01900 813738

Moored in the harbour are **Maryport Steamships**, comprising the
Flying Buzzard and *VIC 96*. These exhibits, under the management of a
charitable trust, continue the maritime theme. Admission charge. Open
in summer, every day 10.00–16.00. ☎ 01900 815954

Back in the town, a short walk to **Fleming Square** will reveal a well
restored former market square bounded by Georgian and Victorian
houses. Continuing uphill, at the top is a substantial building known as
the Battery, once a Royal Naval Reserve Station and now housing the
Senhouse Roman Museum, noted for its collection of Roman sculpture.
Admission charge. Open every day July–September, 10.00–17.00; April–
June and October, Tuesday, Thursday, Friday, Saturday and Sunday,
10.00–17.00; November to March, Friday, Saturday and Sunday 10.30–
16.00. Adjacent to the Battery is the site of the **Roman fort of Alauna**,
an important link in the coastal defensive system which complemented
the better-known Hadrian's Wall. ☎ 01900 816168

From Maryport a different return to Cockermouth may be made by
taking the minor road through Broughton Moor, Great Broughton and
Papcastle, joining the A594 on the edge of Cockermouth.

From the centre of Cockermouth take Station Road and continue up to
the big roundabout on the bypass. Go straight across towards Egremont,
A5086. In 7km.(4.5 miles) turn left to Mockerkin and continue by the
side of **Loweswater** to Loweswater hamlet. The B5289 is soon joined;
turn sharp right to return to Buttermere.

3 THE NORTH

COCKERMOUTH AND BASSENTHWAITE

Cockermouth

Cockermouth is a historic market town, with a charter of 1221. The focal point of the medieval town was, inevitably, the castle, originally mid 12th century, sited close to the meeting point of the **Derwent** and **Cocker** rivers. Most of today's ruins, not open to the public, date from 1360 to 1370. Even earlier in history is the site of a Roman fort, **Derventio**, at **Papcastle** to the north-west of the present town. Main Street is wide, tree-lined and quite handsome and, together with Station Street (there is no longer a railway), is well provided with shops, inns and other refreshment places. The street market is held on Mondays.

At one end of Main Street is Wordsworth House, a well-proportioned Georgian house of 1745, with some 18th-century furnishings, now in the ownership of the National Trust. William Wordsworth was born here in 1770, leaving

Above: Derwentwater from Friar's Crag

on the death of his mother in 1778. Across the road is a bust of the poet.

The impressive statue in the middle of Main Street is the Earl of Mayo, local Member of Parliament in the mid 19th century, then Viceroy of India until his unfortunate assassination in the Andaman Islands in 1872.

All Saints' Church was rebuilt in 1852-54 following a disastrous fire. Wordsworth attended the previous church and his father, John, is buried in the churchyard. There is a memorial window to the great poet. Close to the church is a former grammar school; among its pupils was, inevitably, Wordsworth and also Fletcher Christian, of *Mutiny on the Bounty* fame.

At 7, Market Place, in a niche in the wall, is the 'butter bell' which for many years was rung to signal the start of the weekly market. Behind the market area

PLACES TO VISIT IN COCKERMOUTH

Wordsworth House, Main Street. National Trust.
Childhood home of William and Dorothy. 18th-century furnishings. Garden and terrace. Restaurant. Open late March to end of October, weekdays, and Saturdays in high season and before a Bank Holiday Monday. Admission charge (discounted combined tickets with Dove Cottage and Rydal Mount are available). ☎ 01900 824805

Jennings Brewery
Long established brewery at foot of castle mound. Public tours, usually at 11.00 and 14.00 each weekday mid March – late October; Saturdays April – September and Sundays mid July – end of August. Also Bank Holidays. Gift shop. Admission charge. Group bookings are invited.
☎ 01900 823214; fax 01900 827462

Aspects of Motoring
The Western Lakes Motor Museum. Housed in the maltings at Jennings Castle Brewery. Collection of vintage motor cars, with slide show, video presentation and interactive computer station. Coffee and souvenir shop. Open daily 10.00–16.00. Closed February, Christmas Day, Boxing Day and New Year's Day.

The Printing House
102 Main Street. Working museum of printing. A permanent exhibition of historical printing equipment. Admission charge. Open Monday–Saturday, 10.00–16.00.
☎ 01900 824984; fax 01900 823124

is the site of the former Fletcher Old Hall, now used for car parking. Here, on 17 May, 1568, the wealthy local merchant Henry Fletcher received Mary, Queen of Scots and a handful of followers as they fled from defeat in Scotland. According to legend, Fletcher provided Mary with material to replace her tattered clothing.

Kirkgate is a narrow turning to the right from St. Helen's Street, close to the Market Place. The narrow street soon opens out into a surprisingly attractive area of small but gracious houses with horse chestnut trees and a cobbled forecourt. The Bitter End Inn claims to be Cumbria's smallest brewery

A little way from the town centre, to the left of Station Road as it climbs towards the by-pass, is Harris Park. Here a little statue commemorates the childhood of William and Dorothy Wordsworth.

Cumberland Toy Museum
Banks Court, off Market Place. Mainly British toys of the present century, including model railways. Admission charge. Open daily from 1 February–30 November, 10.00–17.00. ☎ 01900 827606

Castlegate House
Opposite the entrance to the castle. Listed Georgian house and garden of 1739. Original paintings, ceramics, sculpture and glass. Private home, but with monthly exhibitions. Programme available on request.
☎ 01900 822149

Lakeland Sheep and Wool Centre
By the roundabout on the A66 on the edge of town. Exhibition based on live sheep of many different breeds, including shearing and sheepdog displays four times each day. Theatre, and CUMWEST exhibition and visual show, concentrating on the western lakes and coast. Restaurant; gift shop; Disabled access. Admission charge. The centre includes overnight accommodation. Open daily all year round. Shows at 10.30, 12.00, 14.00, 15.30 every day from Easter–mid November, and from mid February–Easter each day except Mondays and Tuesdays. ☎/fax 01900 822673

Cockermouth Golf Club Embleton. ☎ 017687 76223

Cockermouth Sports Centre and Swimming Pool ☎ 01900 823596

Tourist Information Centre ☎ 01900 822634

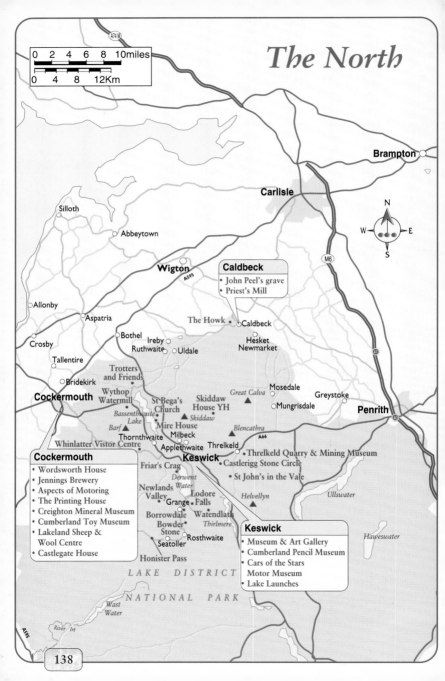

The North

0 2 4 6 8 10 miles
0 4 8 12 Km

A74 M

Brampton

Carlisle

Silloth

Abbeytown

Wigton

A595

Caldbeck
• John Peel's grave
• Priest's Mill

M6

Allonby

Aspatria

The Howk • Caldbeck

Bothel

Ireby

Ruthwaite

Uldale

Hesket
Newmarket

Crosby

Tallentire

Bridekirk

Trotters
and Friends

Mosedale

Greystoke

Cockermouth

Wythop
Watermill

St Bega's
Church

Skiddaw
House YH

Great Calva

Mungrisdale

*Bassenthwaite
Lake*

Mire
House

▲ *Skiddaw*

Penrith

Barf ▲

Thornthwaite

Milbeck

Blencathra

Whinlatter Vistor Centre

Applethwaite

Threlkeld

A66

Friar's Crag

Keswick

• Threlkeld Quarry & Mining Museum

• Castlerigg Stone Circle

Cockermouth
• Wordsworth House
• Jennings Brewery
• Aspects of Motoring
• The Printing House
• Creighton Mineral Museum
• Cumberland Toy Museum
• Lakeland Sheep &
  Wool Centre
• Castlegate House

*Derwent
Water*

Newlands
Valley

Lodore
Falls

• St John's in the Vale

Helvellyn

▲

Ullswater

Grange

Borrowdale

Watendlath

Bowder
Stone

Thirlmere

Keswick
• Museum & Art Gallery
• Cumberland Pencil Museum
• Cars of the Stars
  Motor Museum
• Lake Launches

Seatoller

Rosthwaite

Haweswater

Honister Pass

LAKE   DISTRICT

NATIONAL   PARK

*Wast
Water*

River Irt

A595

138

Above: Watendlath.
Below: St Bega's Church, Bassenthwaite.

Bassenthwaite

Bassenthwaite Lake

From Cockermouth, the road to Keswick heads towards Bassenthwaite Lake. Though not the most spectacular in Lakeland, it is a fine large sheet of water with the distinction of being the only lake in the district which is actually called Lake (All the others include 'mere' or 'water' in their names, rendering the addition of the word 'lake' superfluous.) Despite the rather intrusive presence of the main A66, Penrith, Keswick, Cockermouth and west coast road along the western shore, Bassenthwaite is maintained as one of the quieter lakes, with emphasis on wildlife, particularly waterfowl. It is best appreciated from the eastern side, where the Keswick to Carlisle road, A591, keeps well away from the lake and the tiny but historic and evocative church of St Bega stands lonely by the shore.

PLACES TO VISIT IN BASSENTHWAITE

Bassenthwaite village
With inn and village green, has a peaceful situation a little to the north of the A591, reached only by minor roads.

The Whinlatter Pass
Leaves the A66 at Braithwaite, to the west of Keswick and climbs gently over to the Vale of Lorton, for Crummock and Buttermere. Much of the Whinlatter area is covered by commercial woodland owned and managed by Forest Enterprises, with a visitor centre a little way short of the road summit.

Thornthwaite
Small village with a well known craft gallery situated on a minor road parallel with the A66.

Whinlatter Visitor Centre
Well-equipped forest centre and park, with displays, shop, refreshments and information. Open all year, summer 10.00–17.00, winter 11.00–1600. ☎ 017687 78469

St Bega's Church
By the shore of Bassenthwaite Lake, reached only on foot from the Mirehouse area. Much rebuilt but partially pre-Norman structure on a legendary site. The circular churchyard is a strong clue to an Anglo-Saxon church here. Associated with St Bega, daughter of an Irish chieftain, who landed at St Bees in the 7th century and who may have ministered from an abbey on this site. Melvyn Bragg's *Credo* is based on the St Bega legends. Outside the church is a modern cross where open air services are occasionally held.

Mirehouse

A small stately home situated between mountains and lake a few miles north west of Keswick by the A591 Carlisle road. Since 1688 the house, with its gardens and grounds, has been passed down through inheritance. Still occupied by the Spedding family, it has a wealth of literary and artistic connections. Tennyson stayed here when working on his *Morte d'Arthur*, gaining inspiration from the Bassenthwaite lakeside and St Bega's church. Woodland adventure playgrounds. Varied gardens. Walks over private grounds to lake shore. Tearoom in former sawmill nearby. Admission charge. Gardens and tearoom open daily 10.00–17.30, April–mid October. House open Sundays and Wednesdays (and Fridays in August), April–mid October, 14.00–16.30 (last entry).
☎/fax (house) 017687 72287; (tearoom) 017687 74317

Wythop Watermill and Woodworking Museum

In the hamlet of Wythop Mill, at the entrance of Wythop Valley, 1km (0.6mile) from the A66 and 2km (1.5 miles) from the Pheasant Inn. Signposted from the main road. Vintage woodworking tools and machinery powered by an overshot waterwheel. Victorian kitchen, wheelwright and blacksmith displays. Local history exhibition. Admission charge. Open daily except Mondays from Good Friday–end of October, 10.30–17.30. ☎ 017687 76394

Trotters and Friends

Coalbeck Farm, Bassenthwaite. By the foot of the lake, close to Armathwaite Hall and the Castle Inn. Collection of farm and other animals, including rare breeds. Play areas; teashop; picnic area; gift shop. Pony and tractor/trailer rides during school holidays. Admission charge. Open daily from late March–early November, 10.00–17.00 (last admission), Saturdays and Sundays from November–March (daily during Christmas holidays), 11.00–16.00 (last admission). ☎ 017687 76239; fax 017687 76220

KESWICK, BORROWDALE, THE VALE OF NEWLANDS, THRELKELD AND CALDBECK

Keswick

Sometimes known as the 'Queen of the Lakes', **Keswick** is a very popular small market town beautifully situated between the foot of Derwentwater and the soaring height of Skiddaw.

The oldest part of the town, at **Great Crosthwaite**, is now off-centre. Here, the splendid church is dedicated to St Kentigern (or Mungo) who was active in Cumbria in the 6th century, when there could well

Above: The Pencil museum, Keswick. *Middle*: Market day, Keswick. *Below*: The National Trust Centenery Stone at Derwentwater.

Events — The North

COCKERMOUTH
Cockermouth Show Early August. Small local agricultural show.
☎ Tourist Information Centre 01900 822634.
Lorton Sheep Dog Trials and Hound Show Late July.

AROUND KESWICK
Keswick Jazz Festival Mid May.

HESKET NEWMARKET
Hesket Newmarket Show Traditional local agricultural show. Late
August. ☎ Tourist Information Centre at Keswick, Penrith or
Cockermouth, see page 218.

PLACES TO VISIT IN KESWICK

Cumberland Pencil Museum
Home of the world's first pencils. Easy to find by the side of Main
Street, close to the bank of the River Greta. Historical displays; video
shows and audio tours; children's activities; gift shop. Admission
charge. Open all year, 09.30–16.00 (last admission), closed
Christmas Day, Boxing Day and New Year's Day. ☎ 017687 73626

Keswick Museum and Art Gallery, Station Road.
Fascinating local history and curio collection, including a scale model
of the Lake District, made in 1834. Original manuscripts and
memorabilia from the Lakes Poets in 'poets corner'. Admission
charge. Open daily Easter–end of October, 10.00–16.00.
☎ 017687 73263

Cars of the Stars Motor Museum, Standish Street.
Celebrity television and film vehicles. Admission charge. Open
10.00–1700, Easter–New Year, weekends only in December,
February half-term. ☎ 017687 73757; fax 017687 72090

Tea Pottery, Central Car Park Road.
Offshoot from a similar workshop in Leyburn, Yorkshire. Specialised
manufacture of strange and whimsical teapots, free of charge to
visitors. Gift shop. Open daily, 09.00–17.00, winter 10.00–16.00.
☎ 017687 73983

(cont'd…)

(Keswick cont'd)

Hope Park, Lake Road.
Attractive gardens, pitch and putt, putting and obstacle golf. Games
open from late March–early November.

Fitz Park, Station Road.
Spacious recreation area. Bowls, tennis and putting. Children's
playground. Games open from May–September.

Keswick Golf Club, Threlkeld Hall, Threlkeld.
Visitors welcome. ☎ 017687 79010

Keswick Leisure Pool, Station Road.
Pool with wave machine and water slide. Café, sunbed and beach
area. Disabled facilities. Open daily (closed Mondays and Tuesday
afternoons in winter).

Theatre by the Lake
A fine new theatre on the site formerly occupied by the makeshift
Century Theatre. Good quality theatrical and musical productions
throughout the year. ☎ 017687 74411

Alhambra Cinema, St John's Street.
Traditional cinema open from February to November.
☎ 017687 72195

Lake District National Park Information Centre
Moot Hall, Market Square. ☎ 017687 72645

Keswick on Derwentwater Launch Co. Ltd
Timetabled service of launches calling at total of seven landing stages
around the lake, alternately clockwise and anti-clockwise at half-hourly
intervals. Daily from mid March–end of November, 10.00–20.00
(earlier in low season). In winter, Saturdays and Sundays only, six
sailings only. Boats for hire. ☎ 017687 72263; fax. 017687 73013

Nichol End Marine, Portinscale.
Windsurfing, boats for hire, Canoeing. ☎ 017687 73082

Castlerigg Stone Circle
2.5km (1.5 miles) east of Keswick, reached by the A5271, the A591
(Penrith) road for a very short distance, then a signposted right fork
direct to the stone circle. Finest of all Lakeland prehistoric stone
circles, with unrivalled mountain backdrops in all directions.

Armathwaite Hall Equestrian Centre, Coalbeck Farm, Bassenthwaite
Lake, Keswick. Variety of horseriding offered, including tuition.
☎ 017687 76949; fax 017687 76220

have been a first church on this site. His symbols – tree, bell, fish and bird – are displayed in the churchyard entrance gate. Today's structure is mostly 15th century, with just a little Norman work remaining from a church of 1181. Large scale restoration in 1844 has fortunately left a dignified and spacious church .

Inside is a well carved 14th-century font and a striking white marble memorial to the poet **Robert Southey**, a native of Keswick for many years. The epitaph was written by William Wordsworth, his successor as Poet Laureate. **Canon Rawnsley**, one of the three founders of the National Trust, is buried in the churchyard.

As the centre of a great sheep farming area, Keswick became a notable wool town for several centuries, part of the widespread domains of Fountains Abbey.

In the 16th century industry also came to Keswick. Queen Elizabeth I founded the Company of Mines Royal and experienced German miners opened up the Goldscope Mine in the Vale of Newlands, with rich deposits of copper. Other mines followed and furnaces were built at Keswick. Later, graphite was discovered near Seathwaite, in Borrowdale. This valuable mineral had a variety of uses, eventually becoming the foundation of the world's first pencil industry. Mining activity ebbed and flowed until early in the 20th century.

In the second half of the 18th century Keswick became the Lake District's first tourist destination, visited by most of the early travellers of the Romantic period, such as John Dalton, John Brown and Thomas Gray. Fortunately, several of these travellers set down their impressions of the district, which now make fascinating reading. Not far behind in discovering the beauty of the Keswick area were the first **Lakeland Poets**, Coleridge, Southey and Shelley; Wordsworth was a frequent visitor from Grasmere.

The great and the famous were followed by lesser mortals in considerable numbers after the branch line from the main railway line at Penrith was opened to Keswick in 1865. The town's role as a holiday destination had begun in earnest. Sadly, the railway closed in 1972 but Keswick's popularity has in no way diminished.

The present town centre is mainly of 19th-century buildings, not particularly distinguished, but with a pleasant bustle around the Market Place, where the prominent Moot Hall of 1813 now houses the Tourist Information Office. Plentiful hotels, inns, shops and restaurants all contribute to the holiday atmosphere. **Derwentwater** is Keswick's own lake, truly beautiful, and normally so tranquil that nearby mountains such as Cat Bells are mirrored in the water. The road into the Borrowdale valley skirts the

Above: *Great Calva between Lonscale Fell and Blencathra.*

Below: *Skiddaw House and Great Calva.*

Above left: Castlerigg with the view to Matterdale Common.
Above right: The tarn at Watendlath.
Below: Derwentwater from near Ashness Bridge.

eastern shore, with parking and picnic areas, whilst the Grange in Borrowdale to Portinscale road on the west side provides gallery-like viewpoints over lake and town. At the Keswick end of the lake are extensive boat landings, beyond a huge car park and the Century Theatre. A little way further along this shore is **Friar's Crag**, a viewpoint beloved of John Ruskin, from which the mountains along the sides and at the head of Borrowdale, seen across the water, are truly picturesque. Close to Friar's Crag are a memorial tablet to Canon Rawnsley and a John Ruskin memorial stone.

The lake has four islands, all owned by the National Trust. Of these, the 7-acre **Derwent Island** is inhabited. In the 16th century it was the home of some of the German miners employed locally. They cleared the dense tree growth and constructed a range of domestic buildings. After their departure the island changed hands several times. One notable late 18th-century owner was Joseph Pocklington, who built a large house and a miscellany of other structures including a mock church, a boathouse in the style of a Gothic chapel, a pseudo-Druid circle and a small fort. The porter's lodge was also fortified and was used in the 'naval battle' annual regattas which Pocklington organised from 1787. Understandably, Wordsworth ridiculed Pocklington's

excesses. The island was later purchased by the Marshall family, Leeds-based industrialists, who acquired several estates in Lakeland. The house was much altered and, with diversified tree planting, the effect is now much more tasteful. The family gave the island to the National Trust in 1951; it is now tenanted. In recent years, with the tenant's co-operation, the Trust has organised a limited number of visits to the island, including entry to parts of the house.

St Herbert's Island is believed to have been the home of a religious hermit, possibly as early as the 6th century.

Borrowdale

From Keswick and Derwentwater the Borrowdale valley penetrates to the very heart of Lakeland, with dramatic mountain scenery all the way contrasting with the woodland, water and green fields, to give Borrowdale its high scenic attraction and its popularity among the favourite valleys of Lakeland.

In travelling from Keswick, the first village reached is **Grange in Borrowdale,** with its fine double bridge over the River Derwent. A little further are the **Lodore Falls,** close to the Lodore Hotel, where the Watendlath Beck tumbles abruptly down the precipitous valley side.

Moving 3km (2 miles) from the head of the lake, the valley sides squeeze the road and the river tightly together for some distance in the **Jaws of Borrowdale**, a very scenic part of the valley, with Castle Crag trying to make up for its lack of real height (299m – 980 ft) with its aggressively steep upthrust. Fairly close to the roadside, the **Bowder Stone**, a huge detached boulder 9m (30ft) high and weighing 1,900 tons, has been an object of awe and wonderment since the arrival of the first travellers. In those far-off days sensitive souls were known to have drawn tight the curtains of their carriage windows when passing through this savage and frightening scenery. There is now a ladder to the top of the stone.

After the 'jaws', the valley opens out to an area with a few riverside fields, which have been subject to serious flooding from time to time. Here, centuries ago, the 'Kings of Borrowdale' reigned supreme over their tiny domain. **Rosthwaite**, with inns and post-office stores is the largest settlement, with other hamlets at **Stonethwaite**, just off the main road, **Longthwaite**, with youth hostel, and **Seatoller**, with tourist information and restaurant, the terminus of the valley bus service. The farmstead of **Seathwaite** provides the end of the road car parking for those heading on foot to Styhead Tarn, Great Gable, and/or Scafell. Seathwaite is also the proud possessor of the gauge which consistently records the maximum rainfall in England – about

365cm (144 inches) per annum.

As the valley head is approached, it seems to be impossible for the road to be anything but a cul-de-sac, petering out at the foot of uncompromisingly steep and high mountains. But this is not so; a turn to the right, through Sea-toller, exposes a gap between Honister Crag and Dale Head which allows a vehicular escape over the **Honister Pass** (356m – 1176 ft in height) to Buttermere. Despite 25 per cent gradients this is not a difficult pass to drive. **Honister Slate Mine Visitor Centre** offers tours of the mine several times each day. ☎ 017687 77230

Situated at the end of a no through road in a side valley is **Watendlath**, a tiny farming hamlet prettily set beside its tarn among the mountains. There is a strong literary association with Hugh Walpole's *Rogue Herries* novels, which have a firm base in Borrowdale; his heroine Judith Paris lived in Watendlath. The little road climbs steeply from the side of Derwentwater, passing a famous 'surprise view' and traversing Ashness Bridge, probably the most photographed in Lakeland.

Vale of Newlands

Despite its proximity to Keswick, Newlands is one of Lakeland's quieter valleys, much less visited than its neighbour, Borrowdale. This comparative neglect has nothing to do with the quality of the scenery. Cat Bells and its ridge,

Dale Head, Hindscarth and Robinson, and the grouping of Causey Pike, Sail and Grizedale Pike, form a superb mountain arena, whilst the valley itself has bright green meadows spread around centuries old farming hamlets of weathered stone. The lack of a lake or other particular focal point is probably most significant.

There is only one road of significance in the valley, climbing high on the western flank to Newlands Hause (333m–1,093ft.) before descending steeply to Buttermere.

Newlands Church is tiny, charming and well kept. At one end of the building was the former school room.

Threlkeld

A pleasant but rather workaday large village a few kilometres to the east of Keswick, along the main A66 Penrith road, superbly situated at the foot of Blencathra (Saddleback). The village has inns (one of the 17th century), and a post office/store.

South of the village is **Threlkeld Quarry and Mining Museum.** It is reached from the St John's in the Vale Road, a right turn to the south off the main A66. Exhibits include a history of mining exhibition and museum of artifacts. There is an underground mine trip and a water-wheel is under construction plus a shop with minerals, mining, geology and mineralogy books, gemstone jewellery and original paintings. This attraction

is still under development and a short train ride and a nature trail are to be added. Admission charge. Open 10.00–16.45, summer (until end of October), for winter opening contact Tourist Information Centre, Moot Hall, Keswick. ☎ 017687 / 79747 (day), 01228 561883 (evening).

St John's in the Vale

An attractive farming valley with a minor road (B5322) leaving the A66 near to Threlkeld and connecting with the A591 Windermere to Keswick road at Legburthwaite hamlet, which has a youth hostel in the former school and a small chapel. To the east of the valley, Clough Head and Great Dodd are heights at the northern end of the long Helvellyn ridge. Castle Crag, near Legburthwaite, has long been esteemed as a Romantic scenic feature. The much lower hills of High Rigg and Low Rigg form the western boundary of the valley, with a very minor cul-de-sac road climbing between them to the church of St John's in the Vale, rebuilt in 1845 from a much earlier church, strong on scenic location but weak on likely congregation.

Further south, near Sosgill Farm, St John's Beck is crossed by Sosgill Bridge, an old packhorse bridge.

Thirlmere

For more than 100 years Thirlmere has been a major supplier of water to Manchester.

150

The former Manchester Corporation dammed the lake at its northern end, raising the level by about 15m (50 feet) and constructed a pipeline all the way to Manchester. Part of a hamlet at Wythburn, including an inn patronised by Wordsworth, was demolished and submerged. At the same time, for water quality reasons, vast numbers of regimented coniferous trees were planted and the public was excluded from as much of the catchment area as could be contrived. In short, Thirlmere and its valley for many years constituted a sad hole in the heart of the district; a place to travel through along the main Windermere to Keswick road rather than to linger and enjoy.

Fortunately, more enlightened attitudes now prevail and the successor water authority and company have diversified some of the tree planting, opened up footpaths along the valley sides and provided access points to the lake, with car parking. At the south end, the simple little church at Wythburn survived the raising of the water level and can readily be visited; there is a car park behind.

Scenically, the valley is dominated by Helvellyn, third highest of the Lakeland mountains.

Caldbeck

The area north of the Skiddaw and Blencathra mountain groups is without doubt the quietest and most remote part of the Lake District, although it is just within the boundary of the national park.

As the mountains diminish progressively towards the Solway Plain, sheep farming dominates and there are only two settlements which are of general interest to visitors, and even these villages attract only a tiny fraction of the attention given to, say, Grasmere or Elterwater.

Caldbeck is the main centre of this spacious area, sitting attractively in a shallow valley, with village green and duckpond. Since the 13th century the nearby hills have yielded a variety of minerals in commercial quantities; wolfram and barytes were mined until the early 1960s. In Elizabethan times the imported German miners re-opened several mines which were already old.

Closer to the village, woollen, paper, corn and bobbin mills all made use of the water power available from the Cald Beck and its tributaries.

Today, Caldbeck is best known as the resting place of **John Peel**, the relentless huntsman who ran a pack of hounds for more than 50 years. Peel became famous because the words strung together by a close friend and applied to a local tune or 'rant' were later set to a better tune by the conductor of the Carlisle Choral Society. Despite the dubious literary and musical merit, this refrain has ensured immortality for a man whose sole achievement in life was to pursue foxes a little harder and, presumably, more successfully than most of his fellow huntsmen.

The story of **Mary, Maid of Buttermere** is related elsewhere. After the heady excitement and fame of her youth Mary, apparently none the worse for her experience with 'Hon. Augustus Hope', spent the remainder of her life in Caldbeck as a farmer's wife and a mother. She is buried quite close to John Peel.

From a total of six at the time of peak activity, one inn remains, together with a post office/store/petrol station and two tea/coffee shops.

PLACES TO VISIT IN CALDBECK

Caldbeck Parish Church
Like the church at Crosthwaite, Keswick, this church is dedicated to St Kentigern (or Mungo), exiled Bishop of Glasgow, who promoted Christianity in the northern part of Cumbria in the 6th century. It is likely that there was an early church on this site, but the present building is largely of the 16th century, with a Norman porch doorway, Victorian windows and other features spread over the centuries. The churchyard contains the graves of John Peel and Mary Harrison (née Robinson), Maid of Buttermere. Both are close to the west wall of the churchyard.

St Kentigern's Well
By the packhorse bridge over Cald Beck, close to the church. St Kentigern is reputed to have preached and baptised here.

Priest's Mill
Last used as a mill in the 1930s, now restored and used as a craft workshop, bookshop and restaurant.

Old Smithy Behind the Oddfellows Inn, now a craft centre and teashop.

Near to Caldbeck is **Hesket Newmarket**. Now just a peaceful, unspoilt, village, with inn, shop, market cross and bull ring, Hesket Newmarket did have ambitions 200 years ago. A market charter was granted in the mid 18th century and for about 100 years a market was held. Although a fair amount of trade was generated, this extended role was never entirely successful and Hesket reverted to its previous status as a quiet village.

WILLIAM WORDSWORTH

Ask any visitor the name of a famous poet associated with the Lake District and, even from those who have never read a poem in their lives, there is only one possible answer – William Wordsworth. Indeed, there is no other name in any walk of life which is so indivisible with the District; Beatrix Potter, John Ruskin, Canon Rawnsley and A.Wainwright must all compete for second place in public recognition.

Childhood

Wordsworth was born in 1770 at Cockermouth where his father John was lawyer and agent to Sir James Lowther of Lowther Castle, who became the first Earl Lonsdale in 1784. The Lowther family were long established and immensely powerful throughout Westmorland and Cumberland and Sir James was largely responsible for the profitable development of the rich iron and coal deposits of West Cumberland. Despite the family wealth, Sir James owed a considerable sum of money to John Wordsworth for many years, recovered by William after the death of his father in 1783.

Of the four other Wordsworth children, William's sister **Dorothy**, 21 months his junior, was much the most significant. The family home in Cockermouth is a handsome Georgian house of modest size in the main street, now in the care of the National Trust. As small children, whilst living with relatives in Penrith, William and Dorothy attended Mrs. Birkett's dame school, beside the churchyard; Mary (later to marry William) and Sara Hutchinson were fellow pupils. The building is still in existence as a coffee shop.

Schooldays and Cambridge

In 1778 his mother died and William's education continued at Hawkshead Grammar School where, with his brothers, he was a pupil from 1778-87. Dorothy was sent to live with relatives in Yorkshire. The grammar school, for about 100 boys, had been founded in 1585 by Edwin Sandys, Archbishop of York, who had strong Hawkshead connections. The school is open to visitors, its prime exhibit being the desk upon which Wordsworth carved his initials. Whilst at school here William lodged with Ann Tyson whose cottage in the village centre can still be seen, although it is not open to the public.

Outside school hours young William took to roaming around the surrounding countryside and fells, often well into the night, absorbing the sights, the sounds and the smells, his sensitive character deeply appreciating the wholeness of nature, storing up a vast well of experience from which he would draw for inspiration for the rest of his long creative life. Works

Above: Priest's Mill, Caldbeck.
Middle: Bust of William
Wordsworth, Cockermouth.
Below: Caldbeck.

WILLIAM
WORDSWORTH
1770 - 1850

inspired particularly from this period include his autobiographical masterpiece *The Prelude,* and the *Ode on Intimations of Immortality* from *Recollections of Early Childhood.*

After Hawkshead he went on to study at Cambridge, without in any way distinguishing himself. His father having died in 1783, he was financially supported by two uncles. On leaving Cambridge William was something of a wanderer, without any clear idea of what he wanted to do in life and with quite radical political opinions. This was, after all, the era of popular revolution in Europe and, after a walking tour in France, for a while he became an admirer of Napoleon.

A second French visit in 1791–2 had far more personal significance in that a love affair with Annette Vallon in Orleans resulted in the birth of a daughter, Caroline. Although, mainly because of opposition from Annette's family and the long drawn out Napoleonic War between Britain and France, marriage was not possible, William always acknowledged his responsibility and over the years provided a good deal of financial support for Caroline.

Dorothy and Marriage

On returning to Britain, William was reunited with his devoted sister Dorothy, beginning the lifelong relationship in which her role as his closest friend, soulmate and provider of much of his inspiration has constantly intrigued biographers and others. Dorothy's journals continue to provide the closest insight into William's personality and make fascinating reading, particularly sections such as that describing her reaction to William's marriage. After several years in the West Country, William and Dorothy returned to the Lake District for good in 1799, taking the tenancy of Dove Cottage, a small former inn at Town End, Grasmere. The first poems had been published in 1793 and in the now highly conducive surroundings William was soon in full spate, producing what is widely regarded as his finest work. He married Mary Hutchinson in 1802, producing five children in a comparatively short space of time whilst Dorothy remained as part of a happy triumvirate. Dove Cottage, largely in its original state, and the adjacent barn conversion to form the Wordsworth Museum, are now administered by the Wordsworth Trust as a compelling visitor attraction.

By 1808 the extended family had outgrown the cottage and moved to Allan Bank, a substantial house above Grasmere village of which, ironically, Wordsworth had earlier expressed disapproval as being intrusive in the landscape. He did plant some extra screening trees in front of the house. From 1811–13 the Wordsworths lived in the

Parsonage opposite Grasmere church. This turned out to be a most unhappy period as the house was dark and damp and two of their children – Thomas (6) and Catherine (4) died. The final move of house was to Rydal Mount which William rented from Lady le Fleming of nearby Rydal Hall in 1813, living here until his death in 1850. The house is open to visitors.

As his fame spread, so William's youthful ardour mellowed and he became more of an establishment figure, to the dismay of many youthful admirers. The ultimate accolade was the award of the Poet Laureate title in 1843, on the death of his friend Southey. For many years he courted the patronage of the Lowther family, from whom he obtained the moderately lucrative post of Distributor of Stamps for Westmorland, later adding Cumberland. This undemanding job was concerned with the payment of duty on various legal documents. The office in Ambleside which he occasionally used is in Church Street, beside what is now Stampers restaurant.

With the Lakes Poets

Wordsworth's relationships over the years with other poets and writers – The Lakes Poets – are second in importance only to his relationship with Dorothy. Having met and greatly admired Samuel Taylor Coleridge during his years in the West Country, the two were reunited in Lakeland in a brilliantly creative association until disagreement largely over Coleridge's use of drugs and alcohol led to the latter's final departure in 1810. Another acquaintance was Thomas De Quincey, an opium addict who, after admiring Wordsworth from afar for many years eventually succeeded him as tenant of Dove Cottage

Of all the 'Lakes Poets' the most enduring bond was that between Robert Southey and Wordsworth. Southey, with his large family, lived at Greta Hall Keswick for 40 years until his death in 1843. William often made the long walk from Grasmere or Rydal over to Keswick to visit his old friend. Another regular visitor to the Wordsworths over a period of years was the great Scottish writer, Sir Walter Scott.

Wordsworth's enduring fame is based firmly on his massive output of poetry whether the vast 14-volume work *The Prelude,* or the many shorter, more accessible, pieces such as 'I wandered lonely as a cloud' (describing the 'host of golden daffodils' by the Ullswater shore at Gowbarrow Park) or 'The Rainbow' which includes the immortal line, 'The child is father of the man'.

Guide to the Lakes

However, in his own lifetime, his prose work *Guide to the Lakes* was far more successful from a sales point of view than any of the published poetry. This work started life as an anonymous preface to a volume of sketches of selected views of the Lake District by Rev. Joseph Wilkinson. William did not even like the sketches. Suitably revised and with added chapters on geology and botany (the former by the celebrated Professor Adam Sedgewick of Sedbergh) this preface eventually became a book in its own right.

The fifth edition of 1845, as republished with an introduction and notes by Ernest de Selincourt, is still available. This is very much a guide book of its time. The information which helped visitors to find their way around the district is quite perfunctory, followed by long sections setting out Wordsworth's strong views on matters such as the iniquity of planting foreign species of trees, particularly larches, the colouring of buildings and the inferiority of alpine scenery when compared with the Lake District.

The de Selincourt edition also includes William's eloquent letters to the editor of the *Morning Post* concerning the proposed construction of a railway to Windermere and beyond. Two themes emerge strongly from the guide, including these letters. Firstly, that by today's standards Wordsworth was highly opinionated and had what we would call a snobbish view of the ability of the lower orders of society to appreciate the beauty of the finer things of life such as Lakeland scenery. Secondly, and more to his credit, he emerges as a true, probably the first, Lake District environmentalist, at that early stage recognising the fragility of the local landscape and almost uncannily foreseeing the adverse effects which unsuitable development and mass tourism could have on that landscape. In response to today's environmental problems, over 150 years later the National Park Authority and the many other conservation orientated bodies are echoing many of Wordsworth's views. A prophet indeed!

Together with several members of his family Wordsworth lies at the far end of the churchyard in Grasmere, where the soothing murmur of the waters of the River Rothay would have pleased him greatly. The headstones on the graves are commendably simple.

Above: Dubs Hut above Honister Pass.
Below: Stockley Bridge over Grains Gill.

Above left: Grange in Borrowdale.
Above right: John Peel's gravestone at Caldbeck.
Below: Sprinkling Tarn and Great Gable.

AROUND BASSENTHWAITE

1∧
•••

Mirehouse and St Bega's Church 5.25 km (3.25 miles)
A fairly level walk on good tracks, including both woodland and more open country close to Bassenthwaite Lake.

Start at the Forest Enterprises car park by the Old Sawmill café, across the road from the Mirehouse entrance.

Walk past the café, bearing right to a footbridge over Skill Beck. Turn sharp left after the bridge following blue and yellow waymarks for a short distance, then go uphill to join a surfaced roadway.

Turn right then, in a few metres, turn left to take a forest track which rises steadily, with Ullock Pike above. There are occasional glimpses of the lake as height is gained. Join another track and bear left. The way here is level but it soon rises again.

After narrowing and beginning to descend, Sandbeds Gill is crossed. Continue downhill on a broad track; keep left at a fork and head for the Ravenstone Hotel, in view ahead. Join the road and turn right, pass the hotel and Ravenstone Lodge, and turn left immediately after the Lodge at a public footpath signpost in the hedge.

Go through a gate/stile and cross a meadow on a lightly worn path to a kissing-gate.

Cross the next field towards a group of trees and bear left to a tiny stream and a stile over a fence. The path is now obvious among oak trees, going through more kissing-gates to reach an electricity sub station.

Cross a minor road to a gate/stile and follow the sign to St Bega's Church along a farm track. A gentle descent along the edge of Highfield Wood leads directly to the church and the modern cross. Continue from the church by returning for 50 metres, then turning right immediately before a stream to follow the line of the stream and an avenue of great oaks towards Mirehouse.

Go through metal gates and keep to the designated footpath through the grounds. Turn right by some outbuildings to take a gravelled drive-way, reaching the public road by a gate to the right of a roadside house. Turn left for 40 metres and cross the road to return to the car park.

2∧
••••

Barf
A mountain of 513m (1,536ft) which rises steeply above the shore of
Bassenthwaite Lake on its western side, providing a wonderful
viewpoint over the lake to mighty Skiddaw. Distance is 3km (2 miles) up and down. Apart from one short rocky section, the path is good but the ascent is unremittingly steep. The ascent of Barf may be extended by continuing over **Lord's Seat,** 552m (1,811ft) and returning through the Whinlatter forested area, a circuit of 12km (7.5 miles).

Close to the route is the **Bishop of Barf**, a white painted large rock which marks the spot at which an Irish bishop is said to have died. The bishop, possibly for a wager and possibly after drinking unwisely, was attempting to ride his horse directly up the mountainside. Not surprisingly, the animal fell, killing itself and rider. Repainting of the rock is traditionally carried out by the landlord of the nearby inn.

From the car park at Powter How, on the minor road 1.5km (1 mile) north of Thornthwaite, cross the road and turn left. Very shortly fork right, then right again to follow an obvious path, soon rising by the side of Beckstones Gill.

The path climbs steeply throughout and there is one rocky section to be negotiated. Most of the ascent is in woodland. Near the top of the valley bear right across open land to reach the summit of Barf. and enjoy the reward for all the hard work.

If a longer walk is required, continue along the path which heads to Lord's Seat in about 1km (0.6 mile). Stay with the path after Lord's Seat; route finding becomes more complicated as the forestry land is entered and there are many forest trails. Additionally, felling and replanting of trees quickly outdates the Ordnance Survey maps. A plan of the forest, available at the Whinlatter Visitor Centre, is very helpful. The route is broadly to the west, bending south west after 1km (0.6 mile). Darling How Farm is passed, well to the left hand, before the road is reached, close to the top of the Whinlatter Pass.

Turn left, along the road. In about 1.5km (1 mile) by an informal car park, fork right to use a forest track parallel to the road for almost 2km (1.25 miles). As this track bends away to the right, turn left to descend by a minor footpath to rejoin the road. Turn right to walk to the Visitor Centre.

Leave the centre on a forest trail descending gently towards Thornthwaite. Look out carefully for a bridleway descending to cross Comb Gill. Join another forest trail which follows round the contours to pass above Thornthwaite village. This trail becomes a minor roadway, staying roughly parallel with the public road and rejoining the outward route close to the car park.

AROUND KESWICK

The Keswick and Borrowdale area has a tremendous variety of walks, both mountain and lowland, including some of the best in Lakeland. The following suggestions are just a small sample of what is available.

1ʌ **Skiddaw** 17.5km (11 miles). At 931m (3,053ft)
England's fourth highest mountain, Skiddaw soars above
••• Keswick, its triangular shape being distinctive from most
angles. From Keswick area it is the obvious challenge for those who
want to climb a high mountain which is near at hand. The standard
route is not difficult or exciting, just a long steady plod but with the
compensation of the magnificent views over Derwentwater and
along Borrowdale. By using the car park at the end of Gale Road,
above Applethwaite, the ascent is considerably reduced and the
distance there and back is only 10km (6.25 miles).

Leave Keswick by the Cumbria Way footpath, with its bridge over the
bypass road. Skirt around the flanks of Latrigg, partly in woodland, rising
to the car park at the top of the no through road. From here the Jenkin
Hill route, broad and well-used, wends its way, climbing behind the
summit of Little Man to reach the top of the mountain.

Return can be made by the same way but there are options. The
designated 'Allerdale Ramble' descends over Carl Side, a subsidiary
summit. This path forks 500m after Carl Side; left is a direct path to
Millbeck hamlet, whilst right heads for the forest before a sharp left turn
reaches the minor road just west of Millbeck.

In either case, from Millbeck take the footpath parallel to the minor
road, on its south side, to **Applethwaite**, then turn right to follow the
Allerdale Ramble back to Keswick. To return to the high car park, rejoin
the road at Applethwaite and fork left by the hotel to walk up the lane for
about 1.5km (1 mile).

2ʌ **Cat Bells**
Another great Keswick favourite. Beautiful circuit of almost 6km
•••• (3.75 miles). The shapely peak rises above Derwentwater to a
height of 451m (1,490ft). Quite steep in places, but easy underfoot,
with well-used footpaths.

From the small car park by the side of the Portinscale to Grange in
Borrowdale road, a well-marked path starts the ascent of the long northern ridge of Catbells. No route finding is necessary; just follow the path
up the ridge for nearly 2km (a little more than one mile).

From the summit continue along the ridge to a depression and a
meeting place of paths. Turn left here, downhill. Most of the way down,
at a major junction turn sharp left, towards Keswick. A lovely path, with
gallery-like views over Derwentwater and Keswick to Skiddaw, goes
straight back to the car park.

3ʌ **Derwentwater Shore** 3.5km (2.25 miles) (extendible).
The timetabled service provides several opportunities for lake shore
•••• walks with a return to Keswick or other starting place by the use of

the launch, a most enjoyable combination. The following walk starts at the major car park close to the boat landings area in Keswick. Virtually level and easy underfoot apart from one section of stony ground along the lake shore.

From the car park, turn left along the road to the boat landings. Continue along the shore, passing the memorial tablet to Canon Rawnsley. The island close on the right is **Derwent Isle**. The celebrated **Friar's Crag** viewpoint is soon reached; close by is the John Ruskin memorial stone. From Friar's Crag back track a short distance and bear right down a flight of steps to follow the lake shore around Strandshag Bay. Continue along the edge of marshy woodland, over a footbridge and through a gate at the far end of the wood. Turn right.

Lord's Island is now close as the track heads for Calf Close Bay, with Rampsholme as the next island. The path is squeezed between the lake and the Borrowdale road, with some up and down which can be avoided by walking over the stones of the lake shore. Ashness Gate jetty follows this section. The anti-clockwise launch provides a short sail back to Keswick.

To extend this all too short walk, continue along the shore of Barrow Bay to the Kettlewell car park. Cross the road and take the broad track opposite, through Strutta Wood, avoiding nearly 1km (0.6miles) of road walking. On rejoining the road, cross over to a roadway leading directly to the Lodore jetty. Alternatively catch the bus back to Keswick. This extension adds just over 1.5km (1 mile) to the distance.

4 ∧ Borrowdale
•••• There are many lovely walks by the side of the River Derwent. The bus service facilitates a linear walk which is appropriate to a long, narrow, valley.

The following suggestion is almost level and is generally good underfoot. 4km (2.5 miles).

There is a small amount of parking space at **Grange in Borrowdale**, close by the river, with a superb picnic spot to hand. Walk into the village and turn left at a signposted bridleway to Rosthwaite. There is another small car parking area along this bridleway. Shortly after passing the National Trust Hollows Farm sign, turn left to follow a gently rising stony track. Keep left, towards the river, after passing a camping site.

At a footpath sign to Rosthwaite keep left. A stony section of path climbs before reaching a gap in a wall. Turn left again and continue through woodland to yet another left turn just over the crest of the rise, heading downhill to a cairn. At a quarry spoil heap on the right, a short diversion uphill leads to a rock face with interesting mineral colouration and a large rock arch.

Cross the River Derwent on a stone bridge or, if the water level is not too high, continue for a further 300m and cross by stepping stones, more fun than the bridge. In either case, a lane leads directly to **Rosthwaite.** The return bus service is not very frequent.

5 Blencathra (Saddleback)

A fine and very distinctive mountain when viewed from anywhere to the south, east or west, rising steeply above **Threlkeld** village to its height of 868m (2,849ft). There are many routes of ascent, including the celebrated Sharp Edge; the following is recommended for those who enjoy a little, safe, scrambling.

Park in the village car park, Blease Road, Threlkeld.

Go uphill from the car park, forking right at once to take a good track by the side of a stream. In about 300m turn right and walk across to Gategill. Turn left and commence the climb of the Hall's Fell ridge on an obvious track. Gate Gill, below to the left, has a waterfall and the remains of lead mining. No route finding is necessary; the higher part of the ridge has some steep rock but there is no danger for the average walker.

The ridge has the great advantage of heading straight for the highest point of the great plateau which is the summit of Blencathra.

Turn left and walk along the edge of the plateau towards the Blease Fell end of the mountain. The well-used path slants downhill towards the Blencathra Centre but, to return to Threlkeld, look out for a left turn more than half way down, aiming towards Blease Farm and the top of the stream-side path along which the walk started. Turn right to return to the car park along this path.

AROUND CALDBECK

1 The Howk

Very short and easy. A gentle stroll of only 2km (1.25 miles) to a celebrated glen-like wooded gorge which was Caldbeck's concentrated water mill area. Some parts of the track can be muddy and there are steps which need care.

From the village centre car park head for the green. Turn left, then left again. In a short distance turn right at a sign 'The Howk' to pass between farm buildings.

The way ahead is now straightforward, with the beck cut deep into the limestone, rushing over falls and rapids past the remains of a bobbin mill, where a huge water wheel once powered the machinery.

Go a little further up the valley, cross the beck on a bridge, and turn left to pass through woodland and across fields to the B5299 road. Turn left to return to Caldbeck.

FROM COCKERMOUTH

1A **•••** From bases in Cockermouth and the Bassenthwaite area destinations on the west coast can easily be reached. A good example is the following 32km (20 mile) circular ride to **Maryport,** also visiting several of the more interesting villages.

From Cockermouth head west along Brigham Road through a residential area, to the main A66, crossing almost directly into a minor road to **Brigham** *or head straight up to the main road and turn right for one kilometre(0.6 mile) to reach the Brigham road on the left.* Turn right in Brigham to head for the main road. Turn left, then right in a short distance, cross the River Derwent, and reach the large village of **Great Broughton**. Proceed through Broughton Moor to Maryport.

Leave Maryport on the A596, Carlisle road, forking left on the B5300 in 1.5km (1 mile) This road is part of the Cumbria Cycle Way. Turn right in 3km (1.9 miles) to **Crosscanonby** where the church is Norman, with Roman stones built into the walls. There are also pre-Norman memorial stones, including a hogback gravestone. Rejoin the main road at Crosby, turning left At Crosby Villa leave the main road by turning right, to **Greengill**, **Tallentire** and **Bridekirk**, where the ruined chancel of a Norman church stands close to its replacement. The new church has two Norman doorways from its predecessor, a fragment of a Roman altar and a very finely carved font, probably of the 12th century.

From Bridekirk head south to the A595 and turn right to reach to the large roundabout just outside Cockermouth. Turn left here to return to the town.

From a start at Bassenthwaite, add a few kilometres to the overall distance of the ride; use minor roads either to the north or to the south of the A66, to reach Cockermouth as appropriate.

2A **••••** A circuit visiting **Loweswater**, extendable to Crummock and Buttermere if desired. Basic route 30km (19 miles).

Leave Cockermouth by the B5292, Lorton Road, passing under the bypass, and continue along the beautiful **Vale of Lorton** on the B5289. At Low Lorton turn right to take the very minor road through Thackthwaite hamlet, heading for Loweswater hamlet, with inn and church.

Bear right to cycle along the edge of Loweswater, prettily set beneath Holme Wood.

Unless a steep climbing road over Mosser Fell, on the right, appeals, go on to Mockerkin. Turn right for Pardshaw and Pardshaw Hall. Keep right then left to Brandlingill. Fork left here to reach a T-junction. A left turn now reaches the main A5086, with a right turn back to Cockermouth or a right turn, then a left turn, crosses the River Cocker and rejoins the outward route, with a left turn back to base.

From a start in Bassenthwaite use the minor road through **Wythop Mill**, to the south of the A66 to reach Lorton Vale, or, from the southern end of the lake, ride over the **Whinlatter Pass** to High Lorton and Low Lorton, joining the main route at the latter.

Extension of the ride to Crummock and Buttermere is achieved by keeping to the B5289 along the Vale of Lorton.

3▲ Caldbeck
••••

A ride through some lesser known but still beautiful Lakeland country-side to the northern outpost of Caldbeck, approximately 40km (25 miles).

Take the minor road which leaves Cockermouth to the east, St Helen's Street/St Helen's Road, keeping left at a fork just out of town, then climbing past Setmurthy Common before descending to Higham Hall. Keep left to Ouse Bridge, where the River Derwent leaves Bassenthwaite Lake and continue to the road junction by the Castle Inn.

Go almost straight across and climb below the mound of Binsey before descending to **Uldale** After an initial climb from the village, the road becomes unfenced, crossing Aughertree Fell on its way to join the B5299 and reach Caldbeck. **Hesket Newmarket** is another good village just over 2km (1.25 miles) further along the road.

The return can be varied in several ways. A right fork from the B5299, followed by a left turn, leads to Ireby, a former small town which is now nothing more than a large village. From Ireby head south through **Ruthwaite**, home of the huntsman John Peel, immortalised in the famous song, then keep right at a junction to reach the A591 at Bewaldeth.

Go straight across to take the road to **Iselgate.** St.Michael's Church, Norman and with many interesting features, is nearby. Turn left to cross the River Derwent, then right to pass Hewthwaite Hall and return to Cockermouth.

FROM KESWICK

1▲ Circuit of Derwentwater
•••

A very easy ride of only 16km (10 miles), with possible extension along the delightful Borrowdale Valley (see above). Wonderful views and lakeside picnic spots.

From Keswick head south along the B5289, Borrowdale, road. After passing the far end of Derwentwater, turn right over the double bridge into **Grange in Borrowdale,** where refreshments are available. Bear right to follow the minor road towards Portinscale, with elevated views over lake and town to Skiddaw and Blencathra.

Weave through **Portinscale** to the main A66 road and turn right to return to Keswick.

Above: Bowscale Tarn.
Below: Hesket Newmarket.

2ᴬ Circumnavigating Skiddaw and Blencathra
••••

A longer and more demanding ride of 48km (30 miles). Leave Keswick by the A591 Carlisle road, passing **Mirehouse**. At High Side fork right to take a very minor road which rises and falls around the edge of Skiddaw, passes Orthwaite, and joins a more important road on Aughertree Fell. Turn right, join the B5299, and continue to **Caldbeck**.

Keep right to ride to **Hesket Newmarket** where refreshments are available. Head south on a minor road, keeping as close to the mountains (High Pike and Carrock Fell) as possible. This is another hilly road, largely unfenced, heading for **Mosedale**, followed by **Mungrisedale**. The latter village has an inn.

Turn right in less than 1km (0.6miles) to head for **Scales** along the base of Souther Fell. At the main A66 road turn right to return to Keswick.

1ᴬ CARLISLE AND AROUND
•••
Carlisle

From any base in the Cockermouth, Keswick or Caldbeck areas, a visit to Cumbria's 'capital city' makes a very worthwhile excursion. From Keswick the approximate distance of the return trip is 95km (60 miles), a little more from Cockermouth and less than half that distance from Caldbeck.

Despite its long and turbulent history as a border fortress city, not so long ago Carlisle was widely regarded as a rather dull place. Improvements in the past few years have resulted in a happy blend of the ancient and modern, the castle, the cathedral and the Lanes shopping centre. One day spent in Carlisle will hardly be enough to permit visits to all the interesting features and a selection from the following will have to be made: The castle (and Regimental Museum of the King's Own Royal Border Regiment); Tullie House – a 17th-century town house, now one of the finest provincial museums in the country; the Cathedral; tithe barn; St Cuthbert's church; citadel; railway station; market hall; Lanes shopping centre. The pedestrianised central concourse (Greenmarket), with the market cross, old town hall (housing the tourist information office) and guildhall is an attractive combination.

From Keswick take the A591 Carlisle road, passing Mirehouse before joining the A595 at Bothel. Turn right to follow this former Roman road all the way to Carlisle. From Cockermouth, cross the river in town and head north to join the A595 at a major roundabout. Turn right for Carlisle. From Caldbeck head for Thursby to join the A595.

For a less direct but more scenic return from Carlisle, fork left from A595 into the B5299 Dalston road. Although now largely a residential area, **Dalston** has a green and some Georgian properties. Continue to **Caldbeck** and **Hesket Newmarket**. From Hesket bear right to go south along a minor road, hugging the foot of the mountains (High Pike and Carrock Fell) to **Mosedale**, a tiny hamlet with a restored Quaker meeting-house also doing duty as a tea and coffee shop, and Mungrisedale.

Join A66 main road and turn right to return to Keswick.

Should a longer tour be desired, the historic little market town of **Brampton** is just a few kilometres along the A69, to the north-east of Carlisle. **Talkin Tarn Country Park** is reached by A689, south-east of Brampton and **Birdoswald Roman Fort** and Visitor Centre is along a minor road running north-east from Brampton, towards Gilsland. This road passes through **Lanercost**, with its famous priory.

2ᴬ THE MOUNTAIN PASSES, HONISTER AND WHINLATTER OR NEWLANDS

Full circuit 45km (28 miles). Shorter circuit 36km (22 miles).   Wonderful mountain scenery throughout.

From Keswick head south along the B5289 Borrowdale road, passing Derwentwater and the villages of **Grange in Borrowdale** and **Rosthwaite,** both with refreshment opportunities. The road bears right to **Seatoller,** again with refreshments, before the steep but straightforward climb to the summit of the Honister Pass at 363m (1,190ft.). Here, the remains of large scale quarrying are evident. There is also a long established youth hostel.

Descend towards **Buttermere** with Honister Crag towering above on the left and Dale Head to the right. At the foot of the pass Gatesgarth is an ancient valley head farmstead. Buttermere hamlet has two inns and a café. Continue past Crummock Water and along the Vale of Lorton. Turn right at Low Lorton, pass High Lorton and ascend the Whinlatter Pass, at 318m (1,043ft.) one of Lakeland's easiest passes. The comprehensive **Whinlatter Visitor Centre** is soon reached, on the left. Continue to the main A66, joined at Braithwaite, and turn right to return to Keswick.

For the shorter route, turn right at Buttermere to climb steeply past the

church and over the Newlands Pass (334m – 1,096ft). The descent of the **Vale of Newlands** is altogether scenic, with Skiddaw looming large ahead. Join the A66 at Braithwaite and turn right to return to Keswick.

3 ∧ MARYPORT, SILLOTH AND ABBEYTOWN
····

A drive of 105km (65 miles) from Keswick, largely along the Cumbria coast, returning across the Solway Plain. From a Cockermouth base, the distance is reduced.

From Keswick, drive to Cockermouth, either along the main A66 or the A591 Carlisle road, turning left at the Castle Inn, near Bassenthwaite village. From Cockermouth go direct to Maryport. Head north from Maryport along the coast road, B5300, to **Allonby**, with its long, sandy sea front and views across the Solway Firth to the Scottish hills, and Silloth. In Victorian times Silloth had pretensions to be a popular seaside resort, particularly after the construction of a branch railway line in 1857. However, the situation on a windswept coastline and the comparative remoteness ensured that the town posed no threat to Blackpool. The railway is long gone and Silloth is now a quiet backwater, with gardens down to the sea.

Turn right, inland, along the B5302 to Abbeytown. Here, St Mary's Church is a surviving part of the former Holm Cultram Abbey, a 12th-century Cistercian foundation. Some of the scattered former abbey outbuildings also remain, though adapted for other uses. Continue along B5302 to **Wigton**, for many centuries an undistinguished market town, with a 19th-century fountain in the Market Place. Wigton is probably best known as the home town of Melvyn Bragg, many of whose books have a Cumbrian setting.

The B5304 links Wigton to the main A595 road, about 2km (1.6miles) distant. Join the A595, turning right. This road goes direct to the roundabout on the fringe of Cockermouth; for Keswick, turn left at **Bothel** (Bothel shares the use of the church at **Torpenhow** – a diversion of just under 2km (0.6mile) to the east) on to A591, to return via Mirehouse.

4 THE EAST

PENRITH AND AROUND ULLSWATER

Penrith

Strategically placed between the Lake District and the Eden Valley, yet really belonging to neither, is the ancient market town of Penrith, very much the centre of the area covered by this chapter. Easy access from north and south brought the Romans and, nearly a thousand years later, several centuries of sporadic raiding by the Scots, not finally checked until 1603. The original defensive pele tower of 1397–9 grew into a sizeable castle,

which is now a meagre ruin, its stones taken as ready-to-hand building material by 16th-century vandals. A visit by Bonnie Prince Charlie at the head of his army in the 1745 rebellion, the A6 trunk road, the west coast main railway line and, latterly, the M6 motorway have all resulted from the same geographic considerations.

William and Dorothy Wordsworth lived in Penrith as young children, attending a little 'dame' school close to the church, (see below) also attended by William's

Above: Ullswater.

future wife, Mary Hutchinson.

Despite its historic and strategic importance, Penrith has never grown into a big town; it remains compact and friendly, a good mixture of old and new, with winding streets and yards and some of the best of its sandstone buildings clustered around the parish church. Old signs distinguish several shops in which the same business has been carried on for up to 200 years. These old shops are supplemented by an attractive small modern pedestrianised shopping area at Angel Lane behind the Market Place, and by the Devonshire Arcade.

Ullswater

Favourite lake of many residents and visitors, this large and beautiful sheet of water has just about everything in its favour, not least the fine ring of mountains around its head, including St Sunday Crag, Fairfield and mighty Helvellyn. To sail on the lake 'steamer' or to walk along the lake side path from Howtown to Patterdale is to experience Ullswater at its best.

At the foot of the lake is **Pooley Bridge,** a pleasant village with inns, shops and cafés, right at the foot of Dunmallard Hill, a concentric little mound with

PLACES TO VISIT IN PENRITH

Street Market
Held each Tuesday in the wide space of Great Dockray. Original charter granted in 1223.

Cornmarket
A covered market cross by one end of Great Dockray.

George Hotel
Market Square. Provided lodgings for Bonnie Prince Charlie in 1745.

St Andrew's Church
The 13th/14th-century tower is the oldest surviving part of the building. The nave was rebuilt between 1719 and 1722 after fire damage. The architect is believed to have been Nicholas Hawksmoor, pupil and colleague of Sir Christopher Wren. The Georgian style, with wide balconies, is certainly similar to that of several of Hawksmoor's City of London churches. There is an interesting exposed clock mechanism near the west door.

The churchyard has a very fine and unusual monument – the 'Giant's Grave'. This is constructed from the remains of two stone crosses and four Viking 'hogback' tombstones. A Tudor house dated 1663, by the churchyard, was the former school attended by William and Dorothy Wordsworth and Mary Hutchinson.

Penrith Castle

Sited on a mound in Castle Park, facing the railway station. Ruins only, with deep ditch. Free public access.

Castle Park Tennis, putting, crazy golf and bowls.

Swimming Pool, Southend Road, at southern end of town. Indoor, with indoor climbing wall. ☎ 01768 863450

Penrith Golf Centre and Driving Range ☎ 01768 892167

Penrith Golf Club On northern fringe of town, ☎ 01768 891919

Tourist Information Centre and Museum

Housed in the former Robinson's school, an Elizabethan building altered in 1670, used as a school until the early 1970s. Museum open June–September, Monday–Saturday 09.30–18.00; Sunday 13.00–1800; October–May, Monday–Saturday 10.00–17.00. ☎ 01768 864671 Tourist Information Centre ☎ 01768 867466

Eamont Bridge

1.5km (1 mile) south of Penrith on the A6 road, at the crossing of the River Eamont which was formerly a county boundary. Many inns used by drovers and travellers are now converted into houses. Two great Neolithic henge monuments – Mayburgh Henge and King Arthur's Round Table.

Brougham

2km (1.25 miles) south-east of Penrith. Site of Roman fort of Brocavum. Adjacent are the ruins of Brougham Castle, one of the northern strongholds of the remarkable Lady Anne Clifford in the 17th century. Close to Brougham Hall is St Wilfrid's, a chapel of ease rebuilt by Land Anne in the 17th century when she inherited the Brougham Estate. The chapel is a simple low sandstone building, with exceptionally good medieval carved woodwork.

Rheged

The Village in the Hill – Europes largest grass covered building – a major visitor attraction with permanent and temporary exhibitions, shops and cafe. ☎ 017687 868000

the site of an iron age fort on top. Halfway along the east shore of the lake, **Howtown** is a tiny hamlet, important only as the sole intermediate calling place of the scheduled boat service.

At the head of the lake **Glenridding** and **Patterdale** are both popular visitor centres, not only for lake-related activities. The former was for centuries a busy mining village; the Greenside Mine, up the valley behind Glenridding, closed as recently as the 1960s. The best routes to climb Helvellyn start at

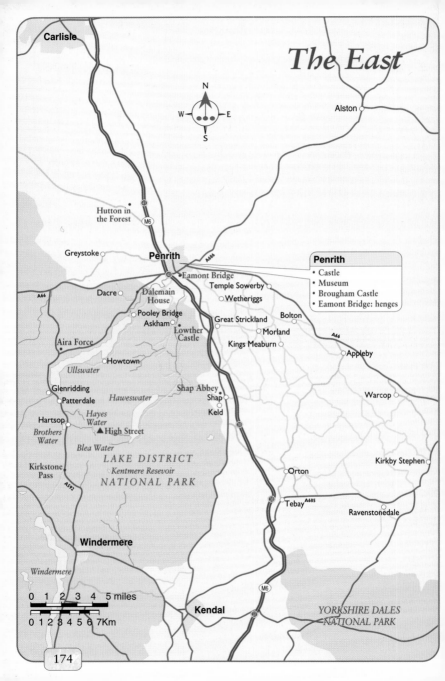

The East

Carlisle

Alston

N
W   E
S

Hutton in the Forest

M6

Greystoke

Penrith

A686

Eamont Bridge

Penrith
- Castle
- Museum
- Brougham Castle
- Eamont Bridge: henges

A66

Dacre

Dalemain House

Temple Sowerby

Wetheriggs

Pooley Bridge

Great Strickland

Bolton

Askham

Lowther Castle

Morland

A66

Aira Force

Kings Meaburn

Appleby

Howtown

Ullswater

Warcop

Glenridding

Shap Abbey

Patterdale

Haweswater

Shap

Hartsop

Hayes Water

Keld

High Street

Brothers Water

Blea Water

Kirkby Stephen

Kirkstone Pass

LAKE DISTRICT

A592

Kentmere Resevoir

Orton

NATIONAL PARK

Tebay A685

Ravenstonedale

Windermere

Windermere

0 1 2 3 4   5 miles

0 1 2 3 4 5 6 7Km

Kendal

M6

YORKSHIRE DALES
NATIONAL PARK

Above: Ullswater.
Middle: Dalemain House.
Below: High Street.

Patterdale, as does the walkers' route to Grasmere by way of Grisedale. The name Patterdale is derived from St Patrick who is said to have preached in the dale. By the roadside, almost opposite the refreshment hut, is St Patrick's Well.

From Patterdale the A591 climbs long and hard to the summit of the **Kirkstone Pass,** at 454m (1,489ft.) one of the highest in Lakeland. Close to the start of the climb, the charming hamlet of **Hartsop** has a range of old traditional Lake District houses, including the odd 'spinning gallery', which allowed home spinning of yarn to continue in good light, but under protective cover, during bad weather.

NORTH OF ULLSWATER

Greystoke

Greystoke is just outside the National Park and a little off the beaten track. It is a fine village, with charming houses round the green and an ancient market cross. **Greystoke Castle** is comparatively modern, its predecessors having twice been burned

---

PLACES TO VISIT IN ULLSWATER

Ullswater Motor Yachts
The motor yachts *Lady of the Lake* and *Raven* have more than earned their keep plying between Glenridding and Pooley Bridge for well over 100 years. The former was built in 1877 and the latter in 1889. Originally steam powered, both were converted to diesel in the 1930s. Sailing all year except Christmas Eve and Christmas Day. ☎ 017684 82229

Aira Force Waterfall
One of Lakeland's finest and most accessible falls, close to the main road along the west shore of Ullswater. Café and large National Trust car park.

Howtown Outdoor Centre
Water-based activities during the summer. ☎ 01768 486508

Glenridding Sailing Centre
Close to the steamer pier at Glenridding. ☎ 01768 82541

Mountain Painters Gallery at Patterdale. ☎ 017684 82131

Pooley Bridge Information Centre ☎ 017684 86530

Ullswater Information Centre Glenridding. ☎ 017684 821414

down. As it is surrounded by a large expanse of parkland without public right of way, it can hardly be seen. Of much more interest to visitors is **St Andrew's Church**, approached along Church Road, where an ancient 'sanctuary stone' has been preserved. Passing this stone on the way to the church was sufficient to claim sanctuary from pursuers. St Andrew's is a spacious former collegiate church, the college having been closed at the time of the Reformation. A modern experiment to reinstate the church as a pre-theological college lasted only from 1958 to 1979, owing to the shortage of suitable candidates. The village has an inn, shop and swimming pool.

Dacre

A 14th-century defensive pele tower, Dacre Castle, now used as a farmhouse, is the outstanding feature of this quiet and attractive village. Even older is the church of St Andrew. According to Bede there was an Anglo-Saxon monastery here, but the present structure is of the 12th to 14th centuries, with 19th-century restoration including rebuilding the tower. Inside, the tower archway into the nave is original Norman. In the chancel window there is a fragment of a carved Anglian stone cross shaft and, on the floor, a 10th-century Viking period stone, also carved. There are monuments to the Hasell family, owners of nearby

Dalemain for more than three centuries. Sir Edward Hasell was steward to Lady Anne Clifford; the south door has a large lock and key dated 1671 and inscribed 'A.P.' (Anne, Countess of Pembroke). The churchyard houses the four famous Dacre Bears – carved stone creatures, one by each corner of the church. There is also a small, cat-like animal present in two of the carvings. Starting at the south-west corner and moving anti-clockwise, there might be a simple story sequence.

Dalemain

To the east of **Dacre**. A basically Elizabethan building with a Georgian façade, Dalemain has evolved piecemeal over the years. Home of the Hasell family since 1665. Fine furniture and portraits. Westmorland and Cumberland Yeomanry Museum. Gardens with many rare plants and collection of more than 100 old-fashioned roses. Attractions for children. Licensed restaurant. Gift shop. Facilities for the disabled. Annual craft fair. Admission charge. Open daily except Fridays and Saturdays, 11.15–17.00. ☎ 017684 86450; fax 017684 86223

AROUND SHAP AND HAWESWATER

This area, much of it poised along the eastern boundary of the district, is the part of Lakeland generally least known

177

Above left: *Heading for Howtown from Patterdale along Ullswater.*
Above right: *Greenside Mine on the path to Helvellyn from Glenridding.*
Below: *Brotherswater, on the road to Kirkstone Pass from Patterdale.*

Above: Haweswater.
Middle: The Cloisters, Kirkby Stephen.
Below: Boarding the steamer at Glenridding.

Events

PATTERDALE AND PENRITH

Patterdale Sheepdog Trials
Late August. ☎ Tourist Information Centre, 017684 82414

Penrith Show
Broughton Hall Farm. Local agricultural show. Late July.
☎ Tourist Information Centre.

APPLEBY
Appleby New Fair
Early June.

LOWTHER
Lowther Horse Driving Trials and Game Fair
Lowther Park. Major three-day event, usually held on the second
weekend in August. ☎ 01931 712378

to visitors. There is good hill country, leading to the rugged east slopes of High Street, there are attractive villages such as Askham, and there is the **Lowther Leisure and Wildlife Park**. The main reasons for the comparative neglect must be the lack of a focal point town, village or lake and the remote access by road, well away from the rest of the district.

Shap

Stretching for some distance along the main A6 road, Shap is the biggest village but it has no pretensions to tourism, although several inns remain from the days when the village was a noted staging post on the route to Scotland, the highest point on the road which climbed laboriously over the bleak moorland. In the mid 19th century the railway builders also had problems in constructing what is now known as the West Coast main line, and in the days of steam power, **Shap Summit**, a little way to the south of the village was reached only after a long, hard struggle up the steep gradient, particularly from the south. The depot at Tebay housed several locomotives specifically for the purpose of 'banking' – pushing from behind – particularly heavy trains.

There is a good deal of prehistory of the Late Neolithic and Early Bronze Ages in the Shap area, largely disturbed by the construction of the railway line and by local farmers. Most notable was an avenue of standing

180

stones, now represented by a few isolated specimens such as the **Goggleby Stone**.

Large operational granite quarries dominate the approach to Shap from the south.

West of the village is **Shap Abbey**, reached along a sign-posted lane from the road to Bampton. Dedicated to St Mary, this abbey was founded early in the 13th century by the Premonstratensian or the order of White Canons. It was home to about a dozen of these brethren, who ministered in surrounding parishes in addition to their monastic duties. The only sub-stantial surviving part is the 15th-century tower, but there are plentiful ruins revealing various phases of construction. Although Shap was never an enormously wealthy foundation, the monastic land holdings, both locally and throughout Westmorland, were consider-able. Dissolution came quietly in 1540, followed by centuries of steady decay. The abbey is now in the care of English Heritage and is open to the public without charge.

Keld Chapel is about 1.5km (1 mile) from Shap village, to the south-west and reached by Keld Road. Probably of the 15th century, this is a most interesting example of an unrestored pre-Reformation chapel, with many original features, including four of the five windows. The east window is similar to a window in the tower of Shap Abbey. In more recent years the building was used as a cottage, hence the fireplace, chimney breast and chimney. The roof had to be renewed following the collapse of the original some years ago. The simply furnished chapel has for some years been in the care of the National Trust and is open to visitors without charge. The key is kept at the house across the road, usually hanging in the porch. The chapel remains consecrated, a service being held in August each year.

North-west of Shap is **Askham** a charming village with more of the character of the Yorkshire Dales than of the Lake District. Spacious greens are fringed by trees and by houses of the 17th and 18th centuries, with two inns and a post office-stores. **Askham Hall** is a privately owned former defensive pele tower of the 14th century, converted into an Elizabethan mansion in the 16th century. The parish **church of St Peter**, close to the River Lowther at the bottom end of the village was constructed in 1832 to the design of the architect of nearby Lowther Castle.

The latter is not a real castle, but a mansion in a castellated style, built between 1806 and 1811. By the 1930s it was becoming too expensive to maintain and was abandoned. The great façade remains as a spectacular sham but there is no public access.

St Michael's Church stands on a a very early Christian site, opposite Lowther Castle. The

Painters of the Lake District

The great surge of poetic writing which played such a prominent part in the age of English Romanticism was inevitably accompanied by corresponding activity in the visual arts. The 'Discovery of the Landscape' went hand in hand with the 'Discovery of the Lake District'.

Painters flocked to observe and to record this unique combination of the picturesque (serene and beautiful) and sublime (horrid and fearful) and, if in their estimation necessary to create a good picture, to rearrange and to exaggerate the various elements. For painters and for some other visitors it was considered to be essential to carry a 'Claude glass', named after the great landscape painter Claude Lorraine. In this glass a 'picture' of any portion of an observed landscape could be composed and framed.

Of the really great artists, **Turner, Constable** and **Joseph Wright** of Derby visited Lakeland. John Constable (1776–1837) came only once and did not like the district very much, perhaps not surprisingly in view of his great love of the flat East Anglian countryside. A pencil drawing of the lower fall at Rydal is at the Abbot Hall, Kendal. Wright (1734–97) was rather more active; he, too, painted the fall at Rydal among several other works. Much more significant than either of these was the contribution to Lakeland painting by J.M.W. Turner (1775–1817).

Of locally born artists, **George Romney** (1734-1802), born in Dalton in Furness, has pride of place, though he was strictly a portrait painter.

Among the many lesser but still important painters working in the district from about the mid 18th century, **Salvator Rosa** was at the forefront of the 'sublime' movement, closely followed by **P.J. de Loutherbourg**, whose *Belle Isle in a Storm* and *Belle Isle in a Calm* may be seen at the Abbot Hall.

A more realistic view of the landscape as inherently friendly, 'a garden where men and nature become one', was depicted by **William Green**, who settled in Ambleside. He is featured at the Armitt Collection. Also living nearby was **Julius Ceasar Ibbotson.** His painting of his home at Clappersgate is one of several attractive and interesting works. Extremely prolific and useful in portraying middle class domesticity of the time was **John Harden.** Other painters of the late 18th – early 19th centuries who made a significant contribution to the illustration of the district include: William Harrell, James Burrell Smith, William Westall, John 'Warwick' Smith, William Henry Pyne, John Glover, Thomas Austin, Philip Reinagle, his son Ramsey Richard Reinagle, John Varley, William Collins and Francis Wheatley. Edward

Lear, of the mid 19th century, is well represented at the Abbot Hall gallery in Kendal.

Later in the 19th century, the multi-talented **John Ruskin** promoted Turner and produced many Lakeland paintings of his own, whilst **Beatrix Potter** was, in her early life, a botanical artist of great talent, as can be seen from the Armitt Collection in Ambleside.

In the present century **Kurt Schwitters** was an immigrant, living in Ambleside for many years, producing largely rather avant-garde work, but with some local scenes such as his *Bridge House, Ambleside*. More

Lakeland has long been famous for its light, bringing painters from far and wide. Here is Ullswater at the end of the day.

recently, **Sheila Fell** produced local work of power and originality until her early death in 1980.

The **Heaton Cooper** family have, for many years, been a local institution. Alfred, his son Heaton, and several of the third generation, have produced attractive landscape paintings and other works of art, many being reproduced in large numbers for sale at their Grasmere studios as a commercial operation.

The Abbot Hall Gallery in Kendal has a limited selection of paintings from the Romantic period, Schwitters, and a considerable number of Romney portraits in its permanent collection.

early 13th century, with many later additions, principally of the 17th century. Evidence of earlier worship here is provided by Norse hogback gravestones of about 950 AD and a cross of the 11th–12th centuries outside. There are good Victorian windows on the east and a modern carving depicting the Last Supper. Close to the church is a sizeable mausoleum, built in 1857 for the Lowther family. Although the site is now isolated, until the 17th century Lowther village was adjacent to the church. It was then moved to a new site 1.5km (1 mile) away.

Haweswater

The only large sheet of water in this part of the district, Haweswater is about 6km (4 miles) in length and a little less than 1km (0.6 mile) in width. Until 1940 Haweswater was a much smaller lake, with the village of Mardale, including church and inn, at its head. Manchester Corporation then constructed a large dam, raising the water level by 29m (nearly 100ft), dramatically increasing the size of the lake and drowning the village. In extreme drought some of the remains become exposed, although all the buildings were demolished (and the bodies from the graveyard were re-interred at Shap) prior to flooding. Haweswater is not a particularly pretty lake, but the scarred eastern slopes of High Street and adjacent heights do provide an impressive valley head.

PLACES TO VISIT AROUND SHAP

Lakeland Bird of Prey Centre
In the walled garden of Lowther Castle. Flying demonstrations daily, 12.00, 14.00 and 16.00. Tearoom. Garden. Admission charge. Open daily, March–October, 10.30. ☎ 01931 712746

AROUND ULLSWATER

1 Λ Helvellyn
●●●

Full circuit 13km (8 miles). At 950m (3,118ft), the third highest mountain in England and probably the most visited of them all. Fairly bland on its western (Thirlmere) side, but wonderfully ice-scraped into dramatic cliff scenery on the east, hence the preference for ascents from Patterdale and Glenridding. The route below includes Striding Edge, in good weather not quite as spine-chilling as some might believe, but not a place for the faint hearted or for unsupervised young children. A good deal of rock scrambling.

Car parking for the ascent of Helvellyn may be found along one side of the lane from Grisedale Bridge; there are also a few spaces by the George Starkey Hut, a little further towards Patterdale. Start by walking along the lane at Grisedale Bridge (not far from the church), pass the entrance to Patterdale Hall, and turn right, uphill, at a junction. At the next junction turn right to cross the river and ascend steeply up the opposite hillside.

Turn left at the top and then bear right to follow the path which climbs diagonally across the steep side of Grisedale. At the top of this section is the 'hole in the wall'. The near end of Striding Edge is soon reached. In high season the edge is likely to be congested. Cross the edge on foot or whatever other part of the anatomy seems to be appropriate; at the far end there is an awkward 'step', a mini rock-face to be descended before scrambling up the shoulder of Helvellyn proper. The summit is a broad, flattish expanse with a rough shelter.

Turn right, and in about 200m look carefully for the start of the track which descends steeply towards the shapely outlying peak of Catstye Cam. Cross Swirral Edge, less sharp than Striding Edge. Before the track rises to Catstye Cam, bear right to continue the descent, towards the outlet of Red Tarn in its hanging valley below.

Cross below Red Tarn to head towards the 'hole in the wall'. The outward route can be rejoined here or, for a varied return, keep left along a path with a wall on the right. Stay with the wall as it bends to the right, now descending quite steeply. Keep left at a junction to follow Mires Beck on its way down to Glenridding, ignoring cross paths to right and left.

Turn right at a junction just before Glenridding Beck and follow the beck into the village. Turn right along the side of the road. There is a roadside path for most of the way back to the parking place.

For a longer but easier return, turn left at the summit and follow the broad track which passes by Nethermost Pike and Dollywagon Pike before descending to Grisedale Tarn. Turn left to go all the way down Grisedale back to Patterdale.

If Striding Edge does not appeal as part of the ascent, go right at the 'hole in the wall', pass by the outlet of Red Tarn and ascend the less spectacular Swirral Edge (the reverse of part of the return route above).

2▲ Glenridding to Howtown
●●●●

With a return by 'steamer'. One of the best loved walks in Lakeland. 11km (7 miles) of delightful footpath, never far from the shore of Ullswater, but rising and falling, into and out of woodland, with many picnic opportunities. The return sail on the lake faces the great ring of mountains at the head of the lake.

From the car park by the steamer pier walk across the adjacent field to reach the road by the refreshment hut. Turn left and use the roadside footpath for rather more than 1km (0.6 mile) towards Patterdale. By the George Starkey Hut, a substantial stone building, turn left into a lane to cross the valley to Side Farm. Turn left. The well-used path is now continuous and easy to follow. After passing a camping field there is a fork; keep left here to avoid unnecessary ascent. On reaching a surfaced road just short of Hallin Fell, turn left and then right to follow a footpath sign to Howtown. Cross Sandwick Beck on a bridge and continue by the lake shore.

As Howtown is approached, turn left down a flight of steps and follow the signs to the pier, where there is usually a timetable inside the shelter building.

3▲ Pooley Bridge and Ullswater
●●●●

There are several pleasant walks from Pooley Bridge. This gentle little ramble of about 3 .5km. (2.25 miles) includes a length of the shore of this lovely lake. Entirely easy underfoot.

Use either of the public car parks in Pooley Bridge. From the car park on the village side of the river, go through a small gate opening on to a lane and turn left. In a short distance keep left along a surfaced driveway, soon reaching the outbuildings of the large 18th-century house, Eusemere, frequently visited by William and Dorothy Wordsworth, who were friends of the first owners, Thomas Clarkson and his wife.

As the drive bends right, turn left through a gate with a public bridleway sign and cross a meadow, angling towards a gate obvious on the far side. Go through a kissing-gate and turn right to follow the Pooley Bridge to Howtown road, usually quiet and pleasant to walk.

Waterside Farm, on the right, is reached in a little more than 1km (0.6 mile). Turn right here, at a public footpath sign, between farm buildings, to reach the lake shore. The way back along the shore of the lake is now entirely obvious, passing the slipway where the two old 'steamers' are sometimes pulled from the water for overhauling.

4 ∧ Hartsop
•••• A varied circuit visiting the hamlet of Hartsop and the beautiful Brothers Water with its adjacent woodland. No significant ascent and no problems underfoot. 7km (4.5 miles).

Use the signposted car park at the point where the Windermere to Patterdale road bends right and crosses the Goldrill Beck at Cow Bridge, opposite Hartsop hamlet. From the car park, cross the beck and, by the National Trust information board, go through a kissing-gate. Turn very sharp right to follow a concessionary footpath towards Patterdale, keeping generally close to the road.

Rejoin the road at a gate and cross over to take another concessionary footpath signposted 'Patterdale via Beckstones'. Cross the valley bottom, then the beck on a farm bridge, and rise to join a bridleway. Turn sharp right towards Hartsop. The route is now straightforward, nicely elevated to give enhanced views across to Fairfield and its neighbours. Pass Angle Tarn Beck with its leaping falls and rapids and continue to the road which leads to Hartsop. Turn left to ascend the street through the hamlet.

At the car park at the far end, go through the gate and turn right to follow the signpost to Pasture Beck. Cross a bridge and turn right to return along the side of the stream. Bear left into an unsurfaced lane which continues to join the main road. Go straight across to a gate with a National Trust 'Brothers Water' sign and bear left along a narrow, winding, lakeside path. At the far end rise steeply to rejoin the road. At Sykeside by the Brothers Water Inn, turn right and follow the driveway through the camping site, crossing the valley bottom to Hartsop Hall, one of the oldest farmsteads in Lakeland.

Go round the back of the Hall and return to the car park along a lovely lakeside track.

EASTERN LAKELAND

1 ∧ High Street
••• At 828m (2,718ft.) the highest of the far eastern group of fells, the top of High Street is a wide, elongated plateau, its main interest being the line of the Roman road from which the name is derived and its former use as a high-level race course. However, the eastern side of the mountain and its neighbours has been shaped by the retreating glaciers into rocky faces and long ridges, with deep corries in between, such as those holding Small Water and Blea Water, the latter being the deepest tarn in the district. The walk described does make the most of these fine features without being in any way difficult for the average walker.

There is a small car park at the end of the road by the head of Haweswater. Set off to the right, crossing above the lake. Cross Mardale Beck on a bridge and turn right towards the Rigg, a peninsula with a

wooded tip. As soon as the path allows, turn sharp left to begin the long but generally gradual ascent of the ridge which heads via Rough Crag almost directly to the summit of High Street. There is a path all the way along this fine route and it is impossible to lose the way.

There are three suggestions for a return route:

a. The shortest, at 11.5km (7 miles) for the total circuit, is to turn left over High Street summit, left again at a fork to go over Mardale III Bell, and descend to the top of the Nan Bield Pass. From the top of the pass a well-used track winds down through rock scenery to Small Water, then over the lip of the corrie back to the car park.

b. Turn right at the top, then right again to head for Kidsty Pike, 780m (2,560ft.). The extra ascent is not great. Continue along the top to Kidsty Hawes and bear right to descend to Bowderthwaite Bridge over Riggindale Beck and back to the Rigg. 13km (8 miles).

c. Start from the top as in a) above, but after the Nan Bield Pass take the path ahead, rising to the summit of Harter Fell, 774m (2,539ft.), then Little Harter Fell and down to the top of the Gatesgarth Pass. Turn left here for a descent straight to the car park. 13km (8 miles).

2ᴬ Keld and Shap Abbey
••••

An easy walk of 5km (3.25 miles) visiting the little chapel at Keld (see above) and the remains of Shap Abbey (see above). No long ascents and no problems underfoot.

From the car park with public conveniences, by the Memorial Gardens, turn left along the main road for a little more than 100m. Turn right at a public footpath sign to go through a farm gate. Angle left in 20m, through another gate, with yellow arrow waymark.

A fairly clear path over grass keeps close to the wall on the right. One or two of the stones of the former Shap Avenue may be seen. Go over a stile and bear right along an obvious path. In the middle of a meadow, as the path bends to the right, turn left along a lesser path, leading to a stile over the wall. Go over two more stiles in quick succession, then another, to reach an old unsurfaced lane.

Turn left, towards farm buildings. About 100m short of the buildings turn right into a similar lane. The view ahead is of the hills and mountains around Swindale and Haweswater. Go through a gate and descend gently towards Thornship farmstead. Bend right to pass the farm, join the surfaced access road and continue to Keld hamlet. The primitive chapel is in the angle at the road junction. The key is kept at the house across the road.

From the chapel go uphill along the road for less than 100m. Turn left over a cattle grid at a signpost 'Footpath Shap Abbey' and go along the upper edge of a house garden. Go over a stile and continue along the edge of a rough meadow. At a junction of paths at the end of a wall keep straight on. Climb over the wall on the left at a high stile, turning right to continue the same line to a stile over the wall ahead.

Keep just above a narrow strip of woodland, with the River Lowther below, the Abbey soon coming into view. Go left down a steep bank *or* carry on to the abbey access road, in either case turning left over the bridge to reach the ruins.

From the abbey take the access road up the steep valley side to a cattle grid with a stile beside. Either continue along the road or go over the stile on the left to walk along the edge of the field. The two routes end at the same place. Join the public highway and turn right at once in a narrow lane signposted Keld Lane, which might be a little overgrown. Turn left at a public road (Keld Lane) and, in 100m, turn right into another unsurfaced lane. Turn left in 40m over a waymarked stile.

Ahead is the Goggleby Stone; another of the ancient stones can be seen on the left, close to a wall. The path back to Shap is now entirely obvious, heading straight for the church. Go through a gate into the built-up area. Turn right along a back lane and then left to the main road. Turn right to return to the car park.

Above: Long Meg and her daughters.
Middle: Appleby Church.
Below: Lady Anne's Almhouses, Appleby.

FROM PENRITH

1 Hutton in the Forest, Greystoke, Dacre and Dalemain

••• An easy ride of 32km (20 miles) in pleasant countryside. Leave Penrith to the north, forking right from A6 at the edge of the town on to a minor road which runs parallel with A6 as far as a large roundabout. Go left here, on B5305, cross over the M6 and continue to Hutton in the Forest, a stately home which is open to the public on Thursday, Friday and Sunday afternoons and Bank Holidays during the season. There are also gardens and a tearoom. From Hutton turn left to ride via Blencow to Greystoke. Leave Greystoke to the south, along B5288, but fork left in less than 1km (0.6 mile) into a very minor road. Go straight across the main A66. After Hutton John and Sparket Mill turn left at a cross roads to go direct to Dacre.

Head south from Dacre to join A592, Glenridding to Penrith road. turning left to reach Dalemain. From Dalemain the return to Penrith is by A592/A66.

2 Shap Abbey, Haweswater, Askham and Lowther

•••• 50km (31 miles) of varied countryside, quite up and down but without serious hills, visiting an abbey ruin, a much admired village and the large Haweswater reservoir.

Take to A6 main road as far as Eamont Bridge. Turn right by the great henge monuments to Yanwath, cross the railway, then turn left to ride to Askham. Continue along the road to the south, bearing right at Bampton to visit Haweswater. At Burnbanks some of the original 'temporary' housing constructed in the 1930s for the reservoir construction workers is still in use, though now somewhat modified.

Return to Bampton Grange, cross the River Lowther, and head towards Shap. Turn right to take the signposted lane down to the Abbey ruins.

Return to the road, turn right, then very shortly right again to go to Keld, where the primitive chapel is well worth a visit.

From Keld ride to the A6 main road at Shap village, turning left to head towards Penrith. With the parallel M6 close at hand, this main road is quite reasonable for cycling. At Hackthorpe fork left for Lowther.

Return to Penrith either by rejoining the outward route at Askham, which is just a little way down the road from Lowther, or by using A6.

3 Wetheriggs, Morland, Appleby and Acorn Bank

•••• A ride of 50km (31 miles) to the fine old town of Appleby, also giving the opportunity to visit established attractions along the way. Leave Penrith by heading south along the A6. 1km (0.6 mile) after Eamont Bridge fork left towards Clifton Dykes and Wetheriggs. At the

latter is **Wetheriggs Country Pottery**, with working pottery, rare breed pigs, natural wildlife habitats, children's play areas, country shopping, events, fun days and tearoom. Facilities for the disabled. Free admission. Open all year except Christmas and New Year, daily 10.00–17.30, tearoom 10.00–17.00. ☎ 01786 892733; fax 01768 892722

After the pottery turn right on a minor road, then left before the railway line to reach Great Strickland. Turn left here for Morland, where the Anglo-Saxon church tower is claimed to be the oldest in Cumbria. **The Highgate Farm and Animal Trail** offers a wide range of animal-based activities, including displays by birds of prey. Snack and burger bar, souvenir shop, disabled facilities. Admission charge. Open daily late March–end September, from 10.30 October, 11.00–15.00. ☎ 01931 714347

Head south from Morland, soon turning left to King's Meaburn. Turn right here, then left along a very minor road to Colby and **Appleby**. Once a more important centre and, for more than 100 years, county town of the former Westmorland, Appleby is now a relative backwater, a very attractive little market town in the broad valley of the River Eden. The elegant, wide, Boroughgate is the spine of the town, rising from church to castle, with the historic Moot Hall of 1596 at the lower end and St Anne's Hospital, an almshouse complex of 12 cottages and a chapel built by Lady Anne Clifford in 1653, higher on the left. The fine sandstone parish church has an entrance through cloisters which formerly housed the butter market. Inside, look for the historic organ, the corporation pews and the Clifford monument. **Appleby Castle** has a 12th-century keep, fine paintings and porcelain, rare breed farm animals, parkland, gardens and plant centre, children's play area and a range of special events throughout the season. Tearooms. Admission charge. Open daily, late March–end of September, 10.00–17.00, October, 10.00–1600. ☎ 017683 51402

Appleby explodes into life in early June each year for the Appleby New Fair, when gypsies and other travellers from all over the country gather in and around the town. The main line of the former Midland Railway, the 'Settle and Carlisle', with a station at Appleby, still has a rather limited passenger service.

From Appleby return to Colby, carry on to Bolton and turn right in about 3km (2 miles) to reach the main A66 road near Temple Sowerby. Go through Temple Sowerby to **Acorn Bank**, a National Trust garden with the largest collection of herbs and medicinal plants in the north of England, orchards, mixed borders and roses. A watermill is under restoration. Open daily late March–early November, 10.00–1730. The obvious return to Penrith is along A66; to avoid this busy road means a considerable detour along minor roads.

EASTERN LAKELAND

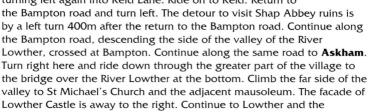

1 Keld, Shap Abbey and Lowther

A short ride of only 28km (17 miles) through pleasant countryside. Up and down but no serious climbing.

From the middle of Shap head north on the main road. Turn left at the top end of the village on the Bampton road, soon turning left again into Keld Lane. Ride on to Keld. Return to the Bampton road and turn left. The detour to visit Shap Abbey ruins is by a left turn 400m after the return to the Bampton road. Continue along the Bampton road, descending the side of the valley of the River Lowther, crossed at Bampton. Continue along the same road to **Askham**. Turn right here and ride down through the greater part of the village to the bridge over the River Lowther at the bottom. Climb the far side of the valley to St Michael's Church and the adjacent mausoleum. The facade of Lowther Castle is away to the right. Continue to Lowther and the **Lowther Leisure and Wildlife Park**.

To return, *either* ride to the nearby A6 and turn right *or* return to Askham and take the very minor road on the east side of the river, via Whale and Low Knipe, rejoining the outward route at Bampton Grange.

2 Appleby and Morland

A ride of about 38km (24 miles) through the pleasantly undulating countryside of the valley of the River Eden, visiting the fine old town of Appleby.

Leave Shap by the minor road just to the north of the church, heading east. The first significant village is **Crosby Ravensworth**, noted for its fine church, some good houses, and a Roman road from Borrowbridge to Kirkby Thore. Head north to Maulds Meaburn, another attractive village, then turn right to ascend to Maulds Meaburn Moor. Join the B6260, turning right to continue to Appleby where, in addition to the features already mentioned, there is an operational railway station on the celebrated Settle and Carlisle line.

Leave Appleby along the minor road heading north west through Colby to Bolton. Turn left in Bolton, then left again in 2km (1.25 miles) to **Morland**. Head south, turn right at Newby, go over the M6 motorway and turn left into a narrow road. Turn right at a T-junction and join A6, turning left back to Shap.

1 PENRITH-ALSTON-PENRITH

A climb over a high Pennine road to an outpost of Cumbria beautifully situated in the valley of the South Tyne. A former market town, **Alston** has a wealth of interest for visitors and a good choice of hotels, restaurants and inns. The cobbled main street has a distinctive market cross. Features include: Gossipgate Gallery, Pennine Pottery and other craft centres, waterwheel at High Mill, the 'Derwentwater clock' inside the parish church of St Augustine. The **South Tynedale Railway**, a narrow-gauge line using some of the trackbed of the former British Rail branch, is claimed to be the highest narrow gauge railway in England. Trains operate between Alston and Gilderdale, generally from Easter throughout the season, with some services in December. The line is in process of extension towards Slaggyford. Recorded timetable ☎ 01434 382828. General enquiries ☎ 01434 381696.

Alston is at the heart of an area which was for centuries extensively mined for lead. A few kilometres to the south-east of Alston, at **Nenthead,** the heritage centre has an exhibition featuring this rich industrial history. The centre is open daily from Easter to the end of October. ☎ 01434 382037

Leave Penrith by the A686, crossing the River Eden close to Langwathby before climbing to **Hartside Cross,** at 580m (1,904ft.) one of the highest passes in England, with its lonely inn claiming a similar distinction. Continue downhill to Alston. Leave Alston to the south east along the A689, soon reaching Nenthead.

From Nenthead a minor road climbs over Nunnery Hill, even higher than Hartside Cross, before descending towards Garrigill. Turn left then right to cross the river, then right again to continue along a minor road to Leadgate. Turn left here to angle up to the main A686, turning left towards Penrith.

For a varied return, turn right into a minor road 2km (1.25 miles) after Hartside Cross, soon reaching Renwick. Turn left to **Kirkoswald**, a charming village with cobbled former market square, close to the River Eden. Although the remains of the former castle are scant, there is a great deal of historic interest in and around Kirkoswald. The ancient church of St Oswald has its bell tower some distance away from the main structure. The most interesting house is The College, instituted as a college of priests in 1523 and home of the Fetherstonhaugh family for 400 years.

Leave Kirkoswald on a minor road heading east of south to Glassonby. Carry on through the village to a cross roads in 1km (0.6miles). Turn right here to visit the stone circle, **Long Meg and her Daughters.** Continue through Little Salkeld and Langwathby to join the main A686, turning right to return to Penrith. Full circuit 87km (54 miles).

2A APPLEBY, ACORN BANK, WARCOP, BROUGH AND KIRKBY STEPHEN

An excursion of 85km (53miles) full of interesting places and possible diversions.

Take the main A66 from Penrith towards Appleby. The first possible diversion is at Temple Sowerby, for **Acorn Bank**. Continue along the A66 to **Appleby**. The main road carries on towards Brough. **Warcop** is a short diversion to the right, a charming village close to the River Eden, with a good bridge, said to the oldest in the former county of Westmorland and a church with 13th-century and later work on Norman foundations. Just a few kilometres further, **Brough** is divided into two separate settlements, Market Brough and Church Brough. The development of Brough is firmly linked to the major crossing of the Pennines via Stainmore, a route in use at least since Roman times when it linked York and Carlisle. Church Brough has the remains of the castle, a Norman structure erected on the earthworks of the previous Roman fort. It was restored by Lady Anne Clifford in the 17th century, and is now in the care of English Heritage. Small admission charge. A medieval village grew up around the castle and St Michael's Church, originally of the mid 12th century but with much 14th- and 16th-century work. From the early 14th century, Market Brough became the dominant settlement when the market traders set up a trading site by the new crossing of the Swindale Beck. Inns and shops flourished, particularly in the 18th and 19th centuries, when the village was a stopping place for many cross country coaches. Old Hall, on Market Street, dating from the early 17th century, is the oldest remaining house in Brough.

From Brough head south on A685 to **Kirkby Stephen**. Continue along A685, fork right for **Orton** with a small chocolate factory, go under the M6 motorway and join the A6 a little way to the south of Shap. Turn right to return to Penrith.

*From Orton, an alternative return route goes north along the B6260, over Orton Scar, forks left to Crosby Ravensworth, Maulds Meaburn and **Morland** (Highgate Farm and Animal Trail). Turn left at Cliburn, soon reaching **Wetheriggs Pottery**. The same road continues, joining the A6 just to the south of Eamont Bridge.*

3A

For a shorter drive, follow any of the cycle routes set out in this chapter.

Fact File

The Fact File provides a summary of useful information, much of it referring to places and activities which have already been described in the appropriate chapter of the guide. The order in which the entries are made in each list coincides with the order of the chapters in the main part of the guide.

REACHING THE LAKE DISTRICT

The Cumbria County Council operates a 'traveline' information and enquiry service for bus, rail and boat timetables at Citadel Chambers, Carlisle, Cumbria CA3 8SG. ☎ 0870 6082608 (Monday–Friday 9.00–1700 Saturday 9.00–12.00,)

Website: http:/www.cumbria.gov.uk/travtour.htm.

By road

Despite the restricted car parking and the limited network of predominantly narrow roads, the majority of visitors will arrive by car. The M6 motorway is the obvious approach road, from both north and south. From the south, junction 36, followed by the A590 and A591 provides a swift and straightforward approach to destinations in the south of the district. The M6 to junction 40, then A66 serves the same purpose for Keswick and other places in the north of the district. From the east, the A66 is the best trans-Pennine route, crossing to Penrith from its junction with the A1 at Scotch Corner. From the southern part of Yorkshire, the A65 via Skipton (bypassed) is the straightforward route.

Long distance coach is another option, generally less expensive than the railway. Stagecoach and National Express operate services to and from the Lake District from Birmingham, London, Manchester, South Yorkshire and the North-east, some passing through the heart of the district, calling at Kendal, Windermere, Ambleside and Keswick. These coaches serve many intermediate towns and cities thoughout the country. Further information on these and local bus services, is available at Tourist Information Centres. Stagecoach Cumberland ☎ 0870 6082608

By rail

There are west coast main line stations at Oxenholme and Penrith. From the former, the Windermere branch line provides a valuable service, generally with connections to and from the London (Euston) services, stopping at Kendal, Burneside, Staveley and Windermere. There are also through trains from Windermere to Manchester and its airport. For the western section of the district, trains to Grange over Sands, Ulverston and Barrow in Furness connect with the London and other main line trains at Lancaster. Also from Barrow there are through trains to and from Manchester and its airport. From Barrow a rather infrequent service runs north along the coast to Whitehaven and Carlisle; the intermediate stations include Ravenglass, Seascale, St Bees and Maryport.

By air

The usual approach to the Lake District is by the international airport at Manchester. There are train services from the airport direct to Windermere and to Barrow in Furness

ACCOMMODATION

Visitors will find accommodation to suit all needs and budgets, ranging from bunk houses and camping barns to luxury hotels; thousands of cottages and apartments are also available to rent. Accommodation can always be booked direct with the establishment or through a Tourist Information Centre on or before arrival in the area. If reserved through a T.I.C. a deposit of ten per cent will be charged; this will be deducted when paying the final bill. If calling personally, it is quite usual to ask to see the available room at hotels or bed and breakfast houses.

Bunk Houses

These vary in character but offer clean, dry, very basic accommodation, sometimes in dormitories, at low cost. Some are situated in towns, others in rural areas. Current details obtainable from Tourist Information Centres.

Camping Barns

A network of stone barns, usually in remote places, owned by farmers but administered as a scheme by the Lake District National Park Authority (☎ 017687 72645 for reservations). The barns provide simple overnight shelter for walkers and cyclists, thus avoiding the need to carry tents. The only facilities are a wooden sleeping platform, table, cold water tap, and w.c. Visitors will need to bring sleeping bags, cooking stove and accessories, and a torch. People under 18 years of age must be accompanied by an adult. Charges are very low.

Camping and Caravan Sites

Because of the impact on the landscape, many restrictions are imposed by the Lake District National Park Authority. Consequently most sites benefit from seclusion and are well screened from the roads and fells. Generally sites open only from mid-March to mid-November but exceptions do occur. Some sites have large static caravans and/or timber chalets to rent on a weekly (sometimes shorter) basis, as well as areas for touring caravans, motor caravans, and tents. Other sites will offer pitches exclusively for tourers and tents or one or the other. Farmers sometimes hold a local authority license to use a small field for tents. The larger touring and camping sites are well equipped with showers, laundry, dish-washing and other facilities. Lists of sites can be obtained from Tourist Information Centres.

The two major clubs, the Caravan Club and the Camping and Caravanning Club own and manage sites in the area. The Caravan Club has sites for touring caravans and motor caravans only, with one exception. It is possible for non-members to stay at all of these sites on payment of an increased over-night charge. The smaller certified location sites administered by the Caravan Club are licensed for members only and are limited to five vans per night; this type of site is frequently found to be a small field on a working farm and most do not have electric hook-ups or toilet facilities.

Details of membership, possible reciprocal arrangements with clubs in other countries and other information may be obtained from:

The Caravan Club
East Grinstead House,
East Grinstead RG19 1UA
☎ 01342 326944

The Camping and Caravanning Club
Greenfields House, Westwood Way, Coventry CV4 8JH
☎ 02476 694995

A Camping International Card, obtainable from caravan and camping clubs in many countries, may be useful.

Youth Groups

There are camp sites which cater for youth groups but reservation should be made well in advance of the proposed visit. Some of the churches provide dormitory accommodation in youth centres – again plan well ahead to ensure that the provision is suitable for the group concerned. Contact a Tourist Information Centre for more details.

Youth Hostels

The Youth Hostels Association has excellent coverage throughout the Lake District. The hostels, always very popular, vary from small buildings in the mountains to those of luxurious standard such as the one by the lake at Waterhead, Ambleside. It must be stressed that hostels are for travellers – young, not-so-young, solo, groups, school parties, families – all are welcome. Booking ahead is always advisable, and is essential for public holidays and in the peak season (July and August). Membership charges are modest – join on the spot at any hostel or write to:

Lake District Booking Bureau
☎ 015394 31117

Membership includes the handbook listing all the hostels in England and Wales with the facilities offered and a location map.

The accommodation offered varies from family rooms to dormitories. Bed linen is provided and included in the modest overnight charge. With few exceptions, all hostels provide meals, usually with a choice of menu and always a vegetarian option. Other diets can be catered for subject to advance notice. Charges for all meals are low and offer good value. All hostels provide a kitchen for those who prefer self-catering and all have a clothes drying facility, especially welcome to walkers and cyclists.

Subject to the availability of beds, there is no maximum or minimum length of stay.

Some hostels have a closed period during the day, usually 10.00–17.00. Doors are locked overnight, usually from 23.00.

Fact File

With few exceptions, hostels can be reached by car and for those travelling by rail to the Lake District, the YHA runs a shuttle mini-bus (summer service only) from Windermere Station to local hostels.

Cottages, Flats and Residential Caravans

There are numerous agents who will offer a choice of accommodation to rent on a weekly basis or sometimes for even shorter periods. The size of the property, its facilities, and the cost will vary considerably. It is also possible to rent properties directly from the owner; these are advertised in the weekend newspapers, magazines such as *The Lady, Cumbria, Cumbria Life*; many are listed in booklets obtainable from Tourist Information Offices.

Bed and Breakfast

Accommodation is offered in private houses or small proprietor-run guest houses in the towns, villages, or rural areas. Standards will vary and this is usually reflected in the price. Look for the B & B sign outside – some will quote the price; otherwise enquire at the door. Most offer at least some rooms with en-suite accommodation and a good standard of cleanliness. The majority do not serve meals other than breakfast but will be able to suggest good local restaurants to suit all budgets. Some of these guest houses will have a residents' lounge; almost all will provide tea and coffee facilities and television in the bedrooms. Remember, you can ask to see the room offered before accepting the accommodation.

Farmhouse Accommodation

Generally similar to the type offered above but in houses attached to working farms. Find addresses from T.I.C.s or guides widely available. Again standards will vary from simple to quite luxurious. Meals, other than breakfast, if available, will sometimes be taken round a large table with the family and other guests. Some farmers will welcome visits to look round the farm and perhaps allow guests to help with the feeding of live-stock.

Country House Hotels

The buildings are usually large houses in extensive grounds. Architecture and decor is frequently de-luxe and service attentive. Such hotels usually have a tranquil setting with attractive views of mountains and/or lakes from the main rooms and from some of the bedrooms. It is customary to reserve a room, breakfast, and evening meal at this type of hotel.

Major and Large Hotels

Throughout the area there are many highly rated hotels. Most offer all the services expected from international hotels. As well as the restaurant, less formal eating areas such as the bar will offer meals and room service is available. Swimming-pools and gymnasium facilities are also available in most hotels of this standard and most will cater for private parties and conferences.

The following lists include premises within each category of accommodation but inclusion does not imply a recommendation. These establishments are merely suggestions from the large numbers available. More comprehensive information is available at Tourist Information Centres.

THE SOUTH

MAJOR AND LARGE HOTELS

The Castle Green Hotel
Kendal
☎ 01539 734000 fax 735522

Stonecross Manor Hotel
Kendal
☎ 01539 733559 fax 736386

Belsfield Hotel
Bowness on Windermere
☎ 015394 42448 fax 46397

Burnside Hotel
Bowness on Windermere
☎ 015394 42211 fax 43824

The Old England Hotel
Bowness on Windermere
☎ 015394 42444 fax 43432

Low Wood Hotel
Ambleside Road,
Windermere
☎ 015394 33338 fax 34072

The Miller Howe Hotel
Windermere
☎ 015394 42536

Rothay Manor Hotel
Ambleside
☎ 015394 33605 fax 33607

Swan Hotel
Grasmere
☎ 015394 35551 fax 35741

Wordsworth Hotel
Grasmere
☎ 015394 35592 fax 35765

Langdale Hotel and Country Club
Elterwater, Ambleside
☎ 0500 051197 fax 37694

Swan Hotel
Newby Bridge
☎ 015395 31681 fax 31917

Fact File

COUNTRY HOUSE AND SMALLER HOTELS

Garden House Hotel
Fowl-Ing Lane, Kendal
☎ 01539 731131 fax 740064

Burn How Hotel
Back Belsfield Road,
Bowness on Windermere
☎ 015394 46226 fax 47000

Fayrer Garden Hotel
Lyth Valley Road,
Bowness on Windermere
☎ 015394 88195 fax 45986

Linthwaite House Hotel
Crook Road,
Bowness on Windermere
☎ 015394 88600 fax 88601

Quarry Garth Hotel
Ambleside Road, Windermere
☎ 015394 88282 fax 46584

Merewood Hotel
Ambleside Road,
Windermere
☎ 015394 46484 fax 42128

Rothay Garth Hotel
Rothay Road, Ambleside
☎ 015394 32217 fax 34400

Wateredge Hotel
Waterhead, Ambleside
☎ 015394 32332 fax 31878

Nanny Brow Hotel
Clappersgate, Ambleside
☎ 015394 32036 fax 32450

Skelwith Bridge Hotel
Skelwith Bridge,
Ambleside
☎ 015394 32115 fax 34254

Gold Rill Hotel
Grasmere
☎/fax 015394 35486

Grasmere Hotel
Grasmere
☎/fax 015394 35277

Britannia Inn
Elterwater
☎ 015394 37210 fax 37311

New Dungeon Ghyll Hotel
Great Langdale
☎ 015394 37213

Old Dungeon Ghyll Hotel
Great Langdale
☎ 015394 37272

Three Shires Inn
Little Langdale
☎ 015394 37215

The Black Bull Inn
Coniston
☎ 015394 41335 fax 41168

The Sun Hotel
Coniston
☎ 015394 41248

The Waterhead Hotel
Coniston
☎ 015394 41244 fax 41193

Queen's Head Hotel
Hawkshead
☎ 015394 36271 fax 36722

Red Lion Inn
Hawkshead
☎ 015394 36213 fax 36747

Tower Bank Arms
Near Sawrey
☎ 015394 36334

Sawrey Hotel
Far Sawrey
☎ 015394 43425

GUEST HOUSES (BED AND BREAKFAST ACCOMMODATION INCLUDING FARMHOUSES)

Higher House Farm
Oxenholme Lane,
Natland, Kendal
☎ 015395 61177 fax 61520

**Lakeland Natural
Vegetarian Guest House**
Low Slack,
Queen's Road, Kendal
☎ 01539 733011 fax 726265

Sundial House
51 Milnthorpe Road, Kendal
☎ 01539 724468 fax 730973

Maggs Howe
Kentmere, Staveley, Kendal
☎ 01539 821689

The Archway
13 College Road, Windermere
☎ 015394 45613

Howbeck
New Road, Windermere
☎ 015394 44739

Laurel Cottage
Park Road, Windermere
☎ 015394 43053

The Beaumont
Holly Road, Windermere
☎/fax 015394 47075

Laurel Cottage
St Martin's Square
Bowness on Windermere
☎/fax 015394 45594

Lingwood
Birkett Hill,
Bowness on Windermere
☎ 015394 44680

Brantfell
Rothay road, Ambleside
☎ 015394 32239

Brantholme
Millans Park, Ambleside
☎ 015394 32034

Laurel Villa
Lake Road, Ambleside
☎ 015394 33240

Riverside Lodge
Rothay Bridge, Ambleside
☎ 015394 34208

Ash Cottage
Grasmere
☎/fax 015394 35224

Beck Allans
Grasmere
☎/fax 015394 35563

Titteringdales Guest House
Pye Lane, Grasmere
☎/fax 015394 35439

Baysbrown Farm
Great Langdale
☎ 015394 37300

Barnhowe
Lane Ends, Elterwater
☎ 015394 37346

Wilson Place Farm
Little Langdale
☎ 015394 37269

**Waterhead Country
Guest House**
Coniston   ☎ 015394 41442

Townson Ground
East of Lake, Coniston
☎ 015394 41272

Orchard Cottage
Yewdale Road, Coniston
☎ 015394 41373

Borwick Fold
Outgate, Hawkshead
☎/fax 015394 36742

Borwick Lodge
Outgate, Hawkshead
☎/fax 015394 36332

Garth Country House
Near Sawrey
☎ 015394 36373

Low Graythwaite Hall
Nr Newby Bridge
☎ 015395 31676

YOUTH HOSTELS

118 Highgate, Kendal
☎ 01539 724066 fax 724906

High Cross, Bridge Lane,
Troutbeck, Windermere
☎ 015394 43543 fax 47165

Waterhead, Ambleside
☎ 015394 32304 fax 34408

Butterlip How,
Easedale Road, Grasmere
☎ 015394 35316 fax 35798

Thorney How, Grasmere
☎ 015394 35591 fax 35866

The Knoll Country Guest House
Lakeside Nr Newby Bridge
☎ 015395 31347

Cobbler's Cottage
Griffin Street,
Broughton in Furness
☎ 01229 716413

Dower House
High Duddon,
Duddon Bridge,
Broughton in Furness
☎ 01229 716279

Newfield Inn
Seathwaite, Duddon Valley
☎ 01229 716208

High Close,
Loughrigg, Ambleside
☎ 015394 37313 fax 37101

Elterwater, Ambleside
☎ 015394 37245 fax 37120

Holly How, Far End, Coniston
☎ 015394 41323 fax 41803

Copper Mines House,
Coniston ☎/fax 015394 41261

Esthwaite Lodge, Hawkshead
☎ 015394 36293 fax 36720

THE WEST

MAJOR AND LARGE HOTELS

There are no hotels in this category in this section; the
nearest is The Seacote Hotel, Beach Road, St Bees.
☎ 01946 822777

COUNTRY HOUSE AND SMALLER HOTELS

Stanley Ghyll House
Boot, Eskdale
☎ 019467 23327

Burnmoor Inn
Boot, Eskdale
☎ 019467 23224; fax 23337

Woolpack Inn
Nr Boot, Eskdale
☎ 019467 23230

Gosforth Hall Hotel
Gosforth ☎ 019467 25322

Wasdale Head Inn
Wasdale ☎ 019467 26229

Low Wood Hall Hotel
Nether Wasdale
☎/fax 019467 26289

Ennerdale Country
House Hotel
Cleator ☎ 01946 813907

**Grange Country
House Hotel**
Loweswater,
Nr. Cockermouth
☎ 01946 861211

Bridge Hotel
Buttermere
☎/fax 017687 70252

Fish Hotel
Buttermere
☎ 017687 70253

GUEST HOUSES (BED AND BREAKFAST ACCOMODATION INCLUDING FARMHOUSES)

Forest How Guest House
Eskdale Green
☎ 019467 23201

Woodbank
Eskdale
☎ 019467 23303

Rosegarth
Main Street, Ravenglass
☎ 01229 717275

**Longacre Country
Guest House**
Santon Bridge Road,
Gosforth ☎ 019467 25328

Burnthwaite Farm
Wasdale Head, Wasdale
☎ 019467 26242

Beckfoot
Ennerdale
☎/fax 01946 861235

Brook Farm
Thackthwaite,
Nr Cockermouth
☎ 01900 85606

Dalegarth
Buttermere
☎ 017687 70233

YOUTH HOSTELS

Eskdale (Boot)
☎ 019467 23219 fax 23163

Wasdale Hall, Wasdale
☎ 019467 26222 fax 26056

King George VI
Memorial Hostel, Buttermere
☎ 017687 70245 fax 70231

Cat Crag, Ennerdale
☎ 01946 861237

Black Sail Hut, Ennerdale
☎/fax 0411 108450

THE NORTH

MAJOR AND LARGE HOTELS

Keswick Hotel
Station Road, Keswick
☎ 017687 72020 fax71300

Stakis Lodore Hotel
Borrowdale
☎ 017687 77285 fax 77343

COUNTRY HOUSE AND SMALLER HOTELS

Trout Hotel
Crown Street, Cockermouth
☎ 01900 823591 fax 827514

Shepherd's Hotel
Lakeland Sheep and Wool
Centre, Egremont Road,
Cockermouth
☎ 01900 822673

Pheasant Inn
Bassenthwaite Lake,
Nr Cockermouth
☎ 017687 76234

Castle Inn Hotel
Bassenthwaite, Nr Keswick
☎ 017687 76401

Swan Hotel
Thornthwaite, Keswick
☎ 017687 78256

**Applethwaite Country
House Hotel**
Applethwaite, Keswick
☎ 017687 72413

Borrowdale Hotel
Borrowdale, Keswick
☎ 017687 77224

**Greenbank
Countryhouse Hotel**
Borrowdale
☎ 017687 77215

Hazelbank
Rosthwaite, Borrowdale
☎ 017687 77248

Scafell Hotel
Rosthwaite, Borrowdale
☎ 017687 77208

King's Head Inn
Thirlspot, Thirlmere, Keswick
☎ 017687 72393

Near Howe Hotel
Mungrisdale
☎ 017687 79678

GUEST HOUSES (BED AND BREAKFAST ACCOMMODATION INCLUDING FARMHOUSES)

Rose Cottage
Lorton Road, Cockermouth
☎ 01900 822189

Stanger Farm
Cockermouth
☎ 01900 824222

Forest Lodge
Beck Wythop,
Nr Thornthwaite
☎ 017687 78396

**Maple Bank Country
Guest House**
Braithwaite, Keswick
☎ 017687 78229

Derwent Cottage
Portinscale, Keswick
☎ 017687 74838

Croft House
Applethwaite, Nr Keswick
☎ 017687 73693

Aaron Lodge Guest House
Brundholme Road, Keswick
☎ 017687 72399

The Dolly Waggon
17 Helvellyn Street, Keswick
☎ 017687 73593

Latrigg House
St Herbert Street, Keswick
☎ 017687 73068

Derwent House
Borrowdale, Keswick
☎ 017687 77658   fax 77217

Hollows Farm
Grange-in-Borrowdale
☎ 017687 77298

Yew Craggs
Rosthwaite, Borrowdale
☎ 017687 77260

**Scales Farm Country
Guest House**
Threlkeld, Nr Keswick
☎ 017687 79660

**Parkend Restaurant
and Country Hotel**
Caldbeck   ☎ 016974 78494

Mosedale Guest House
Mosedale, Mungrisedale
☎ 017687 79371

YOUTH HOSTELS

Double Mills, Cockermouth
☎ 01900 822561

Keswick, Station Road
☎ 017687 72484   fax 74129

Barrow House, Borrowdale
☎ 017687 77246   fax 77396

Longthwaite, Borrowdale
☎ 017687 77257   fax 77393

Honister Hause, Seatoller,
Borrowdale ☎ 017687 77267

THE EAST
MAJOR AND LARGE HOTELS

North Lakes Hotel
Ullswater Road, Penrith
☎ 01768 868111 fax 868291

Glenridding Hotel
Glenridding
☎ 017684 82228

Ullswater Hotel
Glenridding ☎ 017684 82444

Leeming House Hotel
Watermillock
☎ 017684 86622   fax 86443

Shap Wells Hotel
Nr Shap
☎ 01931 716628 fax 716377

Fact
File

Fact File

COUNTRY HOUSE AND SMALLER HOTELS

Brantwood Country Hotel
Stainton, Penrith
☎ 01768 862748

Haweswater Hotel
Haweswater
☎ 01931 713235

Pooley Bridge Inn
Pooley Bridge
☎/fax 017684 86215

Beacon Bank Hotel
Nr Penrith
☎ 01768 863072

GUEST HOUSES (BED AND BREAKFAST ACCOMODATION INCLUDING FARMHOUSES)

The Limes
Redhills, Penrith
☎ 01768 863343

Fellside
Hartsop, Patterdale
☎ 017684 82532

Elm House
Pooley Bridge
☎ 017684 86334

Lattendales Farm
Greystoke, Nr Penrith
☎ 017684 83474

Moss Crag Guest House
Glenridding
☎ 017684 82500

Brookfield
Shap, Penrith
☎ 01931 716397

YOUTH HOSTELS

Helvellyn
Greenside, Glenridding
☎/fax 017684 82269

Goldrill House
Patterdale
☎ 017684 82394 fax 82034

Hire of Cottages, Flats and Residential Caravans

Some Agencies and Associations:

Cumbrian Cottages
☎ 015394 88772 fax 88902

Low Briery Holiday Village
☎ 017687 72044

Heart of Lakes and Cottage Life
☎ 015394 32321 fax 33251

Eden Country Holidays
☎ 016974 76230

Lakelovers
☎ 015394 88855 fax 88857

Clark Scott-Harden
☎ 01768 86900 fax 865578

AGRICULTURAL SHOWS, LOCAL SPORTS AND FESTIVALS

Westmorland County Show
Kendal ☎ 015395 67804

Lake District Sheepdog Trials
Ings, Staveley
☎ 015394 33721

Ambleside Sports
☎ 015394 45531

Rydal Sheepdog Trials
☎ Tourist Information Centre

Grasmere Sports
☎ 015394 32127

Hawkshead Show
☎ 015394 36609

Lowick Show
☎ 015394 36364

Eskdale Show
☎ Tourist Information Centre

Ennerdale Show
☎ Tourist Information Centre

Loweswater Show
☎ Tourist Information Centre

Cockermouth Show
☎ Tourist Information Centre

Hesket Newmarket Show
☎ Tourist Information Centre

Patterdale Sheepdog Trials
☎ Tourist Information Centre

Penrith Show
☎ Tourist Information Centre

Lowther Horse Driving Trials and Game Fair
☎ 01931 712378

CAR HIRE

Avis
Station Road, Kendal
☎ 01539 733582.

Vickers Self Drive
75, Appleby Road, Kendal
☎ 01539 732643

Rayrigg Rover
Shap Road, Kendal
☎ 01539 730060

Mint Motors
Mintsfeet Road, Kendal
☎ 01539 723318

Cumbria Car Hire Ltd
Kendal
☎ 01539 720620

Avis
Belsfield Garage,
Bowness on Windermere
☎ 015394 45910

Rayrigg
Rayrigg Road, Windermere
☎ 015394 42451

Fact File

CYCLE HIRE

Millenium Cycles
Crook Road, Staveley
☎ 01539 821167

Daisy Cycle Hire
Craig Walk, Bowness on
Windermere
☎ 015394 42144

Bike Hire
46, Oak Street, Windermere
☎ 015394 48031

Mountain Trading
Lake Road, Bowness
☎ 015394 44786

David Ashton
Elleray Hotel, Cross Street,
Windermere
☎ 015394 43120

Ambleside Mountain Bikes
The Slack, Ambleside
☎ 015394 33592

Biketreks
Millans Park, Ambleside
☎ 015394 31245

Lakes Pathfinders
Ambleside ☎ 015394 32862
(0374 167 695)

**The Croft Mountain
Bike Hire**
Hawkshead
☎ 015394 36374

Grizedale Mountain Bikes
Grizedale ☎ 01229 860369

Crook Barn Stables
Torver, Coniston
☎ 015394 41088

Summitreks
Yewdale Road, Coniston
☎ 015394 41212

Meadowdore Cafe
Coniston ☎ 015394 41638

Fiat Garage
Lake Road, Keswick
☎ 017687 72064

Keswick Mountain Bikes
Southey Hill, Keswick
☎ 017687 75202

Trackers Cycle Hire
Main Road, Keswick
☎ 017687 71372

Mitchells Newsagents
Near T.I.C, Keswick
☎ 017687 72790

Holiday Lakeland
Portinscale and Ireby
(Offer organised cycling
holidays in addition to cycle
hire.) ☎ 017687 71871
fax 016973 71960

There are waymarked mountain bike routes at Grizedale Forest
and Whinlatter Forest. Details at the forest visitor centres.

Note: Byways (usually unsurfaced roads) are open to cyclists, horseriders and walkers; off-road vehicles may also be encountered.

Bridleways are open to cyclists but horseriders and walkers have right of way.

Footpaths are not available to cyclists.

Open land – there is no right of access for cyclists on fells or farmland without the permission of the landowner.

Always comply with the Mountain Biking Code of Conduct.

EATING OUT

All the large hotels and the majority of the country house and smaller hotels will provide meals for non-residents, though sometimes only in the evening. Almost all inns, including those listed in the accommodation chapter, provide bar food both at mid-day and in the evening.

The following list adds further suggestions for each section of the district, ranging from expensive, high quality, restaurants to more simple premises including tea and coffee shops not open in the evening.

Two exceptional restaurants, worthy of separate mention, are:

The Miller Howe Hotel, Windermere ☎ 015394 42536
The Sharrow Bay Hotel, Ullswater ☎ 017684 86301
Both are also residential hotels.

THE SOUTH

Castle Dairy
Wildman Street, Kendal
(reservations only)
☎ 01539 721170

Déjà Vu
124 Stricklandgate. Kendal
☎ 01539 724843

Duffins Restaurant
54 Stramongate, Kendal
☎ 01539 720387

Farrers Tea and Coffee Shop
13 Stricklandgate, Kendal
☎ 01539 731707

Paulo Gianni's
21a Stramongate, Kendal
☎ 01539 725858

Waterside Wholefoods
Kent View, Kendal
☎ 01539 729743

Magic Wok
2 Crescent Road,
Windermere
☎ 015394 88668

Fact File

Jericho's
Birch Street, Windermere
☎ 015394 42522

Renoirs Coffee Shop
Main Street, Windermere
☎ 015394 44863

Bowness Kitchen
Lake Road, Bowness
☎ 015394 45529

The Porthole
Ash Street, Bowness
☎ 015394 42793

Rastelli's
Lake Road, Bowness
☎ 015394 44227

The Spinnery Restaurant
Kendal Road, Bowness
☎ 015394 42756

Trattoria Ticino
Quarry Rigg, Bowness
☎ 015394 45786

Ambles Brasserie
Lake Road, Ambleside
☎ 015394 33970

Bertrams Restaurant
Market Place, Ambleside
☎ 015394 32119

Dodds Restaurant
Rydal Road, Ambleside
☎ 015394 32134

The Cumbria Carvery
Stock Lane, Grasmere
☎ 015394 35005

Langman's Tea Shop
Stock Lane, Grasmere
☎ 015394 35248

Rowan Tree Vegetarian Restaurant
Stock Lane, Grasmere
☎ 015394 35528

Kirkstone Gallery
Skelwith Bridge
☎ 015394 32553

The Wine Restaurant
Coniston
☎ 015394 41256

The Minstrel's Gallery
Hawkshead
☎ 015394 36423

Whigs
The Square, Hawkshead
☎ 015394 36614

The Café
Grizedale Visitor Centre,
Grizedale
☎ 01229 860011

Boater's Restaurant
Lakeside, Newby Bridge
☎ 015395 31381

Fell Foot Park Café
Newby Bridge
☎ 015395 31273

THE WEST

Brook House
Boot, Eskdale
☎ 019467 23288

New House Farm
Lorton
☎ 01900 85404

Fact File

THE NORTH

Beatfords Country Restaurant
7 Lowther Went,
Cockermouth
☎ 01900 827099

The Lakeland Sheep and Wool Centre Restaurant
Egremont Road,
Cockermouth
☎ 01900 82267

The Norham Coffee House
73 Main Street, Cockermouth
☎ 01900 824330

Riverside Restaurant
2 Main Street, Cockermouth
☎ 01900 823871

Whinlatter Visitor Centre Café
Whinlatter Pass
☎ 017687 78469

Thornthwaite Gallery Tea Shop
Thornthwaite
☎ 017687 78248

Abrahams Tea Room at George Fisher's
Borrowdale Road, Keswick
☎ 017687 72178

Bryson's Tea Room
Main Street, Keswick
☎ 017687 72257

La Primavera
Greta Bridge, Keswick
☎ 017687 74621

The Rembrandt Restaurant
Station Street, Keswick
☎ 017687 72008

The Saw Mill Café
Mirehouse, Nr Keswick
☎ 017687 74317

Yew Tree Country Restaurant
Seatoller, Borrowdale
☎ 017687 77634

Parkend Restaurant
Nr Caldbeck
☎ 016974 78494

Priest's Mill Tea Room
Caldbeck
☎ 016974 78267

THE EAST

Arcade Café
Devonshire Arcade, Penrith
☎ 01768 891240

Cagney's Tandoori
17 King Street, Penrith
☎ 01768 867503

Chataway's Bistro
St Andrew's Churchyard,
Penrith ☎ 01768 890233

Coach House Restaurant
Angel Lane, Penrith
☎ 01768 899544

Heughscar Tea Rooms
Pooley Bridge
☎ 017684 86453

Aira Force Tea Shop
Aira Force, Ullswater
☎ 017684 82262

FISHING

An Environment Agency rod licence must be purchased by anyone wishing to fish in any water in England. (North-west region, north area headquarters, ☎ 01228 25151).

The licence is available from post offices and tourist information centres. In addition, a permit must be obtained from the Angling Association or Riparian owner owing the fishing rights.

However, in the Lake District the following lakes and tarns may be fished by rod licence holders without additional permit, either from a shore where there is public access or from a boat on lakes or tarns where launching is permitted:

Windermere

Alcock Tarn, Grasmere	High Dam, Finsthwaite
Easdale Tarn, Grasmere	Blea Tarn, Boot, Eskdale
Grisedale Tarn, Grasmere	Burnmoor Tarn, Boot, Eskdale
Codale Tarn, Grasmere	Blea Tarn, Watendlath
Coniston Water	Thirlmere - for bait restrictions, refer to the information board at Armboth car park.
Levers Water, Coniston	
Goats Water, Coniston	

Ullswater

Brotherswater, Patterdale

Red Tarn, Helvellyn

Small Water, near Haweswater

Blea Water, near Haweswater

Of the above, Windermere has the greatest variety of fish, including the rare and highly esteemed char. The smaller tarns are generally limited to brown trout, with perch and schelly present in a minority of cases.

A useful leaflet, *Fishing in Lakeland*, produced by Windermere, Ambleside and District Angling Association, is available from tourist information offices.

GOLF

Kendal (pro.)	☎ 01539 723499
Carus Green, Burneside	☎ 01539 721097
Windermere (pro.)	☎ 015394 43550
Keswick	☎ 017687 79010
Penrith	☎ 01768 862217

HORSE RIDING

Hipshow Riding Stables
Kendal ☎ 01539 728221

Holmescales Riding Centre
Kendal ☎ 01539 729388

Larkrigg Riding School
Kendal ☎ 015395 60245

Lakeland Equestrian
Windermere
☎ 015394 43811

Rydal Farm Trekking
Rydal
☎ 015394 34131
(0850 102721)

Crook Barn
Coniston
☎ 015394 41088

Spoon Hall Trekking Centre
Coniston ☎ 015394 41391

Bigland Hall Estate
Newby Bridge
☎ 015395 31728

Armathwaite Hall
Bassenthwaite
☎ 017687 76949

Park Foot Trekking
Pooley Bridge
017684 86696

Rookin House Farm
Ullswater ☎ 017684 83561

GUIDED TOURS

Cumbria Tourist Guides (Association of Registered Blue Badge Guides), Mickle Bower, Temple Sowerby, Penrith, CA10 1RZ ☎ 017683 62233; fax 017683 62211

Nearly 50 qualified 'Blue Badge' guides are listed as available to provide a wide variety of guided tours for visitors. All are experienced in general guiding in the district; additionally, many have areas of particular expertise such as local literature, gardens or religious monuments. Mini-buses and/or motor cars may be provided by the guides. Several languages are spoken.

Fact File

Princess Executive Minicoaches
Kendal
☎ 01539 731894

Mountain Goat Tours and Holidays
Windermere, Bowness, Ambleside, Grasmere and Keswick
☎ 015394 45161; fax 015394 45164

Lakes Supertours
Windermere
☎ 015394 88133

Lakeland Safari Tours
Windermere, Bowness, Ambleside and Grasmere
☎ 015394 33904

GUIDED WALKS

Lake District National Park Authority, Brockhole, Windermere. ☎ 015394 46601

An extensive programme of guided walks is available throughout the year, generally led by a Voluntary Warden, from many centres throughout the district. 'Discovery Walks', with a theme, are led by experts in their particular field. Voluntary Warden walks are free but a modest charge is made for Discovery Walks. Walks are graded easy, moderate or strenuous. The full programme is included in the National Park publication *Events*, produced annually.

South Lakeland Guided Walks - Town, Village and Country
A comprehensive programme of walks exploring the towns and villages of the southern part of the district, organised by South Lakeland District Council. Based on the various Tourist Information Centres in most cases. A modest charge is made. ☎ Tourist Information Centres.

Other Guided Walks
Stanley Ghyll House, Eskdale   ☎ 019467 23327
Glaramara, Borrowdale   ☎ 017687 77222
A charge is made.

LAKELAND WEATHER INFORMATION

Lakes Weather Line ☎ 017687 75757

NATURE RESERVES

Cumbria Wildlife Trust produce a brochure, *Nature Reserves in Cumbria* listing 33 reserves throughout the county. The majority of these are not in the Lake District but could readily be included in a motor car or cycle tour. Those actually in the district are:

Dubbs Moss
1.5km (1 mile) south of Cockermouth. Grid reference, 098282.

Haweswater
At head of reservoir.
G.R. (car park) 469107.

Rainsbarrow Forest
Ulpha, Duddon Valley.
Footpaths start at
G.R. 190925 or 198936.

*****Roudsea Wood**
Near Haverthwaite.
G.R. 330820.

Ash Landing
Close to Far Sawrey.
G.R. 386954.

Dorothy Farrers Spring Wood
Near Staveley. G.R. 480983.

Hervey Reserve
(Whitbarrow) Access at
G.R. 436859.

Latterbarrow
Near Witherslack village.
G.R. (car park) 441827.

Permit necessary (English Nature).

STATELY HOMES OPEN TO THE PUBLIC

Sizergh Castle
Sizergh, Kendal
(National Trust.)
☎ 015395 60070

Levens Hall
Levens
☎ 015395 60321

Holker Hall
Cark in Cartmel
☎ 015395 58328

Leighton Hall
Near Carnforth
☎ 01524 734474

Muncaster Castle
Ravenglass
☎ 01229 717614

Mirehouse
Near Keswick
☎ 017687 72287

Dalemain
Near Pooley Bridge
☎ 017684 86450

Hutton in the Forest
Near Penrith
☎ 017684 84449

Smaller Houses
Townend, Troutbeck
(National Trust)
☎ 015394 32628

Rydal Mount
Rydal ☎ 015394 33002

Dove Cottage
Grasmere
☎ 015394 35544 (daytime)
015394 35651 (evenings)

Hill Top
Near Sawrey
(National Trust)
☎ 015394 36269

Brantwood
Coniston ☎ 015394 41396

TOURIST INFORMATION CENTRES

Kendal, Town Hall
☎ 01539 725758

Windermere, Victoria Street
☎ 015394 46499

*Bowness, Bowness Bay
☎ 015394 42895

Brockhole, Windermere
(National Park)
☎ 015394 46601

*Waterhead, The Car Park
☎ 015394 32729

Ambleside, The Old
Courthouse, Church Street
☎ 015394 32582

*Grasmere, Red Bank Road
☎ 015394 35245

*Hawkshead, main car park
☎ 015394 36525

*Coniston, main car park,
Ruskin Avenue
☎ 015394 41533

*Broughton in Furness,
The Square
☎ 01229 716115

Cockermouth, Town Hall
☎ 01900 822634

Keswick, Moot Hall
☎ 017687 72645

*Borrowdale, Seatoller Barn
☎ 017687 77294

Penrith, Middlegate
☎ 01768 867466

*Pooley Bridge, Ullswater,
The Square
☎ 017684 86530

*Glenridding,
Ullswater, main car park
☎ 017684 82414

Either closed or limited opening hours out of season.

Fact File

Lake Holidays Afloat
Glebe Road, Bowness
☎ 015394 43415

**Windermere Outdoor
Adventure Watersports
Centre**
Rayrigg Road
☎ 015394 47183

Spirit of the Lake
Shepherd's Boatyard,
Windermere
☎ 015394 48322

**Low Wood Water
Sports Centre**
south of Waterhead,
Windermere
☎ 015394 33338

Coniston Boating Centre
☎ 015394 41366

Summitreks
Coniston
☎ 015394 41212
fax 015394 41089

Howtown Outdoor Centre
Ullswater
☎ 01768 486508

Glenridding Sailing Centre
Ullswater
☎ 01768 82541

Balloon Flights

High Adventure, Bowness on Windermere.
☎ 015394 46588

Index

Index

LANDMARK
Publishing Ltd ● ● ● ●

VISITORS GUIDES

* Practical guides for the independent visitor

* Written in the form of touring itineraries

* Full colour illustrations and maps

* Detailed Landmark FactFile of practical information

* Landmark Visitors Guides highlight all the interesting places you will want to see, so ensuring that you make the most of your visit

Guides to Europe & Other Countries

Antigua & Barbuda*	Bermuda*
Bruges*	Côte d'Azur*
Cracow*	Dominican Republic*
Dordogne*	Florida: Gulf Coast*
Florida: The Keys*	Iceland*
India: Goa	India: Kerala
Italian Lakes*	Madeira
New Zealand*	Northern Cyprus
Orlando*	Provence*
Riga*	Sri Lanka*
St Lucia*	US & British Virgin Islands*

Landmark Publishing
Waterloo House, 12 Compton, Ashbourne, Derbyshire DE6 IDA England
Tel: 01335 347349 Fax: 01335 347303
e-mail: landmark@clara.net

*In the USA order from
Hunter Publishing Inc
130 Campus Drive, Edison NJ 08818
Tel: (732) 225 1900, (800) 255 0343 Fax: (732) 417 0482
Web site: www.hunterpublishing.com

Published by
Landmark Publishing Ltd,
Ashbourne Hall, Cokayne Avenue, Ashbourne, Derbyshire DE6 1EJ England
Tel: (01335) 347349 Fax: (01335) 347303 e-mail: landmark@clara.net

Published in the USA by
Hunter Publishing Inc,
130 Campus Drive, Edison NJ 08818
Tel: (732) 225 1900, (800) 255 0343 Fax: (732) 417 0482

ISBN 1 84306 113 9

© Norman Buckley 2004

The right of Norman Buckley as author of this work has been asserted by him in
accordance with the Copyright, Design and Patents Act, 1993.

All rights reserved. No part of this publication may be reproduced, stored in a retrieval
system or transmitted in any form or by any means, electronic, mechanical, photocopying,
recording or otherwise without the prior permission of Landmark Publishing Ltd.

British Library Cataloguing in Publication Data: a catalogue record for this book is
available from the British Library.

Print: Gutenberg Press Ltd, Malta

Cartography: Mick Usher

Design: Samantha Witham

Cover Pictures
Front: Derwentwater and Skiddaw from Ashness Bridge
Back top: The Lakes Steamer approaches Ambleside Waterhead Quay
Back bottom: Wastwater

Picture Credits
Norman Buckley: 11L, 23T, 31B, 34T, 55M, 66L, 66R, 95R, 130, 131L, 131T, 135,
142T, 142M, 154T, 167(both), 178B, 179M, 190M, 190B.
June Buckley: 54T, 79M, 139B, 154B, 159R, 175T, 183, 190T.
SC Buckley: 110B, 142B, 175B, 179T.
RE Dixon: 19B, 110T, 111T, 114T, 131R, 154M.
Lindsey Porter: Front cover, back cover, title page, 6, 10(all), 11R, 11B, 15(all),
19M, 27L, 27R, 31T, 31M, 34B, 46, 54M, 55T, 55B, 66B, 67(all), 75(both), 79T,
86(all), 95L, 110M, 111M, 111B, 114M, 114R, 122(both), 123, 130R, 130B,
139T, 146(all), 147(all), 158(both), 159B, 171, 175M, 178T, 178R, 179B.
Mark Titterton: 43T

DISCLAIMER
Whilst every care has been taken to ensure that the information in this book is as accurate
as possible at the time of publication, the publishers and author accept no responsibility for
any loss, injury or inconvenience sustained by anyone using this book.